To Mary,

Happy

love Kevin

7

So Far, So Good

About the Author

Paddy Barry divides his time between Monkstown in Dublin and his cottage on Mannin Bay in west Connemara.

So Far, So Good

An Adventurous Life

Paddy Barry

Paddy Barry (signature)

The Liffey Press

Published by
The Liffey Press Ltd
'Clareville'
307 Clontarf Road
Dublin D03 PO46, Ireland
www.theliffeypress.com

A catalogue record of this book is
available from the British Library.

ISBN 978-0-9957927-0-8

Printed in Spain by GraphyCems.

Contents

Preface

The runnin' and jumpin' is nearly finished; I was 74 this year, and jogged for 40 minutes along the beaches and grass of Mannin Bay in west Connemara.

I couldn't but feel that this must soon be over; time to walk from now on.

In the meantime, I'll set out some of the story of my life, my family, friends and the times in which we lived.

Family and making a living should dominate, with interests and activities following. But because the former are more conventional and the latter have more colour, I'll write more of adventure, on the mountains and the sea, intertwined with family and work.

Acknowledgements

For the encouragement and criticism, constructive, Theo Dorgan.
For work on the photos, Craig Williams, of Fuji, Blackrock.
For the maps, Copper Reed Studio, Limerick.
For advice on the book trade, Don Roberts.
For the empathetic production, publisher David Givens.

To the Three Pats – Pat Redmond, Pat Colleran and The Patrick –
and Danny Sheehy.
All Gone.

Introduction: A Rough One

Gcoosh, as yet another wave swept over the boat. Ugh, as again the side of the boat was battered, as were we. The five of us were wedged within as the storm, blowing from Cape Horn, raised the seas into a frenzy. It was like being inside a washing machine. How long before we would be beaten to a pulp? How long could our boat stand up to this before being broken and going to the bottom and us with her?

For 36 hours we had been fighting for our lives, the storm raging and the seas in turmoil. Twice already we had been turned over, completely capsized, as we were thrown about. Luckily, in a manner of speaking, we had little room in the cabin for our few things, stove and pots, to turn into projectiles and 'clock' us.

Our timber boat, 23 feet long, was a copy we had built of the one in which Shackleton, in 1916, had made his escape from the Antarctic when his big ship *Endurance* was crushed in the ice. We were doing a rerun, Irish Antarctic Adventure 1997, and going well until this. With 400 miles behind us since Elephant Island and 400 to go to South Georgia, our confidence in success, if not our comfort, had been growing. We could succeed, make the same passage that Shackleton had done and then climb over the unexplored mountains of South Georgia Island to the safety of a disused whaling station. But right now it looked like we were bunched, end of the road. The naysayers had been right: 'Ye should have counted yer children, and stayed at home.'

But we did survive. The combination of a strong boat, steady men and luck saw us through. We did go on to make land and did make the traverse over the mountains, the first to do it since Shackleton.

Later we'll come back to this – its rawness, its suffering and the sinking of our boat we'd called *Tom Crean*. But for now let's go back to the beginnings.

1

Family Background and Schooldays

I was born in Cork City on September 24, 1942. My middle name, Finbarr, came from the city's favourite saint. My Christian name, Padraig, came from my father's side: grandfather Patsy Barry, schoolmaster, farmer and writer of five books dealing with the doings of Bartlemy and Rathcormack in east County Cork.

My godfather, uncle Dennis Barry, had been a lively man. To the chagrin of his family, he had spent nine months in Mountjoy Jail. Apparently the price of beef had dropped hugely in the 1930s. De Valera had stopped paying the Land Annuities to Britain and in response the British had stopped taking Irish beef, with farmers suffering. As a protest against Dev's actions, Dennis and some others cut down the telegraph poles on the road to Watergrasshill. An understanding judge handed down a suspended sentence if Dennis would purge his contempt. But he wouldn't.

Dennis died in a hunting accident in February of 1949. By unhappy coincidence his son, also Dennis, my first cousin, was seriously injured after a fall from a horse some years ago.

My mother, Ursula, was a Ganter from Rathgar, Dublin, of a clockmaking family who had arrived from southern Germany in 1856. Her father, Leo Peter, was a clockmaker trained in Germany and a lovely man, always nice to me. Now elderly, he still used to go to work each day in the family Ganter Brother's shop in 63 South Great Georges Street. If he was a fine man, his wife, my grandmother, was the opposite; she had a small, birdlike presence, with a sharp tongue. The Ganters had come to Dublin from Furtwangen in the south German Black Forest, the *Schwarzwald*, together with a couple of dozen other clockmaking families. At that time there was a surfeit of *urmakers*, clockmakers, in Germany. These underemployed clockmakers, in the mid-nineteenth century, saw in Ireland a surge in the construction of landmark Catholic churches and convents, all of which were to be adorned with a fine clock – work for them.

From our bungalow off the Model Farm Road, my father would cycle to his work on Patrick Street, an Inspector of Taxes. Earlier he had hurled with Bride Rovers and University College Cork. He had left UCC without finishing, having to go to work to help pay for his younger siblings' upbringing.

Horst Kawalski came to live with us just before I began school in September 1946. We both started together in 'Pres' on the Western Road, he without a word of English. In the aftermath of the postwar chaos in Europe, through the Irish 'Save the German Children Society', my parents took him in. This temporary fostering was, I think, unrelated to my mother's background.

I was a normal, happy youngster for the seven years that we lived in Cork. We frequently visited my father's family farm near

First day at school, with Horst, a German who lived with us for over a year

Rathcormack in our black Ford Prefect. And it was on that farm for many schoolboy years that I spent much of my summers.

We moved from Cork to Rosslare in 1949 when our father was transferred to Wexford. The 'we' now included my younger sisters, Maureen and Margaret. These were the days of dipping the nib pen into the inkwell and then padding the wet script down with 'blotting paper'.

Daddy had bought a bungalow on the harbour side of Rosslare Strand, together with a few acres, which he tore into like a demon digging ditches, fencing, repairing sheds. He bought two heifers, strong animals, which promptly broke out. It may have been the steam train from Rosslare Harbour passing by our fields which frightened them. A few days later they were recovered and brought back.

Mammy had day-old chicks in the sheds. For their bedding she shouldered sacks of sand from the beach below.

Schooldays, Tramore and Waterford

In 1951, my father was transferred to Waterford. We lived in nearby Tramore, renting. The in-house telephone must have been coming as I remember asking were we going to get one and getting a cool reply from my Dad. When we did get it it was black with a revolving dial and the number was Tramore 392. Tramore was great for me. The beach, the swimming off the pier, the Sandhills and Backstrand were our playgrounds for myself and Brian Malone. Mam and Dad were busy on committees, he in the Golf Club and Bridge Club and she in the ICA, the Irish Countrywomen's Association. It seems that in small town society neutral personnel are hugely in demand.

I went to Tramore Christian Brothers and got on well, though I still remember one particular Brother in fourth class as a sadist with his cane and leather and I wouldn't have got the worst of it. My younger sisters, Maureen and Margaret, went to the Star of the Sea primary school. Younger brother Fred was born in March 1951.

The Scouts were a big thing for me, the Catholic Boy Scouts of Ireland, as they were at the time, as opposed to the Protestant ones.

As well as learning knots, first aid, how to light fires and what you'd expect, we had 'Popes' Dates', where by rote we had to recite the CV of Pope Pious! The Summer Camp was the big thing, a fortnight away, in belltents, having sing-songs around campfires. In all this, though the sea was never far away and while we did much swimming, there never were any boats involved.

Notwithstanding the apparently frugal times that were in it, our family always had a month holiday away somewhere. Mammy and Daddy would load up the car. It by now was an Austin Ten, with split windscreen and indicators which swung out – real progress from the driver sticking his hand out the window.

It was on holiday in Tramore in 1944, when I was two, that my brother Cyril died, an infant of only a few months old, probably a cot death, as they were called. I obviously have no memory of that and never got an explanation. His grave is there, well kept and clearly marked. When my time comes, I'd like some of my ashes to go in there to keep him company.

Mammy loved singing. On our car journeys she'd lead us all into 'The Bonny Wee Window', 'Clementine', 'The Humour Is On Me Now' and such favourites. However, she had needed a breast operation for cancer, seemingly successful.

After doing the Primary Cert, I stayed on in the Tramore Christian Brothers and went into first year, a natural transition. However Daddy was a great fan of boarding schools so in second-year I was sent, as a boarder, to De La Salle College in Waterford. Once again I felt a stranger and was lacking in confidence. Even my name, Padraig, seemed an embarrassment, so one day in class, when asked by a new teacher, I replied that my name was 'Paddy', as it seemed easier. And so through all the years that has stuck. In family and official stuff I'm Padraig; elsewhere it's Paddy.

Hurling and Gaelic football were games at which I wasn't much use. Apart from anything else I couldn't see well without glasses. But after Easter the Athletics began and it turned out that I was good at that.

All the time I was a year younger than my classmates and in personality I was inclined to be on the quiet side. It didn't matter in the exam results. I was now second or third in class, but could never beat O'Mahony who went on to be an actuary. Mick Considine and Johnny Rooney became my friends. Together we looked over the wall at the gorgeous protestant girls going into their Newtown School. God, you could be expelled for that, or for having bad thoughts or anything, nearly, although no one ever was. (They were actually Quakers, but we didn't know the difference.)

I got Munster medals in the half mile and high jump, a peculiar combination, though I actually preferred the pole vault. High jumping against a nephew of the famous Olympian, Doctor Pat O'Callaghan, I once saw the good doctor putting his shoulder to the bar when his boy was jumping – to steady it! Out of our innocence, we learned.

Meanwhile, in 1957, our family had moved from Tramore to Dublin, to Booterstown Avenue, the top end near Stillorgan Road and Mount Merrion. I stayed on in De la Salle. Mick Considine's family, as it happened, had moved from Wexford to live only up the road in Mount Merrion and it was through him that I got to know some lads around there, Kevin Cronin and Paddy Norris.

During the school holidays, I also knocked around with Louis Hughes, Ronnie O'Donovan and Arthur McManus from Trimleston. The contact there was Louis's mother, who my father knew from playing bridge. In 1967 we four did a three week cycle around Ireland, camping and staying in An Óige Hostels. I had raised the money

Pole vaulting in school sports, aged 16

by working in Phillips of Clonskeagh – £2-10 shillings a week, low wages, even for then.

The girls – there were three now, Maureen, Margaret and Sheila – went to local schools, Sion Hill, and later Loreto on Stephens Green, as boarders!

In The Barn, attached to Mount Merrion Church, there would be (well-supervised) dancing; an initiation to the wide world of 'romance' – much talk, little action.

It was 1959. I got a good Leaving Certificate, six honours, and schooldays were over.

2

University, Dublin and Elsewhere

During the summer of 1959, after the Leaving Cert., I decided I wanted to be an engineer. To get into Engineering in University College Dublin was fairly straightforward: have a Leaving Cert., which included Latin and Honours Maths. One also needed the dosh as fees were £70 per annum. It transpired that I had won a £70 per annum scholarship off the Leaving (which I hadn't known existed) for 'the sons of Civil Servants'. No mention of 'daughters' in those times.

However my father was of the view that, since I only just 17, I was too young and should do another school year. So I went to Monkstown Christian Brothers where my friends Ronnie and Louis already were. This being a rugby school I was introduced to the oval ball and took greatly to it. Though knowing nothing of the rules, I could run and shouted advice which would see me along. But repeating the same school stuff was boring so I persuaded my dad to let me go ahead into UCD. Reluctantly, he agreed, though in retrospect he had been right. In the years that followed I was always younger than my classmates and it sometimes showed in a dearth of street savvy.

In First Engineering they sat us alphabetically. Thus I got to know Mick Cotter and Des Doherty. Mick, who had been to school in Clongowes Wood, seemed to know everyone and everywhere. He took me down Grafton Street to the New Amsterdam Café where, again, he seemed to know everyone though in fact it was just where the Clongowes crowd, and perhaps some from Gonzaga,

9

hung out. Any De la Salle, Waterford classmates who were going on to 'Uni', as it was called, went to Cork. Mick Considine had gone straight to work in Sun Alliance Insurance, of which more later, fate happily intervening.

Engineering was based in the College of Science in Merrion Street, with its ancient workshops, timbered lecture theatres and ribbed central heating radiators on which we warmed our backsides. This was exclusively a male place with brown, black and grey colours and a smell of pipesmoke.

Our lectures on Physics and Chemistry, shared with the medical students, were taken in Earlsfort Terrace, a pleasant walk away, along by Stephen's Green. Earlsfort Terrace was entirely more colourful. Here there were women, not that many, but lending an exotic and well dressed aura to the surrounds. They were unapproachable, of course, to us rustics. We in fact were very busy, attending lectures all morning and doing 'practicals' in the afternoon, including Drawing Office and Workshops.

In contrast, those in Earlsfort Terrrace, doing Commerce and Arts in particular, seemed to live a life of ease, having only a few lectures.

Freshers' Week had a plethora of 'open days' where clubs and societies would vie for attention and new members. A new wide world lay open: History Societies, Fencing, Literary and Historical, Climbing, Sailing. Knowing nobody in them, I joined none, more's the pity.

I continued knocking around with my Mount Merrion friends Kevin, doing Commerce, and Paddy, doing Science, with the latter already showing signs of brilliance. Decades later, working in Houston, he was the one heading the team who guided Neil Armstrong back from the Moon. More importantly back then in UCD, he had access to his Da's car, thus considerably widening our social endeavours, the alternative being the bicycle.

Dances were the thing, to live bands in the tennis and rugby clubs on Saturday nights such as at Bective, Wanderers and Lansdowne where John Keogh and The Greenbeats or The Viscounts played. Everyone jived, with the odd slow one, good for a 'lurch' if you could be so lucky. Ladies Choices were a bit of an embarrassment all round. A really successful night would see you getting a 'coort' while walking her home or in the back of the car. And that was that, nothing more – real sex hadn't been invented yet.

In Second Year – I now was 18 – we started drinking. Not much, just a couple of pints in a pub before going to the dance (there being no drink inside). This also gave a spring to your step if you were getting in over the wall. Lansdowne Road was particularly challenging: climb up, belly it under the barbed wire and jump down, followed by a dash across the pitches before reaching the anonymity of the heaving crowd in the hall. All part of the fun.

In the later student years we took to the Yerrawaddies where upwards of a couple of thousand heaving sweaty bodies would jive and bop in the Olympia Ballroom off Camden Streeton a Wednesday night. The preparation for this was usually four pints of Guinness, at a shilling and sixpence each, leaving from your orange ten-shilling note the necessary four shillings to get in, pockets now empty. Perhaps not entirely so. If things were looking good, one might venture, 'would you like a mineral?'

Strangely, it seems that none of this affected being in time for the following morning's nine o'clock lecture. It may have been different for those lads 'up from the country' living an unsupervised life in Hatch Hall or a flat, but for the likes of myself, living at home, the shadow of parents was present. There never was anything said to me at home, not even after I failed Physics after first year. A notorious Professor Nolan, seemed to delight in his high failure rate. Anyway I got it in the autumn, but it did make a mess of summer having to come home in early August to study to do the 'repeats'.

That first summer I had gone to London, where I shared a two-bedroom flat in Bayswater with Mick Cotter, Dave O'Riordan and Niall O'Higgins, Niall later to become a heart surgeon. As a year earlier, Mick knew it all. He had already been in London and led me around the complications of the Underground, navigating at speed. It took me a while to cop on that he was just following the colour codes of the various lines, District, Circle, Victoria and all. It was the night-shift work that made our room arrangements viable. I worked as a porter in Paddington Station by night and Fortes Cafe of The Strand by day. The money flowed in and the 'overhead' was low, particularly as I would leave Fortes at the end of shift not only well-fed but well-stocked. I surely owe Charles Forte some conscience money.

The second summer I followed the 'canning factory' trail, working a pea-vining job in Boston in Lincolnshire. It was there that the landlady, seeing me with *The Observer*, said, 'Oh, I see you have one of your Oirish newspapers'! On that job, we put in a 16 hour day piking pea stalks from lorrys onto conveyor lines. Even hiding and dossing as much as we could, you'd be whacked at shift end at six in the morning. Getting up in the afternoon, I'd have to put my hands under a tap for five minutes to straighten out my stiff fingers. Later in the summer I went to Smedleys of Peterborough, where we slept in tin 'nissen huts' on the factory site. Such convenient location was very handy for clocking in and getting back for a few hours in the scratcher. Because of the long hours, there was nil social life; only our own *craic* and the odd diversion, such as the night the police arrived, lights already out and now blazing on again. 'Anyone here know anything about stolen bananas?' Not a body stirred; most feigned sleep. You couldn't see the floor for bananas. The Geest Banana Factory down the road had had a visit from some of our 'hungry'.

On our third summer, fellow engineering classmate Sean Mullan, from Williamstown, and myself went to the States. In the airport as we left, we got our exam results and celebrated all the way over. In Idelwild Airport (now John F. Kennedy Airport), we were met by Sean's cousin Jimmy McKee, second generation from Donegal. 'Jeeze, you guys must be thirsty after your journey.' We most certainly were not, but away we went, in his big yellow Chevy convertible, to his local pub where he showed us off. Some sight! Jimmy, fan of everything Irish, put us up in his Queens apartment for two months. We worked, Sean as an elevator operator in Manhattan and myself as a general dogsbody in a Brooklyn warehouse. These were regular jobs, to use the American jargon, with normal hours. So we did have time to see around, Jimmy's world at any rate.

By September we had enough saved and took to the road on '$99, Go Anywhere' Greyhound Bus tickets. For a month around we went, north to Montreal, west to Chicago, Butte, Montana and Seattle, then south to San Francisco, Bakersfield and LA. We'd sleep in the overnight bus, stretched out in the back if we could, and wake the next morning invariably in a kippy part of the town. The bus stations all seemed to be located in Skid Row. We'd do our thing, swimming, Disneyland, whatever. In Niagara we slept in the park, the falls thundering, and were wakened in the morning by an old negro park attendant, our sleeping bags drenched with the light mist.

Going on a long one, 48 hours from LA to El Paso, Texas, I asked the guy beside me, dark-skinned, sombrero low over his eyes, what was that river next to us? Incredulously, he looked at me and said, 'Reeo Grranday'. How could anyone not know? Thousands, maybe millions had crossed it northward from Mexico, striving for a better life in the US. In New Orleans, we went jazzing and later slept by the shore of Lake Pontchartrain; the mosquitoes buzzed and bit all night. In Miami we rented an apartment for a week for seven dollars. Granted, it wasn't in a swanky part of town, but the sun shone as well there as anywhere else.

Too soon we were back in Dublin, summer gone, not a bad one at all with money in the pocket and looking forward to our Final Year in UCD. Decades later, there was to be a subsequent money bonus: the time at work that summer was included in a USA pension benefit.

The dances resumed for us, not just as attendees but now as organisers. We had started the 'Civilkems' the previous Easter of 1962 and got off to a good enough start. For years the 'Ags' had been going strong for the Agriculture Final Year students, and the 'Yerrawaddies' for the Mechanical and Electrical Engineers. We, in the Civil and Chemical Engineering classes, decided to get in on the act. Our main men were Kevin Kelly and Frank Gannon, the latter who rejoiced in visibly carrying around the pink-coloured *Financial Times*. Participation in the Civilkems was voluntary and about 30 of us, three-quarters of the total in both classes, were involved. The Four Provinces Ballroom in Harcourt Street was the venue, an inauspicious choice because of its 'tough' reputation but for us the rent was affordable. To avoid clashes with other dances we held ours on Friday nights, flogging Concession Tickets all week, passing out Complimentaries judiciously, and defacing Dublin city with fluorescent posters.

It worked. A good night would see 500 in to hear the warm-up band and then as the main event one of the big Showbands, The Miami or Capital, would jam the place giving rise to issues with Fire Officers, which the voluble Frank would deal with. We never asked.

Good money, good fun.

The lectures were now being taken much more seriously. The 'practicals' had finished, replaced by 'projects'. My team designed a bridge over the Liffey, located just downstream from the Custom House. (A real bridge has since been built there.)

After First Year the class of about seventy had divided up into Civils, Mechanical, Electrical and Chemical, there being about 30 in my choice, Civil Engineering. I fancied the perceived open air work, waving my hands about and making *big* decisions. While we still had some lectures with the others, we Civils were now a more confined technical group. In all of this there was little of Newman's 'Idea of a University', where students and staff were supposed to mingle freely, discoursing and benefitting from mutual exposure to wide-ranging ideas. Yes, there was a certain amount of discourse, but mostly in the pub!

None of this interfered with the rugby. In First Year I had played with Bective Thirds, then transferred (headhunted, I like to say) to Blackrock, where I knew more people. Sad to say, there I made it only on to the Third As, but it didn't matter. Training was on Tuesdays and Thursdays, matches on Saturdays, either at home in Stradbrook or away in Lansdowne, Terenure, Clontarf or wherever.

My athletics had more or less finished after First Year when I had been UCD Novice Champion, not by reason of much talent or brilliance but because of my wide spread of events.

For all of this my transport was a motorbike, a Francis Barnett 150 cc. Coming home from London, after that first summer away, I had bought a second-hand Royal Enfield 350cc, a beauty, with the exhaust roar of a tiger. My parents were not at all impressed and much concerned for my safety, so this was changed to the demure little new 150 cc job, effective for getting around but certainly not a head-turner.

After Easter of 1963, with the Finals looming, all else was dropped. It was Structures, Foundations, Soil Mechanics, Sanitation and finishing our Bridge Project. With a little help from an *aide memoire* written minutely on the hidden side of the slide rule, I got on well, getting a 2.1 Honours Degree.

The Civilkem Accounts had given us a healthy return, prompting a continental trip for Sean, Kevin Kelly, Diarmuid Gallagher and myself. Diarmuid's mother loaned us her car, a small Daf, into which we just about fitted. From Bonn, in Germany, we drove southwards passing the grassy meadows of Austria and over the Alps. The road through Yugoslavia was cobbled as we rattled south, barely another car to be seen, only the odd horse-drawn wagon. Tito's country seemed decades behind northern Europe, although in Belgrade the trams and coffee shops were busy enough. Blithely unaware of the history of the Balkans and its fragmented ethnic peoples, we continued southwards, staying in basic resthouses.

Greece was our destination, beaches and ancient monuments, retsina and ouzo, our drachmas going a long way. At this time mass tourism had not yet begun in Greece. It was uncrowded and friendly. Each night we would seek out a beach to sleep on, some were good, some gorgeous and some were slimy oil-covered docks. It was only towards the end of our time there that we learned we were using the wrong word for *beach*. We had all the time been using the Greek word for *harbour*!

Kevin played chess with bearded Greek Orthodox priests. We saw sponge divers going down, watched barelegged men loading old timber boats, carrying heavy sacks of grain up springy single planks – almost biblical. We ran round the ancient stadium of Olympia and strolled through the Parthenon of Athens. We ate bread, cheese and fruit by day and concoctions of God-knows-what by night, selected by pointing at the bubbling pots in the tavernas. It truly was idyllic.

We took the ferry over to Bari in Italy. There the mysteries of the *coberto* were a cause of some unpleasantness in our first restaurant. Not shown on the menu pricing, we refused to pay this cover charge, or at least Sean and I did. Amid threats of *politzia* we scampered. I think that Kevin and Diarmuid may have paid for us all for a quiet life.

In Switzerland it rained; time to get home and into the world of work.

3

First Job, First Boat

For engineers, or anyone else, the employment prospects in the Ireland of 1963 were not great. Industry was limited and the 'boat to England' was the common outlet. For newly graduated civil engineers, work in Ireland just might be had with one of the contractors, who built things, or one of the consulting engineers, who designed them. There were also the semi-state companies, like Bord na Móna and the ESB, or the county councils; an unexciting prospect it seemed. Career guidance in UCD had been virtually nil. One's choice, or indeed one's suitability, for a particular type of work was a matter of personal perception, largely uninformed. My father was apologetic in that, from his civil service background, he could offer little advice. I wanted to go into construction, but the conventional wisdom seemed to be that one should first get a couple of years' design experience.

I sent applications to Dublin consulting engineers such as Tommy Garland, who had lectured us in UCD and said that newly graduated engineers were worth *minus* 200 pounds a year, to Jock Harbison of Ove Arup, who didn't reply, and to Nicholas O'Dwyer, who took me on.

Paddy Mehigan interviewed me in their office at 6 Burlington Road. He seemed to be a straightforward, pleasant man and so he proved to be. My Dad was able to tell me, approvingly, that Paddy Mehigan's father had written extensively under the pen name 'Carberry', a good Corkman. I was placed under Kerry O'Mahony to design work on Flesk Bridge in Killarney, then under construction.

17

This was a state-of-the-art prestressed concrete bridge, similar to what my Final Year Project had been. 'Deflection calculations' were required before a very important part of the construction could be undertaken. I beavered away for a month or so, thinking that on the result of my efforts would depend not only the progress of the bridge works, its structural success or failure, but my whole career. As I approached my 'grand finale', O'Mahony casually remarked that the contractor had gone ahead with the prestressing and deflection and all was fine. What price my efforts? Nonetheless, at Christmas I got a rise to £550 a year, up 10 per cent.

It was in Neary's pub off Grafton Street, on Christmas Eve, the pints flowing and crowded good cheer abounding, that Kevin Cronin remarked, 'Wouldn't it be grand to have a little boat?' Buoyed by my new wealth, I went on the search, concluding a couple of months later in Clontarf. There, Ted Chandler showed me his varnished-timber IDRA 14, named *Delos II*, and the many trophies he had won with her. She was a 14-foot timber sailing dinghy and became mine for a 117 pounds and ten shillings, with rudder, centreboard, tiller, shrouds, halyards, mainsail, jib and oars – the oars being the only part I knew the 'what-for'. Through the late spring, with advice from seasoned sailor Ian Cotton, boyfriend of Micheal Considine's sister, I got it all assembled at home in Booterstown.

Socially, the pubs were central to our lives, with the folk scene just beginning, in quiet corners, and the Dubliners and The Clancy Brothers were emerging. Apart from the usual club dances there would be the odd Dress Dance. Monkey suit (hired), chocolates for The Lady, who was collected from her home of course, and then it would be off to The Gresham, Hibernian or Shelbourne Hotel, until an early morning return. At some stage Kevin started 'going out' with Suzanne, whereby we 'lost' a good man on our Saturday night escapades.

In the meantime, at work I had designed the steelwork of the steeple for the new church in Newtown Park Avenue. 'Very refined indeed,' commented my boss, who then promptly doubled the size of its component members.

Doing concrete structures, again by the book, I learned about the concept of 'good practise', whereby one's finely calculated design was invariably upsized. This, I later learned, was not just 'to be safe, to be safe' but to add to fee income, usually a percentage of construction cost.

With my enthusiasm undiminished, monthly I bought and read the British *Proceedings of the Institution of Civil Engineers,* describing the latest advances and works in the profession.

Nicholas O'Dwyer had a strong water-supply arm, being dominant in certain counties, Tipperary being one. The design of these required a survey of pipeline routes, usually starting in the high-ground mountain catchment areas, down to reservoirs and then along roads. Much of the summer of 1964 I spent surveying these routes in the foothills of the Galtee Mountains, the Glen of Aherlow and the pleasant uncrowded roads of Tipperary. I would be the 'brains' with a levelling instrument set up on a tripod and a field notebook, while my chainman (who probably knew more than I did) would carry and place the staff on salient locations for me to sight on and note its readings. Later I would do the sums 'reducing' the levels for later plotting on a drawing.

As with most county council work, the pay was poor, but the mileage expenses were good. I used my Dad's Fiat 124. In addition there was a good Subsistence Rate for nights spent away. As I often camped, after leaving my chainman at his lodgings, this was especially beneficial. Before collecting him the next morning I would make sure to brush away any loose grass from my clothes.

The new dinghy, now freshly varnished, had been 'put to sea' down in Dun Laoghaire's Coal Harbour, with Sean being the main crewman – the blind leading the blind.

One fine day in May the wind blew fresh from the west as rugby player Ronan Wilmot and myself sailed out of the Harbour. Neither of us had a clue about sailing. Nonetheless we were bound for Dalkey Island, a couple of miles downwind. In no time at all we had passed the Forty-Foot, Bulloch Harbour, and Coliemore

Harbour. Then we were there, at Dalkey; now we only had to make the journey back.

Well, that was some epic. The tide had turned, though we didn't know it. The wind rose, the waves washed into the boat, the sails flapped, ropes got tangled. Later I learned that there are no 'ropes' in a boat, only lines, sheets, halyards, painters and endless others. Blown first 'to sea', just Dublin Bay actually, then back into Scotsman's Bay, we were scraping the outside of the East Pier and bucketing water out of the boat with bystanders shouting unhelpfully. Completely wet through, ignominiously, we made it back into the Coal Harbour, from where we had begun.

Both of us much chastened, Ronan said 'enough's enough' and never sailed again. And that might have been 'it' for me too, but it wasn't.

Sean and myself persevered, wet and joyful, the 'gates of hell' being a particular test. This is the gap where the Coal Harbour exits into the main harbour and the wind swirls in all directions. Gradually we got the hang of that and the various other twists and turns of the blowing wind.

Bill Pigott of the Royal Saint George Yacht Club, the 'George', suggested we join in the racing, which was far from our minds – and our abilities. Bill, being Class Captain of the IDRA 14s, was promoting the Class and urged our participation in the Tuesday evening and Saturday racing. We did, learning as we went, both the Rules of Racing and how to make the boat go faster, and even managed to get past some other boats in our class. Additionally, I was introduced to bigger racing boats by Kerry O'Mahony from work. He occasionally took me crewing on his Mermaid class boat, out of the 'Nash', the National Yacht Club, thus widening my sailing knowledge.

After college a few of us had continued running dances. In the Top Hat Ballroom in Dun Laoghaire we once had The Clancy Brothers, *báinín* sweaters an' all, as our Intermission Act. But now that we no longer were students, those full-time in the business took a very different view of us: cancellations would occur at short notice,

Fire Officers would be less accommodating and bands would be unavailable. In other words, we were not wanted. We cut our losses and got out.

After 12 months with Nicholas O'Dwyer, I thought it time to move on, perhaps contracting in England. I went over to various interviews, generally combining them so as to get the travelling expenses 'on the double'. John Laing offered me a position, in the London area as I had requested, as some of my pals were now there. With this accepted offer 'in the bag', at £1,200 per annum, I departed from Nicholas O'Dwyer on the best of terms and with some holiday time to spend.

In Cologne *Jugendherberge*, a youth hostel, an American asked me to drive his Volkswagen to Berlin for him. This was through East Germany and he couldn't do that as he had to fly over that Cold War no-go area. Not a bother on me. I had a grand drive on the autobahn, petrol paid for, not a worry on what might be behind this, no thinking of 'beware Greeks bearing gifts'. As arranged we met on the Kurfusdendamm in West Berlin and he got his car back. The Berlin Wall divided the Russian side of the city from the Western side. I walked for a look around some of East Berlin, going through the Wall at Checkpoint Charlie. This certainly was a grimmer place, with jackbooted, unsmiling guards, grey buildings and hungry-looking people.

Later, back in London, I met Paddy Norris, as previously arranged, and together we flew to Gibraltar. There we hired a car, a little Austin-Healey Sprite, a two-seater convertible, no boot, but very sporty, in our eyes at any rate. A flat battery bode an inauspicious beginning, but the hire guys started it with a push and away we went, up the coast of Spain. In September 1964 tourism was only beginning and that confined to a few coastal places, like Lloret de Mar and Sitges. There we drank the free wine from the town fountains, very tasty but vile hangovers. Food and accommodation were cheap. We ate new stuff such as *paella*. Accommodation was in sparse, white-walled rooms. In one barracks we shared with Franco Youth who, uniformed, went goose-stepping around the parade ground. Near Barcelona the car's head gasket, I think it was, went. Under a tree, a kerbside mechanic fixed it. Along the shore, fishermen worked their boats, adorned with lights at night to attract the fish. Villages of single storey white chimneyless houses dotted the barren brown landscape. These are gone now, replaced by high-rise apartment and hotels. English and German are now the commonly heard languages, the local people being mostly reduced to serfdom as gardeners and cleaners.

We took our little car on the ferry across the Straits of Gibraltar to Morocco, unsure whether this was in order with our car hire providers. In Fez and Marrakesh we were surrounded by youngsters wanting to mind the car. We chose the biggest. The taste and smell of Morocco Gold we found overrated so we stuck to the beer. Returning across the Strait, through Union-jacked Gibraltar, we flew back to rainy London and work, in my case with John Laing of Mill Hill.

4

I Worked for Laing …

'We want you in Abingdon, Berkshire,' said my new boss.
'Okay,' I said, 'but I thought that my first job, where I could find my feet, was to be in London,' I replied.

'Well, it's our London Area, which extends up to Birmingham.'

This wasn't a great start to my relationship with Laing, as I felt I had been slightly 'conned'. In addition to which, Laing being a big civil engineering firm, I had somehow expected to be put to work on something of more substance than a housing site.

Nonetheless, I went the sixty miles or so to Abingdon and introduced myself to the Site Agent, Tommy Dunk. Dunk was a small, miserable man, small in stature, small in mind. He referred to me as a 'student engineer'. I was in turn introduced to the the General Foreman, Jim Davis, an altogether finer fellow, for whom I took an immediate liking, mutual I think.

The job was the site development and construction of a couple hundred houses. My function was the setting out of the roads, drainage and foundations. 'Setting out' is part of every site-engineer's experience, usually for a couple of years. In the meantime the wider experience of construction would be learned, largely by osmosis and observation.

Abingdon was then best known for its car manufacturing, about 1,200 being employed at their Morris factory. More interestingly for me, the River Thames flowed through it. For accommodation, I thought about renting a houseboat of some sort. However, the autumn mists were now setting in, down by the river in particular, making that option less attractive. I chose standard lodgings, an upstairs room in a nearby house, complete with resident landlady.

I got stuck in to the work, enjoying the activity all around. Being new to setting out made it challenging work for me, always a little uncertain. However there was great satisfaction in seeing my timber pegs in the ground, marking the pipeline runs, the road centrelines and the building foundations. The satisfaction would be doubled when, a bit later if not immediately, machines would come powering in, taking lumps out of the ground, excavating, to be followed by the placing of stone and concrete foundations or pipelaying.

Not all of the excavation was by machine. There were about thirty Polish workers who did the building foundations, hand digging with pick and shovel. They spoke no English. Apparently they had been in England since the war and had never gone home. It now was 1964, 19 years later. Maybe they had been from a part of Poland occupied by the Russians? I never did learn.

I got to know a few of the Laing guys who were working on a job in nearby Oxford. They were pleasant enough fellows, but not really my company. The Rusty Rails Folk Club, meeting on a Friday in an old railway station, was closer to my scene. I sometimes thought of doing a song, but held my silence – I didn't really have any half-decent song and anyway was unsure of whether I could make any go of it among strangers.

Many weekends I'd go up to London and stay with Paddy and Johnny Fanning. Johnny, also from Mount Merrion, was now working in advertising. Paddy had acquired a huge white Jaguar, about 15 years old and doing about the same number miles to the gallon. It didn't matter. We all chipped in as we'd take off for pints in the Bunch of Grapes and kick on to a party in some gaff or other to which we might, or might not, have been invited.

Back in Abingdon, I got a lot of post, 'more than the Prime Minister' would say Jim, engineering magazines mostly. The weather grew frosty; snow sometimes fell and stayed on the ground. With gloved fingers in the mornings, adjusting the knurled knobs of the levelling instrument was painful, more so one morning for me when it became apparent that a building excavation was out of square. The concrete had been poured and set, but the foundation formwork, all prefabricated squarely and accurately, would not fit. My mistake. Mr. Dunk would love this in his weekly Report to Mill Hill. 'The student engineer had cocked up.' Not for the last time, I was helped out by a foreman. Quietly, Jim sent the Poles for an early tea break and had a machine come over to widen the trench by about six inches, enough to take the formwork. Tea break over and no one the wiser – except the Poles of course, but they couldn't speak English, and anyway had probably well learned to keep their heads down.

I got fed up with my digs, or more specifically the landlady. She seemed to have x-ray eyes and, through the floor, could see if I had the second bar of the electric fire on. I moved in to Laing's Nissen Huts in Oxford, where the Poles stayed. No 'dreaming spires' here.

On Fridays the two bonus clerks from Mill Hill head office would arrive on site, besuited, standoffish and didn't they get sugar in their tea. On their measurements of work done would depend the bonus to be paid to the men that week. It didn't affect me, I was staff, but the obsequious tipping of the hat to these two who contributed nothing to actual work done did irritate me.

I did in fact get on well with my engineering boss from Mill Hill, though I saw little of him. In early December he offered me 'indentures'. This arrangement, tying me to Laing for some years, would have provided that I be given a wide range of experience, benefitting my career. I thanked him genuinely, but smoked my pipe on it.

I had begun thinking that England was not so great, and that I would go to some brighter place, California maybe. So before going home for Christmas I gave my notice and said my goodbyes.

5

California

My Dad had sold the dinghy for me and with some of the proceeds I got contact lens. A pity they weren't around years earlier; I might have been able to see more of what was happening in the rugby scrums while I waited out on the wing. Later it was Mayo practitioner and friend Mona McGarry who properly fixed me up with contact lens. These were wearable for many days at a time, useful on the 'big trips'.

After Christmas in Dublin, the whole family were out to the Dublin airport to see me off, Mam, Dad, Maureen, Margaret, Fred and Sheila. Fred, nine years younger, had started boarding school in Gormanstown. Sheila, five years younger, was in Booterstown Primary School. Truth be known, I hardly knew Fred or Sheila.

This for me was a more serious going-away than any before. I had no big plan, maybe two to five years away, then possibly return, or maybe not. In Los Angeles I had the name of a Limerick engineer, Mike Punch, who might give me a good 'steer', though I was set for San Francisco. I had liked it when passing through three years earlier in 1962.

It was evening when I landed in LA and put my baggage, mostly engineering manuals, into airport left-luggage. I took a bus out towards where Mike lived, but it was now too late to call. I checked the price of a motel: $10, way too much, even though I had money saved, £400, converted into dollars at three to the pound giving me $1,200. The night being fine and warm, I stretched out in my sleeping bag behind the shrubbery of a building where the street lights wouldn't keep me awake.

The next day I found a diner, ate breakfast and then bought a car. 'Everybody Rides', the sign outside the used car lot said. For $900 I was the owner of a gleaming golden behemoth of a 1959 Chevy Impala. Outside the traffic rolled by on six lanes. I pressed a button, the motor started and the canvas roof rolled up, back and down. The six-cylinder engine hummed throatily as I eased into the traffic and made my way out to visit Mike. He was aghast at where I had spent the night, fine evening or not. 'You could be dead, killed for your shoes in this town,' he said. 'And your money was in your socks!' He furthermore considered that San Francisco was an awful place, 'foggy and damp'. He gave me knowledgeable advice on the engineering scene. Mike was a senior structural designer and knew the scheme of things and the American jargon. 'Seismic' would be my big problem – the San Andreas Fault ran right through California. All new buildings had to be designed and built to withstand earthquakes, of which we in Europe knew nothing. He added a textbook on seismic issues to my baggage in the boot, sorry, the 'trunk', of my car.

Highway 101 took me northwards, passing through Steinbeck country, Salinas, the 'Lettuce Capital of the World' the billboard said.

In San Francisco I booked into the Pink Palace, a transient home for young professionals – an upmarket hostel really – and began my search for a job. The classifieds in *The San Francisco Chronicle* and *Engineering News-Record* yielded little. One helpful person drafted an ad for me: 'British engineer, will travel' – wrong on both counts!

An offer came for an airport construction job in Saygon at $1,200/ month, while the going rate was about $700. 'You mean Saigon in Vietnam. No thanks, there's a war going on over there.'

About a week later I was in business, starting with Bechtel Engineering, a huge worldwide outfit with its headquarters in San Francisco. I would be in their Earthworks Design Division. That I had a US Green Card and Social Security Number, from my student summer of 1962, made the paperwork straightforward. However three weeks or so passed and I hadn't been assigned to any specific job. Asking my boss, a big pleasant Texan, 'what's that about?' his answer was vague. So I gave a fortnight's notice.

'Waal, Pat, in that case you best go this evenin'.'

I was learning the American Way.

A few days later I started with Arthur G. McKee, a mining company. They were located a couple of blocks from downtown Market Street and had five floors, each one having 30 or 40 engineers, mechanical, electrical and process. I was put in their Civil and Structural Floor. No hangin' about here; straight away I was put to work. At the interview they had liked that I spoke good English – a lot of their Asian employees didn't – and that I looked 'clean', whatever that meant. They knew of UCD and also had telephoned Paddy Mehigan, back in Dublin.

In the Pink Palace I had met a few people, none I really took to, but you make do the best you can. This one I took out 'to somewhere there was music'. In the Impala, we pulled up outside some nightclub. A suited attendant appeared saying, 'Park your car, sir?' Mother of God, I had only seen this in the movies. Anyway, little choice now so out I got and skipped up to the club door. No sign of your wan, until eventually she appeared. 'What kept you?' says I. She had been waiting for me to come around and open the car door for her. Not a great start. And the music wasn't terrific either.

A week later, my musical requirements now being better defined, as was my pocket, I was directed to The Drinking Gourd, on 49th Street. Ah yes, this was more like it. Beer in glasses or jugs, and you could stand around or sit and listen to the folk singers. One of these was Irishman Dave Spence, who played Friday nights. His songs were of the Mother Macree type, somewhat Stage Irish, but pleasant nonetheless. He had a voice which was easy to listen to, a nice line of stage chat and was a good guitar player. He would ask for requests. Once I made a particular request. He didn't know it, but asked would I do it. 'Certainly,' says I – must have had a few beers in me. I hopped up on the stage beside him and sang away while he accompanied me on guitar. The crowd stamped and asked for more – they too must have had a few drinks – and subsequently Dave and I became good friends.

Dave was a schoolteacher, living with his American wife Joanne in Los Gatos, some 30 miles down the peninsula. From Newtown-abbey outside of Belfast, he had been out here for four or five years. They owned their house, had a baby, Aran, and were well settled. He loved singing of all sorts, as did Joanne who also sang and played banjo. Friends used to meet in their house for music and song. Dave used to say, 'an ounce of what you do yourself is worth a ton of radio or records'. I probably introduced him to the existence of The Dubliners and the Clancy Brothers, opening up a new world of Irish music for him. He encouraged me to buy a guitar and taught me how to play. I became a regular for one or two songs with him in The Drinking Gourd, doing 'Dick Darby', the 'Lousehouse of Kilkenny' or others from home.

I heard of a farmhouse for rent, $100/month, over in Marin County. Across the Golden Gate Bridge and a few miles northward, behind the village of Sausalito, I turned off and into the hills. The tarmac gave way to a dirt road. Going up Tennessee Valley, with eucalyptus trees and a dusty road, there were a few other houses, some occupied, some not. It had been a long time since any farming was done here. But the object of inspection was fine – timber frame and clapboard, three or four dusty rooms, some furniture, a kitchen of sorts, running water and electric lights. What more could you want! (Since 1972 Tennessee Valley has been incorporated into the Golden Gate National Recreation Area.)

I had in the meantime enrolled in UC Berkeley for a night course in Economics. It wasn't that I had any great interest in the subject, but Berkeley at that time had quite a *cachet* to it and this was a way, a couple of nights a week, of getting into it. Samuelson's book on economics was our bible to which we in the class of about twenty applied ourselves. I stuck with it until the summer evenings grew longer, did the exam, got a medium grade and promptly forgot it all.

Through Dave Spence I met Mark Dowley from Blackrock, County Louth. Like Dave, he was about four years my elder and was probably in the USA for good. Mark, also living 'down the peninsula', had a Ph.D, worked for IBM and was 'trying to find out how the human brain worked'. If IBM could do that, he said, they'd be able to make computers. More relevant to myself, Mark was a keen outdoorsman, skier, trekker and budding sailor. He and his friends took me skiing which I enjoyed so I bought some gear. Weekends we would do the three hour drive, through Sacramento, to the Sierra Nevadas, where we'd ski Heavenly Meadows, Tahoe or Squaw Valley, returning whacked and with faces sunburnt for work on Monday. There would be women with us too, Aer Lingus hostesses and some others who the lads knew. No hanky-panky though, as far as I knew anyway. I took greatly to the skiing, initially falling all over the place. Having recently been playing rugby, hitting the ground was no problem. At least in skiing there was no one rooting at you. Up you'd go and schuus away down the hill.

Mark had bought a sailboat, a two-man Mercury class keel boat, which he had in Richmond on the northeast of San Francisco Bay. Crewing for Mark, I taught him all I knew, which can't have been that much. Nonetheless we started moving up the racing fleet. He would have done that anyway – he wasn't one for 'sucking the hind tit', as he put it, in anything he did. The racing would take us around the Bay, south to Oakland and across to Sausalito on the northwest side. San Francisco Bay is a breezy place, making for bracing sailing, and the water is cold. There's a current that comes in with the tide, cooling the air and causing the famous fog. The tides sweep under the Golden Gate Bridge and around the island of Alcatraz. Rarely do sailboats venture out westward under the bridge.

One day, after racing at the Richmond Yacht Club, I ran into my previous boss, the Texan. 'Waal, Pat, how's it goin'? Friendly as you like and genuinely wondering how I'd been. Not a bother on him, confident, able-bodied, able-minded, this was his America and becoming mine too.

It's because of that cold temperature of the seawater that swimming was never a feature of my time there, even though a walk a mile or so over the hill from where I lived in Tennessee Valley would take you to the coast. With Mark and his friends, though, we did do plenty of walking. With the snow gone and skiing over, we'd do hiking weekends in the Sierras on the John Muir Trail in Yosemite. Smell of pine needles, sunlight through the trees, shorts and tee shirts, cooking steak over campfires.

I was enjoying the work, designing tailings ponds, headshafts, conveyors and the various paraphernalia necessary for tearing out the bowels of the earth and extracting the ore. In the beginning, mindful of my earlier lessons in never under-designing, I came in for some criticism. 'This stuff doesn't have to last forever, ya know, Pat, just fifteen years is the average lifespan of these mines.' However, the structures better not fail, particularly if you're still working there. It was this dilemma, the balance between cost and stability, that made the work hard going for the older engineers with mortgages and families. Indeed, some were having part of their salaries 'garnished', I think, because of court judgements relating to alimony, credit failure or previous business problems. This is 'no country for old men', as W.B. Yeats had put it.

Of automobiles, I now was on my third.

The Chevy was great for the few months it lasted, heavy on petrol, but that didn't matter at thirty cents a gallon. It ran along fine, until one day it didn't. Being an 'automatic' it couldn't be towed and had to be lifted from the side of the highway. Death of the engine was the pronouncement, banjaxed, I forget the details. Goodbye Chevy.

The guy who sold me the '50 Ford' – that's 1950, 16 years old – said it was a 'four on the floor' gearbox. Could I manage that? Sure I could, wasn't I brought up on 'manual'? For a hundred dollars I drove it away, a 'holding job' until I could get more organised.

Next I bought a red TR3, a Triumph sports car, open top, two-seater. 'That's more like it,' said a pal living nearby in San Rafael, who suggested I should buy a nice sheepskin jacket to look the part. No way.

That should have carried me through for years to come. However, one Friday night, after I had been to a wedding, I drove down to The Gourd, misjudged a turn and walloped the sides of a couple of parked cars. The police were very nice about it – nobody else was hurt and I just got a few scratches myself. The TR, however, was a write-off. In the breakers yard, I retrieved my guitar from the trunk. The insurance was good, paid for the damage to the others and a good price for my own. In the subsequent court case I was charged with 'driving over the safe speed' and had my knuckles rapped. That was all.

Happily, I had kept the Ford and, with recharged battery, was mobile again, if not very elegantly.

That spring, Dave was killed. With two friends, he had built a gyrocopter, something like a helicopter, driven by a Volkswagen engine. I wasn't there when it happened but they were at an early stage of flying trials. The rotor appears to have struck the fuselage and down it plummeted, about 50 feet, onto the runway. We were all devastated and Joanne, now a widow, was left to mourn.

That was 1966. I had been in California for a year and a half and was enjoying it. However there were some dark clouds looming. The Vietnam War was going on with Lyndon Johnson trying to combat the spread of communism in southeast Asia. The draft was sucking into the army young men from all over the States. This apparently applied to all, whether one was a citizen or not. If drafted, one was just lumped, a 'private', into bootcamp and onward. I considered enlisting in the Army Corps of Engineers, which would give me 'officer status' and satisfying work, plus a fast track to citizenship. I also looked at going over the Canadian border to Vancouver. And of course out in Tennessee Valley they might never find me!

But they did. I got a letter enquiring as to why I hadn't 'signed on', a mandatory prerequisite. I heard bugles blowing in my ears. Time to 'get out of Dodge City'.

In June of 1965, the insurance money from the crashed TR3 in my pocket, I came back to Dublin, two wedding invitations awaiting.

6

Civil Engineering with Ascon

The first wedding, and that which set the timing of my return to Dublin in June of 1966, was that of Kevin Cronin and Suzanne. They were the first of our lot to be married, so yes, this was a very big thing. It also was, for me, a fine way to meet the lads with whom I had been out of touch for a year and a half. Kevin was by now a fully Chartered Accountant and they were heading for a few years to Sacramento. We could have almost passed each other on the way, me coming, them going.

The other wedding was that of my first cousin Joan Ganter to John R. Sisk, of the building family. Chatting at that wedding to one of the older building guys, it seemed to him that by personality the building/contracting game would suit me. However I was in no great hurry to get working; the Irish summer lay ahead.

Making contact with Mick Cotter, together we bought a '505' sailing dinghy, a flyer. Mick had a car, a nice sporty one as usual for him. He'd always managed to have a car, even back in college days, when we'd all chip in our half-crowns for petrol. Through the summer of 1966 we towed and sailed that boat all over the place, racing and cruising. Yes, cruising. We sailed her from Carraroe, in Connemara, out to Kilronan in Aran, and cruised about there for a week, Mick Considine having brought out our camping gear on a Galway Hooker bringing turf across. I didn't know it then, but the Galway Hookers were later to play a major part in my life.

The 'folk singing' scene was now very much in full swing. The professionals, Johnny McEvoy, The Ludlows, Maeve Mulvanny and

Sweeneys Men, were household names. The Dubliners and Clancy Brothers were filling the Albert Hall in London and Carnegie Hall in New York, while back home every pub and corner would have a singer or two. With gusto I took to this, learning a song a week, songs of love such as 'The Butcher Boy' or 'Love is Teasin'' and songs of patriotism such as 'Henry Monroe' and 'The Foggy Dew'. Through singing I got to know Oliver Mulligan from Annyalla, County Monaghan, a fine performer and the best of company. Like Mick Cotter, Oliver worked in Roadstone, he as an accountant. I also met Mick Dennehy, a car enthusiast, who had to fit his six foot frame into his small racing Mini Cooper. We watched him tearing round Kirkistown in County Down and nearer home in Dunboyne. In one Dunboyne race he came a cropper, exiting through the back window. It was hard to see how anyone could fit through such a small opening but he did – and walked away.

Nearing summer's end, I started writing job applications to building firms. Responses were very few.

Our last outing was to the Rose of Tralee Festival in Kerry. Mick and I towed the dinghy, Mick Considine travelling separately. We were to meet outside Tralee Post Office at a given time. For whatever reason, that didn't happen. Mick and I, in the crowded Brandon Hotel, spied two attractive 'possibilities' and tossed for who'd go for whom. Our approach was distinctly unwelcome and getting us nowhere when Mick Considine arrived out of the blue, greeting one of the girls familiarly and introducing us all round. The one he knew was Mary Cleary, a first cousin and good friend of a work colleague of his in Sun Alliance Insurance, Kay Murphy. The other was an American. We all got on grand for the few days around Tralee and then went our separate ways, taking phone numbers – as one does.

In September I started work with Dublin Corporation, not my first choice but my only offer. They put me in their Building Bye-laws Department in Lord Edward Street.The inside of this musty place was straight out of a Charles Dickens novel, with work arrangements to match. At about ten minutes to ten, a head appeared around the timber partition. '*Tá an uisce beirithe*', water boiling, tea time coming up. It was Dick Morrissey who became a good friend and later introduced me to hill walking.

My given work was two-fold. First I was to make inspections of houses under construction, at three stages, to ensure compliance with building standards and so sign-off, following which the builder could get grant payment.The second part of my work was the 'taking-in-charge'. When housing estates were built, the Local Authority would, after the taking-in-charge, become responsible for the public services – bin collection, drainage, public lighting and pavement maintenance. The builder, naturally, would wish to get this off his hands as quickly as possible. My boss, the senior engineer, explained to me that there was this huge backlog and urged my action on this.

So I bought a few books on house construction. I already knew about drainage and road standards, from my time with Laing, and I consulted a few of the older engineers in the department. Away I then went, out to the housebuilding sites and estates being built in South Dublin, my given area. There were no problems with the 'grant inspections'. That had been jogging along in pretty good order beforehand.

But what a surprise the builders got at my following up their requests for taking-in-charge inspections. With total cooperation they met me and did any completions or repairs which were necessary, the most usual being manhole internals. After six weeks or so, early November, two things happened. First, I got a job offer from Ascon, Swimming Pool Division. Next, I presented a goodly number of taking-in-charge files back to my senior, builders' work done, all in good order. Aghast, he gave me a lecture on the significance to the Corporation of this taking-in-charge, etc, etc. and that it should not be rushed, blah, blah.

I handed in my notice to Dublin Corporation and went to work for Ascon.

In the meantime Mick had taken up with Mary Cleary, in a rather brotherly way I'd say. Mostly we'd go out, all together, Mary not quite knowing who she was supposed to be with. For a month or two, we'd go to the likes of The Brazen Head or The Auld Triangle, for the music and song. Then their interest seemed to fade, but I still kept in touch with her. She was a midwife in the Old Coombe Hospital. On Christmas Day, she was working, but off for a few hours and without a plan. She came out to dinner with my family in Booterstown. In conversation it turned out that her father and mine had been good friends in the Waterford Gaelic League. Still, there was nothing much between Mary and myself, though as the months passed that changed.

Meanwhile my work with Ascon was proving less than terrific. I was overseeing the construction of a swimming pool in Loughlinstown, a job which was not going well. Liam Donnelly, my somewhat pompous boss, was not much help, although his Dutch boss, Mr. Speekenbrick, was capable and charming to clients. In parallel, I was being sent to Northern Ireland to sell our swimming pools. There was little chance that they'd buy anything from what they called the Free State, even if I was anything of a salesman, which I wasn't. One day Speekenbrink called me in and told me I'd have to go, that I'd be better suited to consulting engineering. A couple of days later, Mr. Herlihy, the other director, called me to his office and said they had work for me in Tarbert Island, County Kerry, where Ascon had the contract for building a new electricity power station, one of the biggest civil engineering works in the country.

Miffed at being discarded by the Swimming Pool group, but pleased at the prospect of getting into some real work, albeit inconveniently located, I prepared for Kerry.

I enquired from my uncle, John Gayer, now manager of the Munster and Leinster Bank in Arklow, whether I'd be good for a loan of £300 to buy a car, a second hand Austin A40. 'There's no fool of a bank manager in Ireland who'd give you that,' he said. Nonetheless, when I went in to the Tarbert Munster and Leinster Bank, the manager said, 'we'd be glad to give you £300 on the security of the car, and if you want it, a further £300 on your own good name'.

What a difference. I took the price of the car, a nice green Estate model.

When I crossed the causeway to the site of the power station on Tarbert Island, my new Ascon senior, Liam Bohane, had welcomed me with a direct query: 'How much are they paying you?'

'Twelve hundred,' I said. Much later he told me that he was afraid that I was getting more then he was. Our site agent, Liam's boss, was an unsmiling Dutchman, Rudi Koppen. Ascon were 50 per cent Dutch-owned and 50 per cent Irish-owned by Sisk.

About 12 years earlier, Sisk had been building Wexford Bridge and were in technical trouble; six months into the job and not a pile driven. They sought help from a Dutch firm and successfully completed the job. So well did they get on that they formally joined together and set up as Ascon Ltd.

I was introduced to Gerald Lenihan, Ascon's general foreman, who was heading up the 200 men working for us. Gerald was a grand man, open and friendly. I didn't know it then, but he had been a county footballer. Years later his son Donal played rugby for Ireland. Derek Edge was the other site engineer with me, both of us reporting to Liam. Immediately I felt that this was a good place.

The first fortnight I stayed in the Listowel Arms Hotel, Ascon paying, while I looked around. One fine evening I parked and strolled into a pub. Two men stroked their pints in silence.

'Pint of Guinness,' says I. Long silence.

'Are oo working on the Island boy?'

'I am,' says I. More silence.

'Do oo have a trade boy?'

I paused, and said, 'I do.' More silence.

'Do oo have a car boy?'

The A40 was parked outside so hard to deny it. 'I do.' Long silence.

Then, 'Ood be a great catch boy.' We all burst out laughing. North Kerry wit, laconic and tightly phrased, was enjoyable, once the accent was deciphered.

I rented a cottage half a mile outside Tarbert, one of an attached pair, fairly basic, two rooms with an outside dry toilet. When I told Mary back in Dublin, she gave me a present of a dressing gown 'for outside'. We were now going strong together, my transfer to Kerry being disruptive of that.

In McKennas' of Listowel I bought a bed, a double, a tenner I think it cost. As I was loading it onto the roof of the car I asked whether there was any guarantee going with it. 'Are oo expecting a lot of traffic over it boy?'

The construction of this three-year project had begun a few months earlier and now was approaching full swing. Machines and men tore into it, digging, shuttering, pouring concrete. Vermaat, a big Dutchman, was heading the pile driving; Kavanagh from Wicklow, another big guy, was doing the steelfixing on sub-contract. I tried to hide my surprise, embarrassment perhaps, at recognising one of his men, below in a deep foundation, brown rust covered, who had been boarding in school with me.

I was put to setting-out. Mr Herlihy had said to me that, as a junior, I could learn a lot; the men would talk more openly to you now than later. I sat in on the weekly meetings, where Koppen would lay out the work programme ahead, Liam would organise it and Gerald would agree, or not, on whether it could be done or what was necessary for him to make it happen.

There also was production control, measuring work output and comparing it with The Estimate. Everyone was here for one reason, The Money – the men for the wages, the company for the profit. No getting away from that.

Most weekends I travelled back to Dublin, met Mary and the lads, and sailed with Mick out of the George Yacht Club where we kept the 'Five Oh'. Leaving Booterstown in the A40 on Monday morning at 6.00 am, the first traffic light I'd meet would be in Limerick. Then onward, without hindrance, I'd drive through Askeaton, Foynes and Glin in time to join in for the 10.00 o'clock tea and then get out to work.

Builders' holidays were the first fortnight of August. I managed to swing an extra week. Mick and I chartered a Folkboat out of Kinsale, together with Oliver Mulligan and big Gerry Casey, a fair load for this 25-foot boat which we considered huge. She was charted for West Cork, out to Mizen Head. Surreptitiously we slipped aboard another couple of charts for further up the west coast. I knew nothing about the cruising end of sailing; Mick knew little more. His father had a share in *Estelle*, a Dublin Bay 21, on which Mick had occasionally sailed, and more recently on their *Tryphena*, a magnificent thirty-eight-footer.

Our chartered boat did have a small petrol engine, useful for getting in and out of places, but not having much 'push' otherwise. We sailed all day, westward around the Old Head of Kinsale, past Courtmacsherry Bay, Seven Heads, and past Galley Head (mind the Dhulic Rock, our green *Sailing Directions* book said), pencilling them off on the chart as we went. Anchored in Glandore that evening, we felt that we had sailed the wide world. Next day we again beat to windward, around the Fastnet Rock, taking turns sitting on the bouncing bow of the boat, in sunshine and spray, and finishing in Crookhaven. Rounding the Mizen, we felt the strength of the Atlantic Ocean surging beneath us, sometimes over our deck, but we were used to being thoroughly wet when sailing dinghies so regarded this as normal. There was a 'reefing handle' to reduce mainsail area, but we didn't think to use it. 'More wind, more speed' was our call – wrongly, as we later learned.

I've since sailed that Irish southwestcoast many times, but neverhave I such vivid memories as those on that passage; the long ocean swells, between which our boat would drop below the horizon, the foaming seas running blue on our sidedecks, the four of us jammed on the high side of the cockpit, feet braced on the far side, the Walker Log astern spinning off the miles, the taking of compass bearings on O'Brien's Castle and their plot on the chart as we neared our destination. Our *ultima thule*, Kilronan on Aran, saw the four of us up in the dispensary being treated for burns and salt sores.

Later, big Gerry, never one for understatement, stood stripped to the waist on the pier and scrubbed the salt out of his shirt.

In Bríd Ní Dhálaigh's thatched, low-ceilinged pub, a local asked 'who's that with the scale of the bream in his eye?' With his sharp vision from the side he could see my contact lenses. We made friends with the Mullans from Kilronan, Pat and younger brother Peter. Mary came out on the *Naomh Éinne* ferry a day or two later. We sailed over to nearby Inis Meáin, where her friend Mary Kennedy was newly appointed district nurse. Too soon, in our chartered boat, we turned southward.

I was irretrievably hooked on cruising.

7

Married to Mary

In September 1967 Mary and I got engaged. She now was a midwife in Mount Carmel Hospital in Rathgar. Gladly for me, chocolates from grateful new mammies were invariably waiting when I'd arrive up from Kerry on a Friday evening. More usefully, I now had the benefit of a new company car, reliable mobility thus assured.

Koppen had moved on from the Tarbert Power Station works. Liam Bohane was now agent in charge and I moved upwards in the scheme of things. That was despite a clanger I had dropped, which only Gerald Lenihan and myself were privy to (as far as I knew). As the reservoir we had built was being filled with water, it became evident that there was something amiss at the upper level. This reservoir was the size of a football pitch, so any error was no small matter. I had made a mistake, of some inches, in the level of a stepped wall topping the reservoir. Gawd, this would be evident to all, forever, not affecting the functioning but looking awful. Quietly, Gerald got the overflow weir raised, then continued filling with water, thus hiding my mistake. Forever it remains, but invisible. Liam had long before said to me that 'an engineer is only as good as his general foreman'.

By now I was having much more contact with the clients, the ESB (Electricity Supply Board). Mr. Herlihy had said to me that 'you'll meet all sorts – and have to get on with them all'.

Mary and I were married the following March. 'Best men' were Mick and my brother Fred, with a great turn out of friends and relations. Our honeymoon was spent skiing in the Cairngorms, my preference; Mary would have preferred Paris! Back in Kerry, we moved into a rented house in Ballybunion, adjacent to one rented by an ESB electrical engineer, Hebor McMahon, whose wife Mary quickly became good friends with Mary Barry.

Our rented farmhouse was plagued with mice, traps and poison notwithstanding. But we found the answer: a milk bottle, laid on its side, cheese lump bait within and a half cup of water. The furry fellow would go in after the cheese, but with wet feet couldn't get out of the sloping bottle. Grab the bottle, take it down the field; and sling the craytur out.

That summer we chartered a thirty-foot Kingfisher class yacht out of Lymington in the south of England, five of us lads and Mary, bound across the English Channel for Normandy and the Channel

Mary and Paddy in Ballybunion, July 1968

Isles. The seasickness never diminished for Mary, but gamely she stayed with it. The boat was not great either, the front window being stove in, in a breaking sea off Cap de la Hague.

In September I began building a *Yachting Monthly* Eventide, a 24-foot plywood boat. In Johnny Walshe's shed in Ballylongford, shipwright Joe Culhane and I worked four nights a week and Saturdays. We launched the following Whit, a crowd of friends rolling her down the main street and into the River Saleen, after which I named her, though using the Irish version *Sáilín*. Proud though I was, she was a terrible design, boxy, bilge-keeled and a poor sailor. Her four HP engine, ex-concrete mixer, was of little help. Nonetheless, up and down the Shannon I went, culminating in a holiday time cruise up to Aran where we got hammered in an easterly gale. 'Never again,' said Mary, understandably.

On July 4, 1969, Cathal was born and family life began, nappies and night-time waking, though I played little part of that – woman's work! Liam Bohane had moved on and I was in charge of Ascon's last year on the Tarbert job, learning and doing final accounts, with the associated claims for major extra costs and client delays.

The following year Caoimhe was born. I was transferred to Dublin to work on the construction of Poolbeg Power Station, another big ESB job. I asked Pat Herlihy where I should buy a house. Very reasonably he said that he wasn't going to tell me that, but would tell me where most of Ascon's work was – on a line from Cork to Dublin, generally.

For a house, Mary and I searched the coastal areas between Skerries and Wicklow. In Monkstown, I came across a possibility. It was empty and with ground floor windows boarded up and overgrown gardens. Beneath all that it was of good quality and well located. Going into the auction, I almost turned back, seeing the well-dressed competition. One cavalry twilled gent carried a silver topped cane. In fact, they were only the curious neighbours. I got it

Launch of Eventide, which I had built, in Saleen River, Ballylongford.
Mick Cotter and Paddy.

for £7,050 – 21 Belgrave Road, Monkstown was ours. I rang Mary, still in Kerry, to tell her the great news. We had a solid red-brick semi, built in the thirties, a bit dated certainly but with a big garden, a garage out on to the back lane and Seapoint shore only a couple of hundred yards away.

The Poolbeg Power Station job wasn't nearly such a happy place as Tarbert had been. Industrial unrest beset the country in those early 1970s. We had a strike a month, 'all out', usually over trifling matters. Our own general foreman, a cunning, self-serving man, was little help. Our sequence of management was the same as that of Tarbert, where I followed Koppen and Liam Bohane on the now familiar ground. Our contract this time included the foundations for the massive chimneys, which still dominate the Dublin skyline and which my kids referred to as 'Daddy's Chimneys'.

There was some delay in processing the paperwork on the house, as the previous owner was in state care – an Executor's Sale, I was told. Impatiently, I proceeded with demolition of the old scullery and external coalhouse and toilet in preparation for my new kitchen build. I towed the Eventide on a trailer to Dublin and knocked the rear garden wall onto the lane behind the house to enable bringing the boat into the garden.

However, around now, Mammy's cancer had returned and gradually she had gone downhill, losing the fight in Saint Micheals Hospital, Dun Laoghaire on April 11, 1970.

Mick and I continued sailing the Five Oh. Dave O'Neill began sailing the Eventide with me in the Irish Sea and around to Dunmore East. The house needed doing up and our two youngsters were healthily robust and demanding. Mary and Mary McMahon, with her youngsters, got a particularly good swapping thing going with the kids, allowing them both the freedom to go on holidays. Mary did this also with her sister Anne in Waterford. We didn't have a lot of money, but we had energy and made the time to enjoy it.

We had been looking for a holiday place in West Cork. With the benefit of the company car, Mary and I drove hither and thither, down country lanes to shoresides, up the sides of mountains, even looking out towards Heir Island. There was nothing to be had for our budget so we gave up the quest.

For some years there had been a lovely old timber boat, the Galway Hooker *Saint Patrick*, at Goleen pier in West Cork. Sadly, she seemed to be becoming more decrepit each time I saw her. It was Mary who suggested that since we couldn't get a cottage that I should try to buy her. For comparative purposes, I looked also at another Hooker which was for sale, *Lady Mór*, in Shruthán, Connemara, which had the benefit of being in sailing commission.

At this time I had left the Eventide on a mooring in Dunmore East in the care of one Victor Cobden, who did some chandlery and boat-minding. And there she was lost. He had moved the boat to another mooring from whence it blew off and was totally wrecked. I never did get a convincing account of matters from him but she was insured and I was reimbursed, eventually.

Concurrent with this, my work on Poolbeg Power Station was completed and I was to begin construction of Dillon Bridge in Carrick on Suir, Tipperary. The firm at the same time were awarded a harbour job at Rossaveel in Connemara, onto which Liam Bohane, now living in Cork, was to go. Liam and I agreed a swap, he for geographical reasons and myself because Rossaveel lay in the heart of Galway Hooker country, to which proposal our boss, Herlihy, agreed.

Mary and I, now with a third, Muireann, rented a house in Cashla near Rossaveel. For a year and a half I struggled with this harbour construction job. Little went well. Our dredger, a relatively small machine, bought for work on the sheltered River Shannon, sank not once but twice. Rock blasting proved difficult. Our client, the Office of Public Works, was unhelpful. And the company had underpriced the job because we needed the work. However troublesome matters were, we did get it progressed. At the three-quarter stage of Rossaveel, the company succeeded in winning a major contract for Platin Cement Works in County Meath, a joint venture with John Paul Construction. On to this I was transferred.

Platin was a three-year job because of its size and needed two construction firms to handle it. John Paul was to be the lead partner, whose John Simmington would head the consortium, myself coming next as contract manager and Donal O'Brien of John Paul as construction manager. Each firm then contributed engineers, foremen and machinery as required.

This was, by and large, a happy job, the principal problem area for us being demands by the men for more money, before and during the 'slipforming' of the many concrete storage silos. This form of construction, requiring much planning and preparation, is cost efficient and fast. However it does require continuous, round the clock working. Special pay rates for the operatives are normal and agreed in advance. However the 'bucks' from Meath, steelfixers from Slane in particular, chose to raise the ante while the 'slide' was in progress. This resulted in sleepless nights and difficult times, technically and financially. That period the exception, Platin was a satisfying and happy job.

Daily I would drive to Platin from Monkstown, taking about an hour in the morning, the return in the evening taking somewhat longer. Each summer, the firm would pay for a month's renting of a house nearby, at Bettystown beach, to give me a break from the driving. The kids grew brown as berries.

We got on well with the people of the client, Cement Roadstone, and their engineers Steve Malone and Frank Coffey. Frank's father, as county engineer in Kilkenny, had been a friend of my own father while he was a tax inspector stationed there in the late 1930s. As they say, 'small world'. Steve Malone was our 'opposite number' and older than John Simmington and myself. He had spent years in Burma or somewhere that the 'big whiteman' still reigned unchallenged. Steve was sometimes displeased by our limited respect for his supervising position – all in good clean 'playing of the game'.

That, all in all, was a happy and fruitful job, successfully completed by the close of 1977. What next? I had in the meantime found and bought that holiday cottage, of which more later.

Construction work in Ireland, indeed commercial activity in general, was at a low ebb. Through its parent company Sisk's contacts in Africa, Ascon had tendered for a harbour job in Malawi. And to the surprise of the World Bank, the competing established contractors there and ourselves back in Dublin, it was awarded to us in Ascon. Somewhat to the surprise of Pat Herlihy – we now had four kids, Bairbre having being born in May of 1977 – I volunteered, indeed I requested, to go out to that job.

8

The Galway Hooker *Saint Patrick*

It was about seven on a bright summer morning in 1966 as, out of Greatman's Bay in Connemara, we drifted slowly seawards, bound for Aran. The morning breeze had not yet stirred as the sails of our dinghy barely filled. Then from behind a headland emerged, first a black triangle, then a massive, high-peaked mainsail, overlaying the black hull of a turf-laden Galway Hooker. Slowly she overtook us, working the inshore eddy of the tide, as only a master *bádóir* would know.

For years that memory had stayed, tucked away somewhere in my head, until in Goleen, West Cork, it again was resurrected. Now I beheld nothing so elegant, merely the worn out hull and spars of a boat that had seen better days. Her blocks and rigging were unkempt, her deck and cabin wore a blotched mantle of green verdigris. As she lay against the pier, the tide would partly fill and later empty her, altogether a forlorn sight. Nonetheless, her pedigree showed through, the beauty of her shapely hull, the strength of her framing, the elegance of her mast, bowsprit, boom and gaff spars.

On earlier visits to this pleasant backwater harbour, I had merely looked at this vessel curiously, as with each viewing she seemed more decrepit, with perhaps a heron standing mutely on the far shore. Now, summer 1973, I had decided that I wanted to buy her, to fix her up and to get her sailing, maybe even in the image of that Hooker I had seen in 1966. Her owner, I had ascertained, was Jim O'Meara, a local man teaching in Belfast. He had bought her in Galway a few years earlier, sailed her to nearby Crookhaven, but done little with her, her engine being unreliable and her sails being quite a handful. In looking for a cottage in the area and general mooching around, I had got to know a few people, including the Goleen postmaster. One evening in Dublin I got a phone call from him. 'I think she might be sold. Jim went out to Cape Clear last week, on his honeymoon, and only took his other smaller boat.' And he gave me his Belfast phone number. (These were the days of the wind-up telephone where the post office would put you through, and of course knew every detail of the village and parish around.)

Jim and I spoke on the phone and agreed the deal, or so I thought, arranging to meet a week later in the Ballymascanlon Hotel near Dundalk. There he put me through the ringer, questioning me up, down, around and about as to my intentions and my ability to carry them through. I bit my lip and didn't remark on how unwell he himself had done in that department, although, in fairness, the questioning was probably because he was aware of his own limited success and was ensuring that there wouldn't be a repeat. I wrote a cheque £650 and the boat was mine, and with her all the work, joys and sorrows that followed for the next 29 years.

At that time I was working in Rossaveel in Connemara, building the new harbour but also picking up on the lore of the Hookers, or the *Bád Mhóra*, as they called them. They didn't believe that I had the *Saint Patrick*, or *Bád Conroi*, as they sometimes called her, until one Monday morning I rolled into work, towing my trailer, on which was the massive 19-foot long rudder.

Through the winter, I drove many weekends down to Goleen and worked on the boat to patch her leaks, get her floating and to clean out her insides. The black stinking sludge was thick between her floors. I scooped it out by hand and into buckets, and brought back sails, rigging and parts for repair. I met Micheal Conroy, whose family in Rosmuc had owned her. He told me that, as a young boy in 1912, he had sat on Padraic Pearse's knee as they sailed in this, then a new boat, out to Aran. Pearse, who had a cottage in Rosmuc, was recruiting for the Irish Volunteers. The boat had been built by Pat and Joe Casey on Mweenish Island, out from Carna. A famous boatbuilding family, they had built her for themselves, launching her in 1911 and calling her *Saint Patrick*. A year later she was sold to the Conroys of Garafin, Rosmuc, who ran a substantial shop, goods for which were brought in from Galway by sea. At that time the roads were still very poor and all transport of goods was done by sea. Later she was sold to O Cathain of *An Cheathrú Rua*, Carraroe, who put her into the turf trade, carrying out to Árainn. That lasted until the mid-fifties when she was laid up and then sold in 1958 to a group of young enthusiasts in Galway, who converted her for pleasure sailing. They in turn had sold her to Jim O'Meara, a retired Captain Glanville sailing her south to Crookhaven.

On a fine fresh day in June of 1974, she lay alongside the outer pier in Goleen. Two timber railway sleepers supported her mast at deck level. Her sails of red canvas, freshly mended, were bent on. Halyards, throat and peak were rove through the blocks, ready to hoist the spars and mainsail aloft. Her jib was run out the bowsprit, ready for hoisting. The cavernous insides were empty and the ballast was covered with a few sheets of plywood, with fish boxes for storage. A little Seagull, longshaft outboard engine purred on her stern. Paddy Nolan, brother-in-law, architect, who knew nothing of the sea, only of the river as it flowed through his native Carrick on Suir, cast off the lines as I put the outboard on to full revs – and we barely moved. We were making passage to Crookhaven, about four miles distant, upwind this day. Outside we got the sails up, with great confusion and difficulty. And, hauling in sheets, we got underway. She heeled nicely to the westerly wind and moved broadly in the right direction, out towards the Fastnet. 'Ready about,' I cried. Paddy looked at me curiously. 'We're turning her round, through the eye of the wind,' I explained. After the turn, she took forever to get going and then not very much to windward. Nonetheless, we did tack and tack again until somewhere inside the Alderman Rocks she shuddered to a stop and swung, sails flapping wildly, spars swinging dangerously. We put our anchor out and then saw that our rudder had fouled the line of a string of lobster pots. An hour later, sails down in a heap, we were under tow the rest of the way up the bay to Crookhaven – an ignominious beginning.

Billie O'Sullivan, owner of the pub, offered to keep an eye on the boat and pump her for the few weeks until we would be sailing for Rossaveel. He later told me that he occasionally risked drowning outside boats, but *Saint Patrick* was the only one that he could have drowned *inside*, so much water was she taking. Several times, with crew, and pumps, I came down to sail her away, but either the pumps wouldn't start or they wouldn't prime. The summer passed, Billy pumped – and the plan changed. We'd sail her to Dublin instead. Kevin Cronin, Sean Mullan and myself set off, having a lovely sail across Roaring Water Bay and through Gascanane Sound. There things went distinctly astray as the wind veered, pushing us in towards the cliffs of Cape Clear. We got her away, and into the quay wall at Baltimore, first part of the passage completed. That night, after a happy evening in Bushes pub, we decided to engine over to Sherkin Island, the better to be ready for our departure east the following morning. We must have let the word out because when we got down to the boat, in the lights of the quay, we could see that the deck was covered with people, even some with babies. Relieved I was when we tied to the pier at Sherkin and got them off. If anything had happened!

Next day we sailed to Kinsale and ran her up onto the harbour slip. She was taking too much water. Eddie Hurley, harbour master, said that if she were any other type of boat he would have ordered her sunk at sea. Two weeks later she was lifted on to a low-loader and, over a couple of days, transported by road to Dublin. In September 1974 she was in my Monkstown back garden.

There she stood for almost five years. For the first three, while I still was in Rossaveel and later in Platin, I worked on her, replacing about a third of her frames. I cut and chiselled out old worn black frames, then replaced these with new oak, cut from planks three inches thick, curved and bevelled to follow the inside of the planking. Externally, nothing changed until a couple of months before leaving for Malawi, I engaged master ship-

Saint Patrick *under repair in our back garden, Monkstown*

wright Patsy Whelan from Ringsend. With a helper, he laid into doing new planking, replacing about a third. The new engine went in; I had bought a Perkins 4.236 (with money that might more conventionally have been spent on a new kitchen in the house). The deck and coachroof went back on. By Christmas 1977 she was ready for launching. But I was going abroad and the covers went over her.

Meanwhile, in 1976, unrelated to my working in Connemara, Mary and I had bought a cottage. This was located seven miles beyond Clifden towards Ballyconneely, and then two miles further up an ever narrowing single track road. The last stoney half mile had grass growing high along the middle. She was old style, single story and 'built without regard to expense' as a neighbour put it. On enquiry, that meant that it was a foot longer in each dimension! The beach on Mannin Bay was a couple of fields away. Slyne Head Lighthouse shone in the distance. Water was from the well and light came from paraffin lamps. Perfect. Mary and I loved it, and so did the kids.

Ballyconneely, October 1977, with our kids Muireann, Cathal, Caoimhe and Bairbre. Three months later we moved to Malawi.

9

Malawi

Where exactly is Malawi? I knew it was in Africa, but where exactly? It's called the 'warm heart of Africa'. On its inland side is Rhodesia (now called Zimbabwe) and on its Indian Ocean side is Mozambique. And how had we got a harbour job so far inland? Lake Malawi is bigger than the Irish Sea, about 400 miles long and 70 miles wide. There is much boat traffic on the lake, particularly that of the vessel *Ilala*, which carries cargo and passengers to villages up and down the lake. Chipoka, our harbour to be reconstructed, was the main rail terminus of the *Ilala*.

I prepared, which primarily required the procuring and shipping of everything that would be needed for the construction works – every nut and bolt, machine and tool, because there would be nothing there, certainly nothing that could be relied on. In Bremen the German suppliers were surprised that I insisted on visiting and inspecting the consignment of steel sheet-piles before despatch. 'If they said it would be such-and such, then it would be so.' It was, but I had to be sure. And so it was with every component, the machines and the material. The small stuff went into containers, labelled Ascon–Chipoka in letters three feet high. The crane was broken down to be assembled on site, no part to weigh more than 20 tons, the maximum we could be sure of being handled *en route* by a ship's own derrick. We didn't want to be at the mercy of some broken down port crane in Mozambique, through which all our goods were to be shipped. There was a low intensity war going on at the time, so it was uncertain through which port our

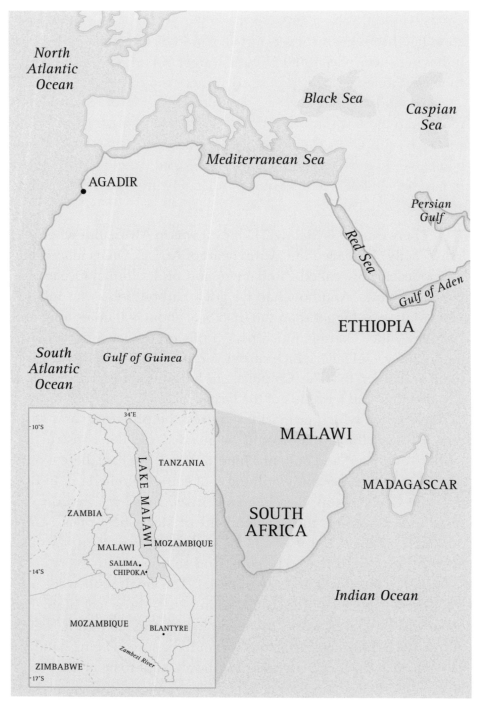

Map of Africa, with inset of Malawi

goods would travel – Beira, Nacala or maybe Maputo. I tried to ensure that through whichever port all would be together – little point in having sheet-piles if the piling-hammer was stuck somewhere a thousand miles away.

Our children were now aged eight, seven, and three and eight months so there was much for Mary to plan. As we could take only so much with us on the flight, the bulky stuff and heavier school-books would have to go in one of the shipped containers. They left in late November. We flew out immediately after New Year, January 1978.

Our plane refuelled in Khartoum, Sudan. Turbaned camel drivers lolled around. Though night-time, the heat was furnace-like. The cool inside of the plane was a respite and the kids were very good. Blantyre is the commercial capital of Malawi. Its airport is of the small, 'walk right on' size. Corkman Pat Power of Sisk's local office was there to meet us and take us to the Mount Soche Hotel, the only one in town. He and his wife Kate were a great help to us for the next few days as we got organised before going 'up-country'. I met the earthmoving sub-contractor and some local suppliers – yes, there were a few.

We met some of the local establishment and ex-pats, including Robin and Pauline Wrixon. Pauline, from Dun Laoghaire, had a wealth of tropical experience behind her. I got a car and loaded up, however my new tropical suit, light creamy linen, hanging by the backseat, was stolen from the car. I had left the window open, just a crack for ventilation, and some enterprising fellow had contrived to get it out. As we drove north towards the lake, the surface of the brown clay laterite road got worse. It was the rainy season, with its daily lashing downpour, followed by quick-drying sunshine. This inundation would corrugate the road surface, or might indeed sweep it away. The couple of hundred miles took us a long day. We had been warned not to stop if we hit anything, animal or human, but to keep going to the safety of the next decent-sized village, where there might be the security of a police compound. Our destination was the Grand Beach Hotel, about 15 miles from Chipoka, where we were to spend a few days before moving into our rented house. This hotel might once have been 'grand', but that was long ago. Now it could have been the setting for a 1920s Graham Greene novel, lost in a forgotten land. The fan in the bar spun lazily and creaked. The small creatures scuttling about the bedroom floor were efficiently disposed of – by the porter kicking them out the door.

Our house, a couple of miles from the Grand Beach, had once been a colonial residence. It was approached by a narrow track running through high maize fields. We drove by a collection of straw huts, termed 'the village'. Passing through a myriad of kids would follow our car. Their mammies, carrying babies on their backs, pounded maize outside their huts, or carried water containers on their heads. This was it all right, the 'real' Africa. The house, in a bushy garden, was extensively elegant and, with the roof overhanging the *konde*, was delightfully cool. Our 'houseboy', Henderson, welcomed us and presented his credentials. His CV and his references went back over 20 years in the service of Madam this and Bwana that. He would be in charge of the staff with himself doing the cooking. He would need an 'assistant houseboy' for the cleaning and kitchen fire, a nanny for our baby, a driver for myself, the Bwana, and a 'garden boy' to cut firewood and 'to keep the snakes out of the house'. What? I baulked, but only at the idea of having a driver. I could do that myself, thank you very much. And best of all, the house fronted on to a sandy beach on the lake. But we were warned not go onto the beach after dark because the hippo then would be dangerous!

Back in Connemara, I had met an Englishman on holiday, a retired colonial administrator for Malawi, a Mr Kettlewell. 'Aagh,' he had sighed, 'Chipoka, terrible place, we used to go there on *ulendo* and I was allowed only twenty porters.' *Ulendo* was the round of tax gathering inspections done by the former British administrators, pith-helmeted whites pratting around, showing the flag, putting manners on and collecting taxes from the local subservient chiefs. These British were backed up by the King's African Rifles, local soldiers with white officers of course.

London Zuma, my general foreman, was a big Zulu from Natal and subservient to no man. He had arrived in Chipoka the previous week. Together we walked the site, or indeed what we could of it for the greater part was marshy, reed-covered ground. A thatched hut village stood on that part where our new railway line was to go. The existing 'pier' was little more than a broken line of boulders jutting out from the sandy edge of the lake. The waters of the lake itself glistened in the harsh light. The sun was almost directly overhead. Now it was mid-summer and our latitude was fourteen degrees south of the equator so it was hot, very hot. London had already got men 'shovel-ready', as we might put it, and I had some Malawian technical staff hired from Blantyre. We marked the perimeter of the works and 200 men were set to work to clear the reeds with panga-knives. For a week, knee-deep in the leech-infested waters, they cut, dragged and cleared the reeds, which would later be put to use as thatching. 'What about the village?' I had said to London. Its clearance had already been negotiated, 'dictated more likely,' I said to myself. Each household was being paid some paltry sum, a few kwachas and tambalas, to move a half mile down the lakeside. Thoughts of the Highland Clearances and our own Cromwellian period came to mind. Our site, about a half mile square, could now be seen and properly surveyed.

It was probably little different from what David Livingstone, Scottish missionary explorer, would have seen 120 years earlier. The local fishermen still cast their nets from dug-out canoes and the *dhows* still sailed under lateen rig carrying cargo and people. Back from the shore was the main village of about 2,000 people. The village had a police station, a telephone – the number was Chipoka 1; later I was to be offered Chipoka 2 – a hospital/clinic and schools, all fairly rudimentary I was told.

Bricks were delivered, with cement and tin sheets, for the construction of the site offices. Mine enjoyed the shelter from the blazing sun of an overhanging baobab tree. London set to work, with men and carpenters, on what could be done without the machinery and materials which we were waiting for from Europe. The delivery of these was my main worry.

At least the earth-moving could go ahead. It was being done by a local outfit, Cilcon, headed by a white ex-Rhodesian police-man. God how I learned to dislike these ex-tobacco farmers and ex-policemen. They were so superior, so critical of the locals, and not much good themselves, to say the least. Most of their own white foremen wouldn't have held down jobs in Europe, but here they lorded it. I overheard a good Malawian mechanic ask how many rubber gaskets he should make. 'Keep makin' 'em, 'til I tell you to stop,' said the white foreman. I cringed then and many times more. The best of the whites were the South Africans. Though incredibly racist and narrow-minded, they were great guys to get things done and didn't at all mind getting their hands dirty.

Meanwhile, back at the house, each evening at about seven Henderson would light the two Tilley paraffin lamps. They gave a comforting soft light and would hiss through the night until dawn, about six-thirty. It now was the rainy season and most nights the thunder would roar, deafeningly, with black clouds blotting out the starry sky. Lightning flashed in vivid white sheets across the sky. Initially the kids would scamper into our bed, cozying up to Mammy, she herself uneasy, terrified might be the more accurate word. I don't know what I felt. That finished with the close of the rainy season in March; it was just that we had arrived in Malawi at a bad time of the year.

Mary would do 'school' for Cathal and Caoimhe from seven to ten in the morning with those books that we had with us. Mary was fine at the reading/writing, but the maths would require some tu-toring from me the previous evening. Muireann, approaching four, couldn't wait to begin her education and be included in the school-room. She, more than any of the others, was picking up words of Chichewa from Henderson and the others. Bairbre spent her days on the back of Emily, strapped up in the African way. The kitchen was a separate, thatched-roof, red-bricked building about 20 yards from the house. Within the kitchen was a wood-burning, cast iron stove, hot-plates on top, on which Henderson cooked all the meals. Garden boy John kept the supply of wood coming in and that fire, as far as I could see, never went out. I couldn't be sure of that as I was rarely there – not my domain.

All the time there were the sounds and the smell of Africa. The smell was that of wood fires burning, smoke curling upwards from cooking fires, not only in villages but anywhere there were people – waiting for a bus, relatives outside a hospital or on the shore, waiting for a boat to arrive. The sounds were particularly noticable at night with the screams of monkeys, the chattering of chicadas and the occasional snort of a big animal, probably a hippo.

Henderson baked bread daily. Vegetables he got locally and John brought in bananas and mangos from the garden. Meat came from the town of Salima, about 20 miles distant. Mary and Henderson would go there once a week or so. It once had been a well stocked place with the shops run by Indians, however Hastings Kamuzu Banda, Malawi's President for Life, had decreed that all Indians must sell up to locals and leave. So now, on one week it might be good for soap-powder and the next week perhaps for coat-hangers. There was this delightful air of uncertainty, adventure almost one could call it. However there was always meat there, usually goat, which, stringy and tough, was best served with loads of onions. Occasionally there would be a pig which would provide a wonderful change in diet. Under Henderson's tutelage, Mary got quite adept at bargaining. Of the fish from the lake, chambo was by far the tastiest, being typically nine or twelve inches long, a heavy-bodied flat fish, not altogether unlike hake. And it tasted all the better knowing that it was probably caught within sight of the house.

The job was not going well. The earth-moving contractor was a pain in the arse, delaying the start and then providing insufficient machinery. He even tried to persuade me that his D4 bulldozer was a more powerful and bigger D6. 'Who're you kidding?' It seemed he'd been getting away with this on the Malawian government for years.

This delay was compounded by a rising lake flooding part of the site. The water had risen eleven feet, an unprecedented seasonal rise in height. Through all of this time our gear still had not arrived. Impatiently, I wanted to go over to warring Mozambique and track it down. All advice, nay instruction, was: 'don't – there are some things more important than job progress'.

The piling foreman Jilles Vermaat and crane driver Jimmy Brady were sent out anyway; they had been hanging about the Ascon yard back in Dublin, impatient to get going. Now together we fumed, waiting. One day, unannounced and almost unnoticed in the sidings of Chipoka railway yard, on wagons being shunted to continue upcountry, were our light green containers, our machinery and sheetpiles. Glory be! At last we could get going, and we did. Six days a week, seven to seven on the job.

Engineer and Cork senior county footballer Tom Creedon came out to assist. Now we were knocking sparks out of this job. The dredging began. For this we had hired a Malawi Railways dredger, very like the one that we had used back home in Rossaveel. Tom Terry McDonogh, from Carraroe, who had driven the machine there, I especially asked for. Later, on the job, Tom would be starting a big eight-inch pump we had, powerful for shifting water but not easy to get going. But Tom had the knack. On the air intake of the engine he would stuff a petrol-soaked rag and put a match to it. Bang, smoke and flame – and away would start the pump. Close around Tom for this performance might be a dozen or so local workers.

'Is that not a bit dodgy?' I asked Tom.

'I do tell 'em to shtand back,' he replied.

We had need of additional pumps. Nello Teer, a Korean road contractor, had some idle in their Blantyre yard. These I tried to hire, spending almost two days being politely given tea and small talk, but getting nowhere. Later I learned that for some Asians hiring out their machines was tantamount to an admission of failure, with associated loss of face.

Not so the pragmatic Italian contractor who had no such qualms and from whom I did hire.

London meanwhile had put his men to work, several hundred; sometimes I wished we had instead a dozen Connemara men. However the work was getting done. One day I went with London into the 'bush' where our stone for the job was being collected. Local men, with their families, were being paid to gather these. This arrangement I had picked up some years earlier when my older colleague in Ascon, Jim Brew, had needed stone in Kilronan, Aran, for a pier job he was doing there. What Jim did was wonderful. He rented a field fronting Kilronan Harbour and through the winter anyone bringing in stone, by the cartload or however else, was paid for it, thus spreading the money around.

London Zuma, meanwhile, would take no backchat from the locals, not even from the Chief in the village of Chipoka. I'd heard that the Chief had sent a complaint about injured men being taken to the hospital in wheelbarrows. 'Tell the Chief,' he said, 'that if I hear any more complaints, I will withdraw the wheelbarrows.' I once heard him chide an old carpenter, 'Hey ol' secondhand, there is no feet an inches on this job, only metres, centimetres and millimetres.' I, too, still somewhat in the imperial measurement mindset of that old carpenter, turned away.

Once a month or so, Mary, myself and the kids would make the trip down to Blantyre. There she would do a 'big shop', the kids would go to the pictures, I would do local business and communicate with Dublin and also buy my supply of reading, two or three books, for the next month. In the local club, we would meet 'ex-pats', accountants and others, living and working an air-conditioned life. When they would complain about their staff I'd bite my lip, mostly. I was invited to join the Master Builders Association and declined on the basis that I wouldn't be around that long. To Robin Wrixon, a Cork accountant running an electrical company there, Everglow, I had confided that I hadn't seen many 'master builders' around. His wife Pauline and Mary became good friends and decades later still are.

Blantyre has a population of about a million, of whom about 25,000 are whites, British mostly. Its name derives from the Scottish town of the same name which was Gaelic in origin. It is one of the oldest cities in Africa, predating Nairobi, Harari and Johannesburg. Its name was given by the missionaries who followed Livingstone.

Back up at the lake on Sundays, Mary would invite our lads, staying in the Grand Beach, and London Zuma, to our place for dinner, a few beers and a chat. Tom Terry and myself built a two-man currach, dimensions from his head of three foot in the beam which was too narrow. If you stopped rowing at all it would incline to tip over – at least the water was warm – but its main problem was that it leaked a lot because we couldn't get proper tar to seal its cloth skin.

There was a family of American Baptist missionaries, the Workmans, in the area. Our kids would visit theirs until one day, it must have been coming up to Christmas, Cathal and Caoimhe came home despondent – 'there's no Santa Claus'. Mary enquired of the Workmans. 'We don't like to tell lies to the children,' they said. That was the end of that neighbourly relationship for us. And there weren't many other Europeans, or Westerners of any sort, around. Of visitors none was more welcome than my father because he took over 'the teaching' from Mary. And on weekends, the back of the construction now being broken and completion in sight, we'd drive to the national parks, staying in tents or grass huts, 'glamping' it would be called now. Sometimes animals could be heard outside, shuffling and snorting.

On one Sunday, while big Vermaat was still around, and on that day we were glad he was, we had driven into a bush village. Anne, Mary's sister, was with us. A village crowd stood around in a large circle within which there was a guy with a wicked-looking head-dress, feathers and blood daubing his bare body. He foamed at the mouth, ran around, his feet clawing at the ground like a wild cock, mouthing incantations, indecipherable even to the locals. We had stumbled onto a Gule Wamkulu, an African Magic Doctor. We got out of there fairly fast.

In late 1978 the job was coming to a close. Our lads, who had been here three months at a time, had gone home. Tom Creedon was lucky to have done so. Strong and fit as he was he had had a particularly bad bout of malaria. Malaria is like a very bad bout of the flu, with fever added. We all had got it, to a greater or lesser extent, and Mary had nursed us through it. But Tom's bout lasted longer and we worried for him. Uncomplainingly, he pulled through, though on returning to Cork he never got back his place on the Cork Seniors.

The rainy season was again in progress when, about fifty miles to the south of us, the railway bridge at Ntaka Taka was washed out. Banana trees, swept down on the river, had blocked the flow, getting caught up in the bridge. Under pressure, the whole bridge and approach embankment had been swept away, leaving only the two rails hanging uselessly in the air. The northern half of Malawi, dependent on the railway, was isolated. We still had our construction machinery, which I was about to put on the market.

Malawi Railways made contact with those civil engineering/ bridge contractors in the country. I was asked to meet the railway people in Blantyre. Approaching their office, I bought a poppy, it being that time of year, and, not being particularly enthused of British soldiery, stuffed it deep into my pocket. At Reception, the nice Malawian ladies, wearing poppies, rang upstairs. 'Yes, I was expected.' Upstairs, a European lady, secretary to the chief engineer Mr McAndrews, also wore a poppy. In the short few steps to his office, I dug down, retrieved the poppy and pinned it to the lapel of my jacket. I walked in the door and was effusively made welcome by McAndrews and his two assistants, also thus decorated. In competition with the UK firm French Kier and the Koreans, Nello Tier, I got the job for Ascon. The railway company had sheetpiles and bridge girders, but needed foundations, abutments and piers constructed, those girders lifted in and rails placed. That was our contract. Rapidly, a few of the guys returned from Dublin.

In 19 days, working nonstop, we built that 150-foot bridge, three 50-foot spans, and made money on it. My one regret was that we had taken it on a 'cost-plus' basis – on a 'tender price' basis we surely would have made more.

During the last few months, in the spring of 1979, there was the final account for Chipoka to be done, the wrap-up and one other small bridge job for Malawi Railways in Penga Penga. Mick Long, from Crosshaven, came out and took over from me on that. I had had enough. My work was done and I was keen to get home. Ascon had made good money out of Malawi, and so had I.

10

Home and Away, Spain

In June of 1979 we were back from Malawi in time to get Cathal and Caoimhe into Scoil Lorcáin before the summer break, and to get Muireann started. The teachers found that they were well up to speed on all subjects, ahead on some and just a little behind on the *Gaeilge*. So, after a year and a half, the 'home schooling' had worked well. My Da, who had babysat our house in Belgrave Road, moved into an apartment. The cottage in Mannin was in good order and I was due accumulated holidays.

As I peeled the covers off *Saint Patrick*, the neighbours might have worried that the back garden was once more to have the look and sound of an industrial boatyard. Not so. Except for the application of antifouling, *Saint Patrick* was ready for her launch.

In the years since I had bought her, there had been a stirring of interest in the Galway Hookers – the revival had begun. While a couple of the old Connemara workboats had remained under sail by their families, *Maighdean Mhara* of Caladh Thaidgh and *Tónai* of Shruthán, the work for the boats was over and most were lying idle and rotting. The poet Richard Murphy had written 'The Last Galway Hooker' and the writer Dick Scott had been assiduous in recording the last of the Hookers working under sail, as had Éamon de Butléir and Joe St. Leger in capturing them on film.

Some had been taken out of Connemara and converted for pleasure sailing. John McCormack, son of the singer, had had one in Dublin, as had Jim Halpenny. Dick Fletcher had taken *Ark* to Dublin, and she had then gone to Ballycotton and later to England.

Denis Alymer had, in 1966, brought *Morning Star* through the Grand Canal to Dublin. *American Mór* had been brought by the Needham family of Comber to Strangford Lough – I sailed on her there in 1976. *Pamela*, then in the ownership of Harry Knott and later Fergus Cahill, was winning races in Dublin Bay. In Cleggan, Richard Murphy had *Ave Maria* and *Volunteer* in commission. *Ave Maria* then passed to Nick Tinne, who kept her in Castletownsend, while his father, Rev. Derek Tinne, kept *Volunteer* in Roundstone. *Hunter* was being sailed in Bertraghboy by Englishman Cyril Saunders. *Connacht* had been brought to Dublin by Johnny King and converted out of recognition. *Saint John* of Cleggan had been brought to Killyleagh, where she lay covered but unused.

In the Coal Harbour of Dun Laoghaire, during the winter of 1975/76, *Morning Star*, now sold to Johnny Healion, was repaired. For next MacDara's Day, July 16, 1976, she was transported by road to Carna, launched and rigged. In Mac Moylett's bar there was much talk of boats, boatmen and the 'race' to be held. *Hunter, Volunteer* and the *Star* were the lineup. I crewed on the *Star*. It was an uneven race, but a mighty event. The *Star*, by far the bigger boat, with bigger sails, ran away with it, but what mattered was the interest it generated. The revival of traditional boats had begun.

In the next couple of years, Con McCann had bought *Connacht*, Mick Hunt *Saint John* and Brian Hussey *American Mór*. In Connemara, *Capall*, which Dudley Bailey had shown me under repair in 1974, was back; others, the smaller gleoiteog mainly, were re-emerging. *Lady*, now in the ownership of Dubliner Tom Kelly, was being rebuilt in Mweenish by Cóilín Joe Bhairbre Mulkerrins.

In the autumn of 1997, following a meeting in the North Star Hotel in Dublin, the Galway Hooker Association was formed.

On July 16, 1976, in Moyletts Bar, I had asked Pat Ceoinín, doyen of *Máistir Bádoir*, what should be the length of mast for *Saint Patrick*. He disappeared for a few minutes and, on return, declared, 'Thirty-seven feet and six inches', possibly having consulted someone. And so, to that precise measurement, I had built the mast and got the sails made.

The crane lifted *Saint Patrick* out of the garden and she was lorried down to Coal Harbour and dropped in, being lifted again briefly for Johnny Healion to caulk a seam that had been missed. With help from Seamus Breathnach of Carna, Johnny and myself got her ballasted, rigged and sailing by the next day.

A few weeks later we sailed for Connemara. In Baltimore, County Cork, the engine wiring shorted and caught fire. Luckily, Sean Mullan was aboard and dealt with it. Christy Collins, cox/mechanic of the Lifeboat, did a repair job, showing us how to start the engine by shorting the starter motor.

While Sean and I were sailing northwards off the mouth of the Shannon, the old binding of the mainsheet block parted, sending the boom swinging wildly. In bouncing conditions we made into the shelter of Kilbaha and carried out repairs, all the while casting a baleful eye over the rest of the rigging. Halyards were still those on the boat as she had lain at Goleen, hairy sun-bleached polypropylene that would skin the hands off you.

At the major MacDara race it was apparent that our sails were too small. Even with the redoubtable Johnny Peter Bailey helming and Johnny Sean Jack piloting, we were left behind. Neither was our return to Dublin a triumphant one. There were three of us aboard, Paddy Norris, Sean and myself. Approaching Blasket Sound from the north, the evening grew darker; the forecast was for a southerly Force 5 or 6. We decided to shelter at the small village of Brandon, on the east side of the mountain of the same name.

Anchored off, at about nine in the evening, Sean decided that he wanted to go ashore. Paddy and I went too, all life-jacketed, into the eight-foot timber dinghy. By now the clouds above Mount Brandon were scudding past at speed and a fair chop was being kicked up. Into it we rowed, as the little boat took more and more splash over her gunwales. About 100 yards from the pier, where we could both shelter and bail her, she filled. By now the dusk had darkened and there was not a sinner around to see us. In the sea, holding on to the gunwales of the dinghy, we kicked towards the shore. Northwards we were swept, away from the village and the pier, but gaining towards the boulder-strewn shore, the waves breaking white. The better to kick the water, we got rid of our boots. About five yards out we shoved the dinghy away and, waves breaking over us, were thrown up onto the shore, breathless and bruised, but not injured.

The lights of the village were distant as we walked barefoot across a field towards a farmhouse, cowshit squelching between our toes, thistles stinging our feet. We shivered. After knocking, the door was opened and we saw a group inside playing cards. We were directed to the 'hotel'. We walked to the village and went into the first pub we met. There we stood, dripping wet, shivering and invisible, for a long time it seemed, before someone copped our appearance. From then on the care we got couldn't have been better.

Lifting Saint Patrick *out of the garden, over the shed, June 1978.*

Brendan O'Rourke, taking in our predicament, took us to his house, dried and fed us and put us up for the night. As the wind outside rose and rose, Brendan, who had a half-decker himself moored at the pier, was himself concerned.

On the national radio the next morning we heard of the Fastnet Race disaster. A full gale had blown up to a violent storm, a depression deepening without warning. Many yachts had been damaged and lost, the number of those drowned was not yet known (fifteen, it transpired). Lifeboats from Dunmore, Ballycotton, Courtmacsherry and Baltimore were all out.

I telegrammed Mary at the cottage in Ballyconneely. '*Saint Patrick* and crew all well.' Only later in the day, as she heard of the tragedy on the radio, did she realise why I had sent such a message.

How lucky we were not to have carried on southward that previous evening, August 13, the night of the infamous Fastnet Gale. In the following week, much chastened, we sailed *Saint Patrick* back to her Dublin moorings on the Liffey.

It was this mooring that made it possible to keep such a big boat in Dublin. I had laid it, with local advice, during 1975. At this time the south bank of the river was fairly empty of boats and moorings. East Link Bridge had not yet been built, nor its approach road. Poolbeg Yacht and Boat Club, 600 metres down river, was in its infancy. The club did not have moorings, these being individually arranged. Since then the club, of which I am glad to have always been a member, has prospered, now with a fine clubhouse and marina.

In the course of the following winter, I put a forty-foot mast on her, other spars in proportion and ordered new sails. This boat had once been the finest in Connemara; she would be that again, or close to it.

During the winter or 1979/80, I had become Honorary Secretary of the Galway Hooker Association, thus affording me a good vantage of the gathering pace of the Hooker revival. More and more boats were being rebuilt or re-commissioned.

On the evening of Friday, June 27, we left Dun Laoghaire for Baltimore. We called into Youghal for pints on Saturday night and made into Baltimore by Sunday evening, where Dermot Kennedy put us on a mooring for a week while we went back to work. Our wives had driven down to do a sailing course with Dermot. Conveniently, we drove back to Dublin in the same car and returned the following Friday evening.

We went to sea at 23.00 hours, Louis Purton, Dave O'Neill, Sean and myself. In terrible visibility and a light southerly wind we went near, too near, the cliffs on the south side of Cape Clear. I had overestimated our speed and turned northwestwards too soon. I had also failed to stream the log, which would have shown our distance run and the safe time to make the turn.

Through the night we motored past Mizen and Dursey, the fog lifting when we were around Skellig about mid-morning. There we had heard breaking seas on the cliffs before we saw them. All was placid that night, as we anchored in Smerwick, walking Béal Bán beach for a pint in the village of Ballyferriter. A wonderful sailing breeze brought us, goose-winged, through Gregory Sound and then into Kilronan, and the following day through Joyce's Sound to Clifden. There it was 'propellor-off', cabin table and spares ashore to lighten her, as for the next five weekends we raced in the traditional regattas. While Roundstone and Kinvara Cruinniú Na mBád were the most convivial, the MacDara race, Craobh Na hÉireann, was the one to win.

Pat Ceoinín must have approved the new sails and rig because he took the helm; thirteen were aboard, way too many. He insisted on bringing his own crew and I was damned if my friends were to be left ashore. A photograph on the front page of the *Irish Press* the next day said it all, being captioned 'Bending with the Breeze'. Flying past MacDara Island, sails full and close-hauled, spray in the air, crew holding tight and the fleet astern, *The Patrick* was back.

At season's end we sailed northwards around Ireland, back to Dublin, taking three weekends to do so, twice being caught in bad weather. The highlight, in a quiet way, was our making into Belmullet from the north side of Broadhaven Bay. There, our red sail catching the last of a light evening breeze, we twisted and turned in the ever shallowing channel, as some knowing bystanders on the shore shouted encouragement and instructions, until we reached the old quay, the first boat of this size to be in for many years we were told.

A good season.

In 1981 we sailed southwards. Feeling that our 'running in' period was now over, from our winter base on the Liffey, we went across the Bay of Biscay to northern Spain. To spice up the trip, we planned some symbolic trading, taking Irish woollens and whiskey out and returning with Spanish wine and cheeses.

On July 2 the moorings were dropped at Ringsend and we went across Dublin Bay to Dun Laoghaire to collect our 'cargo' of woollen jumpers and a cask of whiskey – courtesy of Irish Distillers – and some poitín. The voyage got under way on Friday evening when we sailed out of Dublin Bay in a light westerly breeze. There were six of us on board. If given titles, I was skipper/navigator, Sean was mate and cook, and Danny Sheehy was ship's raconteur and oarsman, for which he was well trained since in 1975 he had rowed around Ireland in a currach. There was also Kevin, in the vital position of financial controller, Fred Barry was graced with the title of spare navigator, and Eddie Naughton as pierhead jumper missed the toss for bunk selection – and emphatically didn't get the bridal suite.

We'd company for the first stage, down the Wicklow and Wexford coast, sailing together with Con McCann's *Connacht*, she bound for Connemara in a round Ireland cruise from her home in Strangford Lough. The log was streamed (which gave us our speed and distance run), we lit the fire in the pot-bellied stove, for it was a cool, damp evening and waited for the forecast northwest wind which never came. So it was our diesel engine which pushed us southward in the dark to good effect, for at nine on Saturday morning we were in open water south of Wexford's Tuskar Rock. We still were motoring, in virtual calm, with a light drizzle.

By early afternoon the wind was filling in from the south. At this stage we wanted to make as much progress as possible, so kept on motoring. Anyway, even as her loving owner, I wouldn't claim that windward work was *Saint Patrick's* favourite point of sailing.

In view of the cruise plan as a whole, it seemed sensible to keep thumping along, particularly as the BBC forecast spoke of southerly wind, Force 6 to 7, possibly 8. Despite the earlier inaccuracy about nor'westers, this time they were bang on. The southerly wind freshened, and as it got up a gale warning for Sea Area Fastnet, to our west, gave the promise of a dirty night. We had a choice of heaving-to or continuing our damp but steady progress under fairly low engine revs. We chose the latter, though it made conditions below decidedly un-yachty. But at least we were getting along, every mile made good was a mile nearer the south, so we gritted our teeth (those who weren't getting seasick) and plugged on.

Around 3.00 am, nobody's favourite time of day, a mighty clattering brought all the ship's company to life. A gas bottle adrift? The engine off its mountings? No, in bashing through an unusually steep sea, the bowsprit had snapped off. For an hour or more, in the dark and with the boat bouncing in the windblown seas, we struggled to get the broken spar and rigging aboard and safely lashed. After checking that everything else seemed okay, we continued our decidedly miserable progress.

The Isles of Scilly were now a definite objective in order to repair the damage. That Sunday was an eminently forgettable day. Plugging along in the driving murk, the succeeding forecasts gave only a slight change in wind direction, from south to southwest. The references to 'occasional Force 8' gave us wry mirth, as it was evident to us that we were in the middle of it. Navigation was difficult, but radio communication with the tanker *Esso Warwickshire*, which stopped nearby to see if we were all right, gave us a useful position fix. Then as the 18.00 BBC forecast was giving further Force 6 to 8 southwesterly, the Scillies were sighted, and by heaven were we glad to see them.

It took two hours to cover the remaining miles to land, but with the increasing shelter from the islands and the anticipation of harbour delights, the atmosphere aboard revived, miraculously. The fire was stoked, the dishes were washed and a lively discussion was in progress as to the hour of 'closing time' in Hughtown, the capital of the Scillies archipelago. We motored in through Crow Sound, while Sean cooked. As the Hooker can comfortably dry out alongside, we went right to the inner end of the pier. There we took the ground, while boats outside pitched to their anchors. It was 9.00 pm. Most of the passage had been tediously under power, but at least we were 200 miles nearer Spain. After a quick demolition job on Sean's dinner, it was to the Mermaid Inn to celebrate. Unlike some of our favourite haunts in the west of Ireland, it closed at a very early hour, our protestations about being *bona fide* travellers being to no avail.

On Monday morning we were glad to be in port, as seas were breaking over the outer wall of the pier and gale forecasts continued. Anyway, we'd work to do. The bowsprit was splinted, ship refuelled, dried and grub re-stocked. The Scillonians passing by were very friendly, even if their rigid adherence to the licensing laws was matched by the neatness of their community, almost overpowering. That evening we left. The wind had eased, though still from the southwest. With reduced sail, two reefs, we were able to lay a course for Ushant on the French side of the Channel. We had intended to clear it by at least 50 miles, but now we were forced by this wind direction towards the busy shipping lane off this island outpost, the turn into the Channel from the Bay of Biscay.

Shortly before midnight we had a decidedly unsettling experience. We almost went between a tug and its tow, a heavily listing vessel about a mile astern of it. Their slow speed alerted us that something was peculiarly odd. It was Fred, consulting *Reeds Almanac*, who identified the lights of a tug and tow. A radio call clarified the situation. Shortly a serious sounding Dutch voice on the radio issued a *Securitay* warning message to All-Shipping.

We had tacked to avoid them and in doing so had started the engine to give us more positive manoeuvring. It hadn't run with its usual confidence, but we gave it no further thought as we switched it off and continued silently under sail. Well, relatively silently. By the small hours of Tuesday the moon was out and we were romping along. This fine progress wasn't to last, as by morning we were slowing. A school of dolphins, playing alongside, emphasised our slow progress. With the knowledge that Spain was still many miles away, we tried to start the engine but could get no life.

This wasn't funny. We were about 30 miles northwest of Ushant, notorious for its dense shipping, and the forecast was for light winds in which we would have limited steerage. To get into Brest for repairs would have been difficult. People in Spain were expecting us and there we could have the engine repaired. We would keep going. For the next 30 hours we sailed close-hauled southwards. We were able to keep outside the ship traffic lanes, at one stage clearly visible, ship after ship in a continuous line. It became warm and sunny, the *craic* was good, the food great and the sea temperature warmed sufficiently for us to make plunges over the side. About midday Wednesday a good breeze filled in, our suntans were going strong, shipboard routine was established and the bashing north of Scillies seemed a million miles away. To cap it all, on Thursday a northwesterly Force 7 blew in from astern, giving us great progress towards our destination. On Friday, the wind had lightened. We got a good position from sunsights on the sextant and were rewarded when at 2.00 am on Saturday the lighthouse of Cabo Major started stabbing its beam in the darkness ahead.

Daylight found us sailing nicely towards the mouth of Santander. There Fernando Pombe, who had been expecting us, came aboard and piloted us in, we now using our big 19-foot sweeps to row to the quay wall. We had logged 700 miles since Dun Laoghaire.

Sean later described the joy of our arrival in this foreign place, the pastel-coloured buildings, red-roofed, being those of a warm continental country to which we had independently travelled in our own little ship.

Our gallant financial controller had some money still available, so as loyal shipmates we adjourned ashore that night to advise him on its disposal. This dutiful fulfilling of responsibility naturally took its toll, being ever so slightly fragile the next morning when we went to meet some of our families at a house which had been rented. Mary, Suzanne and nine children, in two cars, had travelled by road and ferries. During the next fortnight we had a family time, the engine was fixed (dirt in the fuel injector pump) and we tidied ourselves for a reception given by Santander Camareo Commercia Navigation, where our cargo was handed over to them. In return, these kind people gave us brandy, sherry, wines and cheeses.

The holiday period came to an end and it was time to think about returning northwards. Fred and Eddy had left by air, to be replaced by Paddy Norris. On Monday, July 27, we sailed, and had a pleasant three-day passage to Audierne in Brittany. After a short stay, disappointed with French nightlife, we were away, departure time dictated by the strong tides. We went through the Raz de Seine and Chenal du Four, crossed the Channel and tied up outside the Royal Falmouth Yacht Club. The members were amazed at the quantity of booze we carried, Customs insisting that we bring it all on deck for their inspection.

In the following days we called to Penzance and St. Ives before sailing, uneventfully, back to Dublin.

None of this sailing could have been done without the help and good company of many, most notably Sean Mullan and Kevin Cronin. Sean, active rugby man and married to Jane, was nearly always aboard, willing and capable. He had an excellent feeling for weather conditions and a natural way with the complicated ropes and blocks of the Galway Hooker. In addition, he was a very good cook. Like myself, he was inclined to be frugal, though more so. Cheese, long smelly and ready for dumping, would be put on the cabin table, himself the only taker. We wouldn't always know if he was having us on.

Kevin too was stalwart. Though not as 'rope-ready' as Sean, when something needed doing he'd be up and at it. He had a quiet way and was a very good 'people person'. On the occasional difficult times between others, and indeed my sometimes intemperate self, he would be the pacifier. Nonetheless, he was not forgetful of my losing overboard his outboard engine as we were going into Santander. In 2017, when we were going in there again 37 years later, he remarked that we should keep an eye out for it.

11

Busy Times, But ...

Four of us in Ascon were upgraded to contract manager, a new category in the firm and a step up from being site agents as previously. We were Jim Brew, Barry Supple, Liam Bohane and myself. There was probably a three year gap between each, downward in age, among the four of us. Speekenbrink had gone back to Holland and the firm was being run by Herlihy and Tim Teahan, an accountant, who was ambitious and abrasive. Ownership, 'the shareholders' as they were referred to, were 50 per cent each between the Dutch and the Sisks, the Chairman being Hal Sisk.

Civil engineering construction activity had taken a lift while I had been away. Ascon had a won a major job in County Clare, Moneypoint Power Station. I was given several smaller jobs, Ballycoolen Reservoir, Dublin (which was in progress), Ferrycarrig Bridge, Wexford, the Sludge Jetty in Ringsend, St. Patrick's Institution, Mountjoy Jail, the Diving Department and some estimating for new tenders. Instead of being in one location, I was doing a lot of driving, long days, going hard at it. I didn't mind a bit and was well able for it. As a friend, Eugene Magee, had once said to me, very few are so lucky as to have work that they both enjoy and get well paid for.

I had met Eugene through Kevin Kelly, who had been in UCD with me. Kevin was from Newry and Eugene from Irvinestown, County Fermanagh. And it also was through Kevin that I met his friends Jim Harrington and Austin Duke, all of whom, Mick Cotter too, had done a Masters of Business Administration in Trinity.

Through the 1970s, we and others had met on Saturday nights for pints. Mary and I, being early married and the first of those to have a house, would sometimes host dinner, where we drank awful concoctions of Sangria and god-knows-what. Charades, in competing teams, would see 'Napoleon's Army' retreating from Moscow, through the sliding doors and out the front window. Our neighbours must have wondered what we were at.

In 1972 a few of us had gone on holiday to Corfu, exotic stuff. The lads, not yet married, were going to Club Med, an upmarket French activities-based holiday resort. Mary and myself, too poor (or for me, too mean) for that, instead rented a scooter and were to 'B&B it' around the island. Within hours of landing, Mary was in hospital. With her on the pillion, I skidded the scooter on a gravel road and we crashed. I was unhurt, but she, sandaled only, had a badly damaged ankle. A Toyota pick-up brought us to hospital, where for almost a week she was bedridden. The surgeon said that he had 'spooned' the gravel out of her foot. He then was most reluctant to discharge her, and certainly not to Club Med. However the lads had met a Gussie Mehigan, a surgeon from home, who undertook an avuncular medical role, thus allowing us to spend our second Corfu week there. I loved it and should have gone there in the first place, with loads of waterskiing, sailing and tip-rugby by day, and French food, wine and shows in the evening – Mary being carried by all of us, thus ensuring our breaking into the top of any queue. One Vincent Browne, 'correspondent for three national newspapers,' he said (*The Irish Press*, *The Evening Press* and some other we had never heard of) was particularly to the fore.

That Club Med introduction was the first of a half a dozen or so visits that Mary and I had over the following years in various countries, although the nature of their set-up, being isolated from the local community, was such that you'd hardly know in which country you were. As had happened earlier to me with skiing, I thought each trip would be the last and so never bothered to learn much French.

What made these trips, and Saturday nights out, possible for Mary and myself was the availability of childminders. In the case of nights out from Belgrave Road, my Da was always available; in the case of longer away trips, it was the good child-swapping arrangements that Mary had developed with Mary McMahon and with her sister Anne. Our cottage in Mannin, near Ballyconneely, was particularly useful in this regard; so much so that when we returned from Malawi I undertook a two-room extension.

The purpose of this was twofold, though inter-related. First was that we would have room for adult friends to visit. Secondly was to have room for the many children, cousins and others. Malawi had yielded us a bonus of £9,000. With it I planned to build a conservatory in Belgrave Road and an extension in Mannin. Fortunately, I first went for the Mannin job because this exhausted all our funds. For this, after getting planning permission from Galway County Council, I engaged our good neighbour Christy Flaherty to do the job. Since we had bought the place, he had always been willing to carry out any repairs and replace broken and blown-away slates. With him for this extension he had Brian King from Errislannan, across Mannin Bay.

My design, wishing to follow the form of the existing cottage, required the removal of overground rock at the existing gable. Brian and Christy were quite prepared to drill and blast; I demurred, fearing damage to the existing masonry gable, suggesting instead the use of 'plugs and feathers'. This, commonly used, requires drilling using compressed air and insertion into the drilled holes of 'plug and expanding wedges – feathers'. For two weeks they were at this, getting nowhere. I visited each Saturday. They suggested moving the new extension to where there was no rock. This would result in a flat-roofed appurtenance, an awful prospect, though common enough. 'Blast away,' I said.

Not a scratch was put on the existing gable; those men knew what they were doing. At Easter, 1980 we had the 'official opening', two rooms with inbuilt bunks, capable of sleeping twelve – which it sometimes did – in *Seomra Na gCaillíní* and *Seomra na Buachaillí*.

When the Hooker was in Connemara the kids would come on board, not for the racing obviously, but in between, often involving a lot of driving by their mammies. On one occasion, after driving back from Carraroe, Hugh Mullan was missing, shortly to be found asleep on the back window ledge of the car. This was before the days of individual children's car seats – just pack 'em in.

During the summer of 1982, *Saint Patrick* was back in Connemara, again rounding Ireland, the return journey around the north coast again proving difficult. In terms of publicity for the Hookers, the postage stamp was probably the big thing, albeit embarrassing in a technical sense.

As Honorary Secretary of the Galway Hooker Association I had been contacted by the philately section of the Post Office. They were doing a boat series on stamps, which would include a Galway Hooker. 'Would I have a suitable photograph? Certainly I would, or could get one. The Hookers are very photogenic and with the resurgence in traditional boat regattas, the photographers had been many. I had good colour shots of Bailey's *Capall*, the *Mhaighdean Mhara* and the *Tónai* and thought about submitting these for their own consideration and choice. However, my conscience and humility were cast aside; I sent them one of *Saint Patrick*, racing in Kinvara. On September 22, *The Irish Times* reported:

Cruinniú Na mBád, Kinvara
(photo by Eamonn Ward)

> *Asgard II* and a flotilla of Howth 17-footers caused quite a
> stir yesterday when they berthed in Dublin port, but no sight
> was more majestic than that of the Galway Hooker, the *Saint
> Patrick*, as it zig-zagged up from the mouth of the Liffey to
> take its place beside them on City Quay.
>
> The boats were there for the launching aboard *Asgard II* of
> four stamps commemorating them and their smaller relation,
> the currach, performed by the Minister of State ...

A good day, and good publicity for the Hookers. There was,
however, a 'sting in the tail'.

On the stamp, the Hooker, or *Bád Mór*, to give its proper Connemara nomenclature, was described as a 'gleoiteog', a similar, but
smaller, member of the family of traditional boats. A certain 'stirring in the dovecote' ensued, including letters to *The Irish Times*. For
the Philately Department, this must have been particularly embarrassing since not long previously a new Irish stamp had depicted
an Irish oyster, the *oyster edulis*, but upside down. I held my peace,
much appreciated in a letter I received from P.A. Warren of the department:

> You express a very clear view on the matter, and your for-
> bearance in not adding to the controversy at the time is ac-
> knowledged with appreciation by one who worked long in
> the old Department of Posts and Telegraphs.

What had happened, I later understood, was that the department had consulted one of the Conroys of Rosmuc, who was a
translator in the Dáil and whose family had once owned the boat.
He, decades away from Rosmuc and boats, memory dimmed, had
got the name wrong.

During the autumn of 1982, I had heard in the office of a board
meeting agenda which included a Chairman's item, 'Who can
we fire?' It didn't concern me. I was busy tendering for the Nore
Bridge in Kilkenny and the construction of Fiddown Bridge on
the River Suir. I had satisfactorily concluded the final accounts on
Ballycoolen Reservoir and Waterford Bridge Repairs. Indeed, my

negotiations on the Waterford job had got off to a difficult beginning when the consulting engineer, Cyril Roche of Cork, met me off the Dublin train asking, 'Is Pat not here?' Pat Herlihy was coming up to retirement and taking less and less interest; Teahan was now running things. All morning I made the case for the various extra payments I sought, all to nil effect. Travelling to lunch I remarked that 'Pana', Patrick Street, had changed a lot.

'What do you know about Pana?' Cyril asked.

I told him of my youth at Pres. on Western Road, living in Faranlea Park, my uncle Dick Barry, the TD in Fermoy.

'You never told me that,' he said. The lunch dragged on, and on. I had been hoping to get the four o clock train. Back in his office, he picked up my list of 'asks'.

'We can pay you that, that, not that, that and that,' a most satisfactory total. And then he took me to the train, sending his best regards to Pat Herlihy.

I'm sure that, even without my Cork credentials, the result would have been the same, but only very eventually. Blood's thicker and all that.

Anyway, things in Ascon were fine for me. Or so I thought. In the first week of January 1983, I was called to Head Office and told I was redundant.

12

Saudi Arabia or the Council

I was shocked, stunned. I never saw it coming, although the signs had been there if I'd paid any attention to them. A new managing director-designate had been announced before Christmas, without any reference to myself or the next two most senior in the firm, John Craddock and John Pentony, both working in Moneypoint.

Mary was hopping mad, particularly because of what she had done for Ascon's people in Malawi. Business was business, I reconciled. New work was drying up. Ireland was in recession. The redundancy package that I was given, per my solicitor, was in order.

I began painting the house, this apparently a standard reaction. I sold the company car, which I had been let keep, and bought a smaller Peugeot 304, for which I used diesel from our heating tank. I got a business card designed and made up with help from Johnny Fanning and considered what I would do next.

There would be no work to be had in Irish civil engineering or building. Collen Brothers, a strong protestant firm, had some months ago let go Joss Lynham, their very able and well known engineer. This was not a big deal, other than to those involved, but was the first sign of impending trouble. To find work, it looked like I'd have to go abroad, Saudi Arabia or somewhere.

There was, however, another possibility. My friend Dick Morrissey encouraged me to apply to the county councils. I cringed, but did so. In the meantime, I had to get some money coming in. A roofing job in Bray came my way. I took on men, through the *Evening Press*, using first names only and paying cash. They would disappear at dole time and I hoped that I wouldn't meet them in the Labour Exchange, where I too was collecting. I also got work doing a survey and proposal for improvements to the *Sean Céibh*, the old quay in Spiddal, County Galway.

In the yacht club world, where I was a member of the Royal St. George, I kept up appearances, hoping not to run into Hal Sisk. Apart from the Ascon connection, I had done a survey of traditional boats with him for the Maritime Institute of Ireland.

Around Saint Patrick's Day, keeping the sunny side up, Mary and I invited our friends to a 'redundancy party' in Belgrave Road. Great Night!

At Easter I got a job offer from Dublin County Council and took it, with misgivings at being sentenced to this 'graveyard of ambition'.

I wasn't to know it then, but in the succeeding years, when I took every conceivable break from work to go sailing, which the local authority system allowed me and which the commercial world of contracting would not have, I had a lot to thank Hal Sisk for.

13

Brittany, Mostly

Larry Brassil, Deputy County Engineer, made me welcome, said his door would always be open – which later it wasn't – and sent me to take charge of Sandyford Bin Depot, refuse collection. I also would be responsible for a number of graveyards, or more politely called 'burial grounds'. My immediate senior would be a Pat Dullaghan. Reporting to me, as Inspector General, would be Christy Bollard.

On day one, as Christy and I set off in his car from the depot, he said that we *both* would be entitled to whatever mileage (expenses) were clocked up. Oh? And many others were the local matters of 'custom and practise' I got to know as I settled into my new domain. The binmen, on 'job and finish' working arrangements, had their rounds done and were finished their day by about 1.00 pm. The foremen, having seen their men off at about 8.20, would go for a short drive around and be back in the depot in plenty of time for their 10.00 o clock tea.

And my main purpose, as I was beginning to see it, was to sign the wages sheets.

There had been a low intensity 'go slow' in progress when I arrived. Working with Christy, we managed it, minimising disruption to the public. Brassil complimented me. I did do, or tried to do, some useful analysis of the binmen's rounds. I did write some letters to the more extreme abusers of the council's sick pay scheme; for one of which I was hauled up by both the men's trade union and the council's Personnel Department. Bohernabreena Burial Ground was the only active one we had. The others all were old and had been a long time full, our work in those being mainly maintenance, hedge cutting and such. In Kilgobbin, up in Stepaside, we had two stonemasons carrying out repairs to the very old church there. That at least was interesting, if very, very slow moving.

For painting of graveyard railings and metalwork, we had the council's painters come from Swords Depot. Yes, travelling through the city from across the other side of the county (there was no M50 then), starting from their depot at 8.00, or as quickly after as they themselves decided when they had their brushes and paint sorted, and being back by 4.00. Their effective hours on the job were a joke.

I did what I could to move things along, with Christy Bollard being both experienced and helpful. My pay wasn't too bad, particularly with the excellent 'mileage'. I fitted in as best I could and got on with it. At least I had plenty of time to get the boat ready for the season.

Louis Purton and Liam Canavan had become key men in the upkeep of *Saint Patrick*. As Kevin later said, 'We wouldn't have got the boat out of the Irish Sea without them.'

I had got to know Louis Purton through my uncle, Leo Ganter. As a kid I had watched Uncle Leo taking running dives from up high off Spiddal pier stormwall. Louis and he played music together, Leo on accordion and Louis on flute, an odd pair in that Louis was many years his junior. Louis always loved 'tinkering', fixing things. He himself had a boat, a Laser dinghy when first I knew him, later a pocket cruiser, *Clarinda*. This he would tow down to Roundstone, launching and sailing from Ervallagh (pronounced 'erlough'). Liam was a brother-in-law of Louis, his wife Pauline being Liam's sister and the principal of a girls' school.

There was nothing mechanical or electrical on *Saint Patrick* that Liam and Louis couldn't repair, improve or make better: metal spider bands on the mast, and other spars; a trim tab to take the weather helm off the rudder; a pot-bellied stove; a heater piped off the engine; an anchor-chain pawl, a bilge pump driven off the engine; navigation lights; compass lights and a fuel tank. Still, she

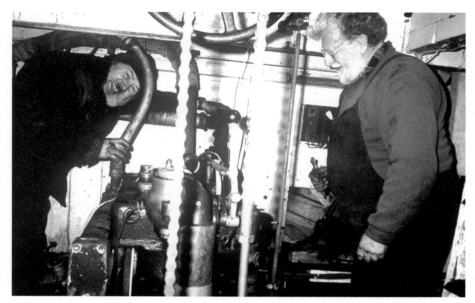

*Liam Canavan and Louis Purton seen here later working
on the Kelvin engine on* Ilen.

remained a relatively simple boat, strong and fairly foolproof. Fresh water for cooking was taken directly by hand pump from a 20-litre drum. The pot-bellied stove ran on sticks, coal, turf or anything else that would burn. The toilet was a black bucket, for privacy taken to the foredeck.

In 1983 we went to Brittany, with family link ups, ourprevious visit being indicative of her attractions. Conn McCann's *Connacht*, the oldest remaining Galway Hooker, was in company with us intermittently. He played fiddle and whistle and had Paraic Ó Tuairisg and whistle player Raphael McIlhone as crew. The weather everywhere was glorious. Basing ourselves in Duarnenez and Concarneau, the best of Breton hospitality was enjoyed. We were treated royally by Bernard Cadoret and friends of the *Chasse Marée* magazine. Their book on French working sailboats, *Ar Vag*, in two volumes, was a delight. Jean-Jacques Guillou of the Societe Nautique de la Baie De Cancarneau was responsible for a fine time had by all.

We made sail by the quayside in Camaret and heard later that Parisiennes on holiday were delighted to see a real 'Breton boat'.

In '84 we again sailed to Brittany, our focus being on the Morbihan and La Trinité, where ourselves and Cronins had taken a house for a month in nearby Carnac. Sailing with me from Dun Laoghaire were Kevin, Sean and Joe Kenny. Joe had never been further offshore than the Forty-Foot, but had his own place in local nautical history as one of the very few to go off the high board in Blackrock Baths on a bicycle during the Sandycove Gala comedy act.

At mid-Friday afternoon, on a warm July 7, we left Dun Laoghaire, the tide due to run against us until 17.00. The wind was as forecast, Force 3 from the southeast. We motored. In Killiney Bay the wind changed, or seemed to, to Force 4 southerly. We set two-man, four-hour watches and streamed the log in a now dirty sea, with the wind blowing over the southgoing tide. At 21.00, determined to establish a civilised regime, we partook of a tot of malt all round. The fire was lit to take the chill off the cabin. We stayed inside the Arklow Bank and outside the Wexford Banks and sighted the Tuskar Light out of the fog at 05.30. Course was set for Round Island, Scillies, and we motored on.

Saturday was another sunny day. A forecast southerly Force 2 to 4 did not materialise. Some sunsights were tried, to get the hand in and the brain working and were found to agree tolerably well with the 'dead reckoning'. At 100 miles off Round Island our radio direction finder (RDF) did not register it at all. However the cooking from a still well-stocked larder was up to an excellent standard. By 17.00 a breeze from the east southeast had filled in. Up went all sail and the engine was gratefully turned off with 110 miles logged. A beautiful evening followed. This was cruising as it should be with regular meals, steady progress, dry bunks and good company. To allow for leeway, we altered course by ten degrees towards the east. Dolphins were jumping about and gannets (according to Sean) were in abundance. An evening sunsight again put us on our dead reckoning line. This really was too much! Saturday evening dinner was washed down with a light red from Quinnsworth as we reached easily at four and a half knots. However the sun set high over a cloud bank to the west and a ground swell came up. The forecast was for a deepening low west of Shannon.

The RDF picked up Round Island before midnight, about five or ten degrees off out port bow. Now the question was whether we would to sail on past the Scillies or pull in? Our records show that we did copious calculations of depths, ETAs and the likes, indicating that the navigator at least had no intention of passing the delights of the Isles of Scilly. At 04.00 on Sunday morning the Round Island light came into sight and the Seven Stones light, over by Lands End, was on our port quarter. We sailed in through Crow Sound and went alongside a crowded Hughtown Pier for a 7.00 am breakfast.

We were shortly afterwards encouraged by Art, the assistant harbour master, to move out to anchor. Over a glass, later in the day when he had more time, he described in loquacious detail the feudal system under which the islands were administered. These are part of the Duchy of Cornwall. In even more lucid detail he described the difficulties pertaining to his own job. In Hughtown the harbour fee for *anchoring* was £3 per day.

Our intended short stay in the Scillies extended to two days, as a southerly gale kept the large international fleet of cruising yachts pinned down. As a by-product we visited many anchorages within the islands using depth sounder, arithmetic and detailed Chart 34. We also visited some yachts and (between us) all the known pubs. By Tuesday we were impatient to get going. The low was moving slowly away and the evening forecast gave a decreasing south/southwesterly. We left shortly after dark. Later, a VHF radio call from a Welsh yacht in Hughtown harbour came on the air, enquiring about sea conditions. They were informed by our watch that the skipper was 'asleep in his bunk'. In his bunk, yes, but sleeping? Unfortunately not! A tough night followed, but not what you might call 'a pasting'. The hand pump blocked a couple of times and was cleared. This is a hands and knees operation on the cabin floor, which is normally guaranteed to unsettle a body. However it is remarkable how a problem is diminished if fed and fit.

By 13.00 the next day, out of the grey a navigation buoy appeared. Glory be! We were 30 miles out to sea northwest of Ouessant, why should there be a buoy? Chart 20, Ile d'Ouessant to St. Nazaire was consulted and, sure enough, it revealed our buoy, more or less where we thought we were. The navigator's star was in the ascendant again, after some temporary doubt.

We later picked up the big Ar Men lighthouse off to port. We rounded the unseen rocksand eased sheets further for Penmarche. Our crew all being in fine fettle, we added a foresail and by midnight had the blaze of lights, which marks this headland, on our beam. Penfren (Glenaan) came in line with its protecting mark by 04.00 Thursday. The wind held up as we bowled along. Belle Isle appeared ahead, on cue, and the foresail was doused to slow us for the tricky Teignouse Passage. Going through, we met an early morning racing fleet and exchanged pleasantries in our best French. We gybed off the lighthouse and across the shoal waters of Quiberon we ran, in showery squalls, to tie up at the outer pontoon in La Trinité Marina at midday Thursday.

Harnesses and oilskins were peeled off as we prepared ourselves for the pleasures of La Belle France. Two of our families had combined to rent a grand maison in nearby Carnac for July. Contact was made. Driven by Mary and Suzanne, they had successfully traversed their party of 12, plus Mirror dinghy, on the car ferry route. Notwithstanding engine problems on the ferry putting timetables out of joint, their trip was fine, with double servings of movies and discos enjoyed by the kids.

Carnac is an old Breton village, overshadowed by the considerable influx of French visitors in the many holiday houses in the area. Life was good there, if a little pricey; putting the Mirror dinghy in the local yacht club was £40 for the month, the house rent was £500 a week. La Trinité-sur-Mer had a well organised yachting centre, under the benevolent control of the municipal authority. For our £10 a day we got a pontoon berth or mooring, 24 hour launch service, security, weather reports and company.

For 12 days we forayed forth *en famille*, generally every second day, to a variety of places. The abiding impression I recall is of anchoring in a couple of fathoms off sandy beaches. The grown-ups would swim ashore. Life-jacketed toddlers would be rowed in the dinghy by some of the older kids, with the picnic consumables. The weather was only middling for sailing, but was great for the beach. Places visited were Belle Isle (Les Grand Sables), Quiberon (Port d'Orange) and, within the Morbihan, Port Navalo, Locmariaquer, Ile Logue, La Bona and the old village of St. Goustan at the head of the Auray River. Happy days, how quickly they passed. The only concerns were fast flowing tides and dinner bookings. Our bachelor crew reported the nightlife as being exotic, but unrewarding.

The local working boats of the Morbihan were lug-rigged and run by islanders called Sinagot. The boats, as far as we could make out, also are known as Sinagot. Alas, we saw only two and those somewhat out of character, having being tarted up. The French all along this coast were interested in old sailing boats. The Société Nautique de la Baie de Concarnneau was one of several active groups along the Brittany coast who host an annual maritime festival, featuring old boats, both local and visiting. The French in general, and in Breton in particular, show an affinity for *Le Irlandais* and their boats. A ferry load of Parisienne holidaymakers were thrilled to see the red sails going up on this old Breton boat. The ferry skipper, that evening, told us that he hadn't the heart to tell them that their Anciens Bateaux Bretagne had been Irish. C'est okay.

While at Quimper we had an evening with our friends from the previous year, Bernard and Michelle Cadoret, who run the magazine *Le Chasse Maree*, which deals with the maritime arts, particularly old working sailing boats. He described to us how the southwest coast of Ireland was well known to Breton fishermen. They used to do a round trip of a fortnight to work the lobster and crawfish during neap-tides. The 1920s 'troubles' in Ireland were apparently good years for the Bretons due to the lack of attention from the forces of law and order ashore, who were otherwise engaged.

It was time to go. Sean had been replaced by Peter White, who came aboard weighed down with ham radio equipment. He was delighted to be on the Maritime Band, now prefacing his many numbers with the letters MM – Mickey Mouse.

And so to sea again we went, homeward bound. On Tuesday the 24th clocks were set to British Standard Time and four watches were set. Watch calls were ten minutes before time. The wind was on our nose. We motored out, and kept motoring all day, arriving at Raz de Seine before dawn on Wednesday. Notwithstanding that this now was the fourth time in three years that we had been through the Raz, we had difficulty with the lights there for navigation. There are so many and the brightest ones are not always the nearest.

We lost a couple of hours getting a positive fix before we punched the neap ebb to go through. We breakfasted in Chenal du Four. Sail was hoisted, but the wind was too light so the motoring continued through Chenal de la Helle, setting course for The Longships off Lands End. Later in the day the wind settled from the east, giving us a good overnight sail across the English Channel to sight The Lizard in the early morning. We sighted Tater Du Lighthouse (*Du* we reckoned being the old Cornish for the Irish word for black, *dubh*.). We passed inside The Runnelstone, not recommended, and outside The Longships to reach St. Ives in hot sunshine.

St. Ives, then as now, is strictly a fair weather port of call, with its drying harbour crowded with small boats and the bay open to any swell running. On Friday evening we took the ground alongside the old stone pier on the west side of the harbour. As I stayed with her, while 'seeing her down', the local brass band played on the pierhead. This was solid stuff, being enjoyed by all in a thoroughly old fashioned way. The Sloop Bar is easily seen from this pier and seemed to be the favoured watering hole of nautical types, both yachting and working. Our Joe reported that at 6.00 am 'the seagulls own this town'.

The last leg of 190 miles was good, a easy westerly wind giving us nice sailing up St. Georges Channel and then the Irish Sea to bring us into Dublin Bay on Sunday afternoon. *Ar Ais Arís.*

I made some notes subsequently on the Galway Hookers, *Saint Patrick* in particular, as cruising boats. The gear is heavy, the helm is heavy. When the sails are full and drawing, life is comfortable, but any change requires knack and muscle, in that order. Reefing down sail is hard work, particularly in the sea conditions in which it mostly is done. Twenty minutes would not be unusual to allow for reefing if in any sort of a seaway. Hookers are a dead loss on a long windward passage. We use the engine on tick-over if close-hauled. If headed by the wind on a long passage, we would down sail and motor into it. The decks leak and we are only moderately successful in deflecting the resulting drips. Against that, they are a stable, sea-kindly boat on which to eat, sleep and navigate aboard. An open coal stove makes life below distinctly cosy. The decks are broad and solid underfoot, a rigid nine-foot dinghy being easily carried. Shoregoing is facilitated by taking the ground alongside wherever possible and storage onboard presents no problem at all. Off the wind, they are a delight to sail, but foremost of all is the aura which they exude, of other days and rocky places.

14

Isla Selvagem and Tenerife

Waiting for us on the harbour wall of Los Cristianos were Catherine Rochford, Suzanne and Mary. It was July 1985 and we had sailed *Saint Patrick* from Dublin to Tenerife, one of the Canary Islands.

A couple of days later we all sailed to the nearby island of Gomera, a day which turned out very differently from that intended. From Los Cristianos, on Tenerife's southwest coast, to San Sebastián de la Gomera, is only 21 miles. A mere puddin' for men who have sailed the ocean wide. Or so we thought. This was to be a nice *promenade sur mer* – or the Spanish equivalent – a sea picnic for our wives and a trio of casual German acquaintances.

Motoring out of the harbour, only an hour and a half after our intended 9.00 am start, life felt good. There was diesel in the tank, wine in stock and sun warming the deck. The almost calm breeze from ahead offered no scruple to our consciences as wind sailors. And so it went for an hour or two. No need for a compass or Walker log as Gomera appeared looming out of the mist. A casual comment on white seagulls in the water ahead went unremarked. About ten minutes later a cry was heard as the first wave ran several inches of water down the towels spread on deck. The next one drenched all on it and the next again ran in the open portlights and hatches. Pandemonium ensued. Oilskin jackets were dragged out of storage, picnic baskets flew, some felt sick. A northerly Force 7 wind had come out of the blue on our starboard bow, with steep, two metre breaking seas. How could this be? We were in about 1,000 fathom depth about midway between the islands. There was nothing for it but to bang on. Weren't we lucky not to have had sail up?

For an hour and a half we crawled forward, praying against fuel blockages and airlocks. The ladies were not amused by salty phrases involving 'heaving to', 'bare poles', 'short sail', 'running for sea room' and so forth. About 3.00 pm we swept into the shelter of the harbour of San Sebastián and tied alongside the wall between two inter-island ferries. One French yacht swung to anchor, a dozen small open fishing boats inside her. We dried out, swam, picnicked and visited the town. We spoke to a resident Dutch yachtsman who explained the wind phenomenon and the eddy of the Canary Current which kicks up the sea nearby.

We lost several of our guests to the ferry, pulled all reefs in the mainsail, put a *barróg* in the flying jib, donned oilskins and harnesses and took off like a Five o Five. The ferry overtook us a couple of hours later as we were taking out reefs. By the time it passed us the wind had dropped to nothing. We tidied and engined back 'home' to Los Cristianos. This was our last sail on a cruise that had taken us 1,900 miles from Dublin Bay in the previous three weeks.

The crew were Sean and Kevin, as usual, Joe Kenny again and Fred Rochford on a first outing, with myself dispensing orders. Johnny Walsh, from the Irish Mountaineering Club and with the benefit of a week's sail training in Glenans, was to join us later. Joe had previously established that he could cook in sea conditions in which no takers could be found to consume. Fred, though not a sailor, was a good all rounder and one of nature's gentlemen. An amount of organisation had been brought to bear on this year's preparations. Joe was in charge of 'first aid'. He and I had taken a nine-week course. Various tinctures, tablets, drugs and syringes had been supplied by a friendly sailing doc, David Thomas, who also supplied a supporting certificate of authorisation for the drugs. Kevin was the cameraman. He had acquired an additional yellow plastic underwater camera, for £39, to capture all those hitherto un-shootable moments. He didn't of course, but that was not the fault of the camera, merely that at those crisis times both his

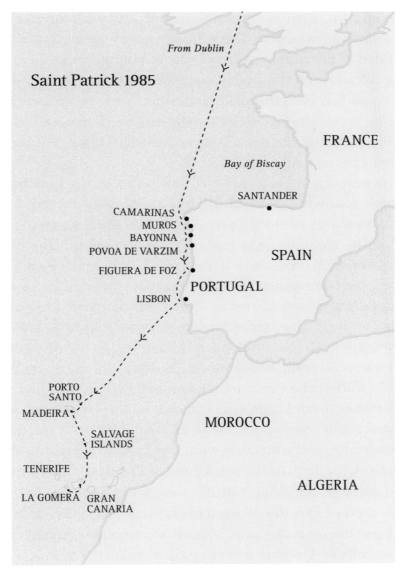

Saint Patrick 1985

From Dublin

FRANCE

Bay of Biscay

SANTANDER

CAMARINAS
MUROS
BAYONNA
POVOA DE VARZIM
FIGUERA DE FOZ

SPAIN

PORTUGAL

LISBON

PORTO
SANTO
MADEIRA

MOROCCO

SALVAGE
ISLANDS

TENERIFE

LA GOMERA GRAN
CANARIA

ALGERIA

Dublin to Tenerife

hands were required elsewhere. Joe had a movie camera, loaned by RTÉ. Sean was quartermaster and chef, a post for which he required no additional training. The navigational gear was supplemented with a proper Kelvin Hughes sextant, loaned by friend Pete Hogan.

The ship herself appeared externally much as she had for the previous 76 years, the rig and sails being unchanged, but bigger. The coachroof had been strengthened and bolted down. Deck sealing had been done, a new Sampson post fitted, five oak frames replaced and six planks renewed. The caulking was hardened. A trim tab was fitted to the rudder. A brake was put on the prop shaft, a sea-water tap taken off the engine water inlet and a gimballed cooker, with oven, had been installed. The ballast was wedged in and the covering floorboards coach-bolted down. The inside received a new coat of cream and the outside several coats of black. We needed a holiday after all that!

The evening of Friday, July 5, saw us motoring quietly down the Irish Sea, with mainsail up, hoping for a favourable breeze. The forecast was westerly Force 3, which as usual was too good to materialise. We quit the charade and off Bray Head dropped sail and motored on. What was it about Friday nights that we always seemed to motor down the Irish Sea? In earlier days, in lighter boats, getting round Carnsore Point seemed to be a justification for use of the engine. Indeed, as unpleasant a night as ever I had had was spent off Cahore Point, in a bilge keel Eventide, waiting to catch the south going ebb at dawn. Poulduff, an uneasy anchorage north of Cahore, had been indelibly impressed on my mind as one of my non-favourite anchorages. Such thoughts passed the night as we went south. We had reviewed the safety drill – 'If you go over, you're dead' – and who takes what if we had to launch the liferaft: Sean, food; Joe, first aid; Kevin, fishing tackle; Fred, water. I'd be doing Mayday on the radio. Watches were set as two-man, four-hour. With a crew of five, this allowed every second off-watch to be eight hours – in theory at any rate. Inshore is hard on the navigator as he can never be easy within soundings, particularly if it is his boat!

A word on navigation: Dead reckoning (DR) is done using a compass to give direction and a Walker Log to give the distance travelled. The Walker Log is trailed behind the boat, with its rotator turning the mileage clock. Starting from a known position, one can then plot on the chart one's progress, making allowance for tidal set and leeway. It is in making such allowances that the 'art' comes in to navigation – as well as the fact that the helmsman may not always have been steering the stated compass course. Other compass allowances are necessary for 'variation' and 'deviation'. Resulting accuracy should be within two or three miles per hundred travelled.

In sight of shore or island features, more precise position fixes are determined by taking angles off known features and plotting the intersection of such lines on the chart. These should spot you to a quarter mile or less.

Astro navigation is done with a sextant, taking sights on the sun or stars. By measuring the angle between the altitude of the sun and the horizon at any accurately taken time, with the use of navigational tables and an almanac, one can plot a 'position line' – you are somewhere on this line. A further sight, taken later in the day, gives another line. Where they intersect, allowing for distance travelled between sights, gives one's position. This should be accurate to within about five miles. This is only attainable on a yacht in good conditions, that is, a steady boat, visible sun and a clear horizon.

By Saturday morning our sails were up and we cleared the Tuskar with the last of the south going tide. The short wave radio, recently installed, was working well on the ham bands, that is, ones that can both receive and transmit. The day continued fine, with fair wind, and that night the stars were up. We were sailing on the eastern edge of a stable high pressure system and all seemed well with the world.

Believe it or not, so it continued until we reached the northwest coast of Spain, five days later. Our plan was to close Cape Finisterre, but keep clear of its offlying shipping lanes. Our sunsight plots had tied in well with any ships that we had spoken to on the VHF radio. We hardened sheets to close the land, in towards the southeast.

Our watch runs had been increasing gradually, with a combination of rising wind and a desire to get to shore. But the wind and sea rose, the foam blew off the wavetops in streaks. We got the mainsail and jib down and with engine and steadying foresail closed the land, still not in sight. The easy alternative of running away southwest, before wind and sea, if it occurred to us at all, was not considered. In a long few hours land eventually appeared through the haze, about two miles ahead. The seas eased and we

Rough weather in the Bay of Biscay (photo by Kevin Cronin)

met a French yacht coming downwind under her headsail. Off Ria de Corme y Lage the trailing log was taken in. That night the village of Camariñas, 18 miles on, was our haven and our heaven.

Anchoring off the pier with four or five other yachts, the restaurant was pointed out to us by people with dark-creased features who wore black and dark blue. Washing and flowers hung overhead in the narrow streets. The restaurant looked like any of the other bars, with its terrazzo and TV, but they took good care of us. Later we watched the sardines being iced and loaded from fishing boats on to lorries. Sean swam back to our boat, which was probably as safe a way as our return in the dinghy. We conked out in bunks, flat out.

The next day we were under sail at ten. The wind falling light we drifted and fished, then anchored off a sandy beach a mile to the north of Cape Finisterre, Playa del Mar de Fora. Later we made for Muros and the next day, foggy at first, for Isla Cíes with its pine woods down to the beach, later sailing eight miles to the town of Baiona. There we tied stern to, our anchor off the bow. Baiona was gorgeous, fulfilling all descriptions and expectations, which unfortunately could not be said of our journey's end the next day in Povoa de Varzim, the Blackpool of Portugal. Skip it, unless stuck for a harbour of refuge. We left it shortly after midnight and the next day had pleasant sailing to Figueira da Foz, altogether nicer. Again we left after midnight, this time under sail. By 8.00 am we were fully reefed-down in a following wind and sea. All day we coasted, passing inside the Berlenga Islands and picking off features on this coast of endless beaches and sunshine. Because of the strong wind, the *Nortada*, we wore tee shirts.

We passed Cascais, intending to anchor, but the wind would have made dinghy work dangerous, so we continued up the mighty Tagus River to Lisbon. A full gale had risen and we were glad to be in.

For three days we 'touristed', visiting the monuments, Maritime Museum, Old Quarter, the lot. Johnny Walsh joined us and now we were bound for Madeira, 500 miles to the southwest.

This *Nortada* had us scared by now and it wasn't all bar talk, where the hazards of the sea are often exaggerated. Since arriving in Lisbon, each afternoon saw a full gale from the north. Lisbon Met. Office said that this would continue, but would be less out from the land. How far out? They couldn't tell us. So we left at dawn, streaming the log off the Tower of Belem and getting under sail at Fort Buggio, the sandbank fortress which guards the great harbour of Lisbon. We cleared with Cascais Radio and were on our way. A course was set to the north of our line in anticipation of the *Nortada*, which never came.

For day after day we sailed without incident, always reefs in, sometimes all. Generally we stayed under-canvassed, and always so by night, shades of the East Indiamen. Without pushing, we knocked off over 120 miles a day. Meals were regular. The sea got bluer, a deep azure, perhaps turquoise. Each afternoon a baking session produced three loaves of soda bread, eaten as soon as they cooled. Oilskins were worn at night to keep off the dew; the harness always worn at night. At 10.00 pm, on our fourth day out, the Porto Santo light flashed on our starboard bow. Five hours later we dropped our anchor in the warm water of the new harbour.

*Better weather going south. Johnny Walsh, Sean Mullan, Joe Kenny
and Fred Rochford (photo by Kevin Cronin)*

In the morning a nominal shore party spent a couple of hours on this little sister island of Madeira. Two yachts swung at anchor. It had the flavour of a tropical version of Aran, with a crowd waiting for the plane from Funchal. It was there that Christopher Columbus, while a young sea captain, had met his bride, the Governor's daughter. For us, a brisk quartering sail closed the thirty mile distance to Madeira. Funchal was beautiful, its people civilised. To attempt to say more might diminish it. For three days we enjoyed its hospitality.

We left for Tenerife, 300 miles to the south, by way of the Salvage Islands, Isla Selvagem. Fifteen miles from Funchal, in a rising wind, while reefing, we had an unmerciful gybe. The 24-foot gaff snapped in two and jammed aloft. The topping lift was torn off the boom and we were in trouble. The seas were knocking the boat about, making a bosun's chair job up the mast not impossible, but certainly hazardous. We couldn't reach the clew of the sail to cut its lashing and brail the sail to the mast. The engine was started and we motored slowly head to wind to consider. Isla Deserta lay about 13 miles upwind. This was uninhabited, with only goats and wild tomatoes. We put back for Madeira. Gradually, the wind and sea dropped. We

Fred Rochford repairing the broken spar (photo by Kevin Cronin)

anchored and made repairs, but held our departure until the next morning. Much chastened we left, the stars still bright in the pinkness of oncoming dawn.

Selvagem Grande rose to meet us 133 miles onward. Three and a half hours later we anchored in Cagarras cove, on the sheltered south side. We were surprised to see people about, as it was supposed to be uninhabited. And there even was a Portugese flag. The holding was poor on a rutted rock bottom, so we shore-partied in two trips. The people were ornithologists; one group of four from the Portugese mainland, the other were English-speaking Madeiranese. Shearwaters abound in these waters and until recently weremuch sought after as a delicacy by fishermen from Madeira who came annually in July. They used to catch them with hooks and barrel them. We walked the island round. It is a volcanic plateau of about one mile in diameter, 500 feet high. There are some signs of former agriculture, with water ditches. There were no houses apart from the two we saw at the landing place, one of which was occupied by two lighthouse keepers, whose duty, they said was to protect the birds, mind the light and to defend the island! We remarked that this might have more to do with protecting fishing and mineral rights than navigation.

These are called Ilheus Selvagem on Portugese charts. Many English references call them the Salvage Islands, but they have always been Portugese and the translation of *selvagem* is 'savage' not 'salvage'.

Captain Kidd's treasure is thought to be lost in these waters. Shackleton had received permission from the Admiralty to search for this when returning from Antarctica. He died before reaching these waters and that was that. We wondered whether he also had asked the Portugese authorities for such permission? Unlikely.

We pointed our bowsprit for Tenerife and a day and a half later sailed into Los Cristianos. For the following week with our wives/ girlfriends we swam, ate well, sailed locally and met some people. The Hooker was lifted ashore in the local boatyard, stripped, scrubbed and washed down. Hot work!

It felt unreal to be back in Dublin airport on a rainy, cold, end of July night.

   ह ह ह

In January of 1984 I had been elected a member of the Irish Cruising Club (ICC), proposed by yachting journalist Winkie Nixon. This club has no premises, no real 'overhead' and so the 'sub' is nominal. It promotes cruising, rather than racing which was well catered for elsewhere, though most of its members would have 'cut their teeth' at racing. It is a 32-county organisation, most of whose people were considered 'better off', though it had a proportion who visibly were not – teachers, technicians and others just making their way and enjoying the cruising.

Through the *ICC Annual*, I read of the doings of others, near and far. The Christmas Lunch became a landmark feature, mighty *craic*, often running into the late late hours. Through the years I contributed to the *Annual*, the primary requirement being a good cruise, with a story well told. Later, for ten years, I was to be its Honorary Editor. From the ICC and associated British and American Clubs I got occasional awards and dined well. But most of all, I met good people. It was to become an integral part of my life.

15

Westward to America

'Are you going west?' my sailing friend John Gore-Grimes had messaged me.

'Yep,' I responded. Always better to tell the truth, but not say too much, in advance at any rate.

In November 1984, Opsail of New York had invited *Saint Patrick* to take part in the Parade of Sail, which would take place on July 4, 1986 to celebrate the centennial of the Statue of Liberty. They had got our name from the Brittany connection. We now were about to put to sea again, bound for New York City.

Danny Sheehy and myself went out ahead to Tenerife in April to get the boat ready. Danny was a woodwork teacher by trade, but now fishing for a living in his home waters around the Blaskets. He last had sailed on *Saint Patrick* in 1981 when we went to Spain. Joe and Fred couldn't come due to work, but Joe maintained that they had in any event 'broken the back of the journey'! The condition of the boat, after the winter in the Canaries, was much worse than we had expected: her paint was peeling and blistered, her seams were opened badly, shakes had shrunk in her spars.

Danny Sheehy preparing for caulking. The long hot winter had badly shrunk the boat timbers.

For two weeks Danny and I worked on her, relieved only by the doubtful attractions of cheap drink and late nights. We employed a shipwright to recaulk her. We located a 25-foot timber pole, not easy in these parts, and made a new gaff to replace the one broken last year. The blocks were greased, the lines end for ended, the sails reinforced in places, the engine serviced and started. Newly painted, we launched and held our breath.

The pumping reduced quickly to a tolerable level. We put aboard 23 five-gallon drums of drinking water and diesel for 400 miles. The distance to Bermuda was 3,000 miles, targeted at 30 days. We carried provisions for a 15-day overrun, plus emergency liferaft rations.

A week after launching, Kevin, Sean, Johnny and Colm Dubh Ó Mealóid arrived. For Colm this was his first passage of any length. However he was from Camus Uachtair in Connemara and had the sailing of Hookers in his blood. He also played the melodeon, or 'the box' as he called it.

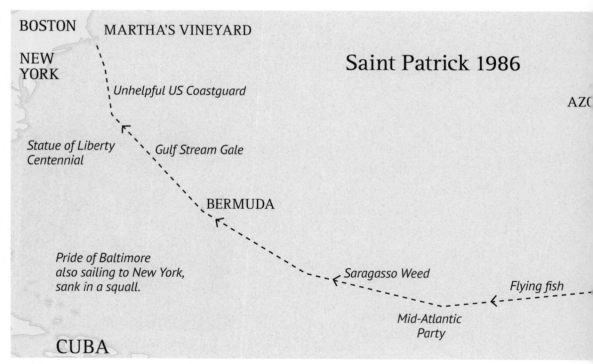

Tenerife to Martha's Vineyard, 1986

On May 12, with a forecast of northeasterly Force 7 at our back, we untied from the harbour wall and faced to the southwest. To get solidly into the trade wind belt we planned to go southward first before turning west. As we reefed to a strengthening wind the evening grew grey and almost Irish. By dusk all reefs were in and both headsails were down. Occasional gusts had threatened our flying jib or the bowsprit. Provided we kept strictly stern to the wind and sea we were in control. At the 10.00 o clock watch change Danny said, 'We'll have to get the sail off her.'

'No,' I said. 'Keep going as we are, we want to get away from these bloody islands, with their currents and downdrafts, as quickly as we can.'

We were doing watches in pairs. Despite being whacked, I couldn't get to sleep. It's always the same for the first couple of off-watches. The boat's gear seemed to be taking a hammering. In my dozing I felt the movement become less regular and the noise of the wind and water seemed to rise. I tried to ignore it. I woke to

LISBON •

MADEIRA

oken Spar

VAGE ISLANDS

TENERIFE ·

ckdown

the sound of a tremendous crashing noise, blocking out all other sounds, and found myself dropped out of my bunk on to the port bunk opposite. I saw the pressure cooker in the air and water flowing solidly through the mainhatch. Rushing towards the hatch, in the oilskins that I had never taken off, I met Colm rising from the port quarter bunk. He had taken the torrent full on. He got the engine started and the belt-driven pump working.

It was three in the morning. The lads on deck were all there, held aboard by their harnesses. The running rigging was in a mess. The mainsail was torn. The wave which knocked us had come from ahead of the beam, Sean said, a wall of water roaring down on us. It took us all an hour and a half to get the mainsail down and the foresail up. In an hour's time, Colm and I would be on watch again. Some first night out!

By the afternoon of the following day the sun was out and the wind and seas were down. We surveyed the damage: torn mainsail, broken VHF aerial, top mastband torn off. The wave had run right over us. All these were fixable, as far as we could see. However, more seriously, the rudder had come loose in its irons. The shrinkage of its timber, aggravated by the heavy battering, had caused that. I considered whether to put back for repairs. 'Carry on,' I decided. Fortunately we were successful in getting all into sailing shape again, due in no small measure to Colm and Danny's work. When there's work to be done, you can't beat good tradesmen.

A couple of days later, on reaching the latitude of 25 degrees south, we made our turn to the west and now felt truly on our way.

Day followed night, night followed day. The fresh provisions were mostly gone and the green tomatoes and bananas were starting to ripen nicely. We cooked in pairs, by rota, every third day.

Reefing the mainsail in rising wind (photo by Kevin Cronin).

Breakfasts were *ad hoc*, lunch was prepared by the cooks, usually a rice salad or the like, and eaten on deck. One bottle of wine, between us, would wash it down.

All had agreed that a fairly robust approach would be maintained towards keeping our speed up, tempered of course with prudence. Our ship was, after all, nearly 80 years old and for 50 of those years had worked cargo for six months of the year. This was considerably more service than any yacht of similar age might have seen. The men who built her, Pat and Joe Casey of Mweenish near Carna, were masters of their trade. There never was a boat that came out of that family's yard, over three generations, that wasn't sweet and strong. *Saint Patrick* hadn't let us down. It was up to us to play our part.

And so we changed her sail area up and down, as the wind dictated, without waiting for the change of watch. Reefing was a four-man job; the pair due on the next watch would be called to make up the four. At the end of the first week we had covered daily 65, 109, 111, 86, 94, 105 and 132 miles, a total of 702. Those early days had slowed us, but our target of 30 days looked attainable.

We were discovering that, at this time of year, so called southeast trades actually blow more from the east. For the Hooker a wind from dead aft is a nuisance; the headsails tend to be blanketed behind the very big mainsail. So much of the time we found ourselves tacking downwind to keep the wind on our quarter and so gain speed. By and large, we had too little wind rather than too much.

Each day we baked soda bread in the oven and what a treat that was, with strawberry jam. My own reputation as a poor cook was reinforced by once making an 'Erin' dinner on salt water. Too late I read the instructions – Erin Foods included all the ingredients, including salt. Luckily, both Sean and Johnny were excellent cooks. We looked forward to their 'cooking day'.

The first time we caught a fish on the line we were like children with excitement. 'You'd think we never before had seen a fish,' said Danny. Mind you, Kevin had been nursing the trailing fishing line for a week before this catch. 'Surface fishing,' he described it and his bag was a 'dolphin fish'. This is not related to the mammal dolphin, more like a small tuna. We later caught a barracuda, but the dolphin fishes were our mainstay. About once a week they gave us a change of diet.

The flying fish were a delight, visible two or three times most days, swooping over the waves, translucent with their small wings and sometimes even landing on our deck. They were too small to think of cooking; in any event, it would have seemed unkind.

The days were sunny and warm, the nights starry. By day we were 'sunburn aware', wearing hat, tee shirt and sunglasses most of the time. The recommended clothing for overall sun protection was silk pyjamas – not much in evidence! The nights were a little cooler, not much; a tee shirt was still good enough.

While we steered by grid compass and trailed a Walker Log, our position fixes were by intersection of sunsight lines. Because of sleeping and watch arrangements, normally the first sight would be the noon sight. The second sight, to give the all important longitude, would be in the late afternoon, when the sun had gone round to the west. Thus our daily position plots were 5.00 pm positions mostly. Some days I didn't bother. This navigating thing can be taken to extremes!

By the end of our second week out, the crosses advancing across the chart were approaching the fold which marked midway. Our daily progress that week had been 134, 130, 113, 95, 106, 98, and 104 miles, a total of 780. Engine use, so far, had been six hours. Since leaving Tenerife we had met flying fish, whales, Portugese Men of War, a floating radio beacon, several overflying aircraft and two ships on the horizon. We had kept the boat pumped and, so far, managed to repair the rigging and sails when necessary, which was daily. We had a fairly good card game going, the stakes being in dollars in anticipation of our eventual landfall. We confined ourselves to two bottles of wine a day and, usually, a tot of whiskey after the last night watch. And we hadn't a single heated word. The *craic* was very good most of the time and, at worst, subdued.

We navigated by sextant (photo by Kevin Cronin)

Twice a week we made contact on the shortwave radio with Ireland, giving our position and exchanging news. Only once, in poor conditions in which speech was unclear, did I have to use Morse Code, with its dots and dashes. Salt water dripping on the Morse key was no help.

Now in our third week, the wind seemed to become more fitful. From radio contacts we heard this to be the case over a wide area, even several hundred miles to the south. *Ocean Passages of the World* instructs that a sailing vessel should 'stay south until the meridian of 60 degrees west is reached, when a course for Bermuda may be steered'.

This very westward dog leg adds several hundred miles to a more direct course. Undoubtedly there was very good reason for it, but right then the sailing wind appeared to be no worse on the direct line. And the old sailing ships did not have diesel engines; we did.

So we allowed our track to gradually turn to the northwest. The engine was used intermittently, for a few hours at a time, when we got fed up, in calms, sitting in the same place. About this time we took to swimming on a regular basis, every two or three days.

Occasionally squalls would keep us on our toes. Sometimes we dropped sail, sometimes we kept it up and just kept running before it, hoping for it to blow over quickly. Our action was decided largely by the mood at the time.

The moon, which we had seen grow nightly from slender beginnings to full size and then grow slender again, was now gone from sight. This made for better star watching if only we knew which was which. They were so many, so clear, that the usually prominent ones were lost. Shooting stars and satellites abounded.

Seaweed began to appear on the surface of the sea, every 100 metres or so at first and a couple of days later at about five metres centres in all directions – the Sargasso Sea. These were balls of about 300mm diameter round and down to a depth of a couple of metres at least. The fishing was temporarily suspended, but we persevered with our log line. The watch distances were too important psychologically to capitulate to the weed. Although this led to some over optimistic guesses at 'weed losses', sadly to be corrected by the following sunsights.

Week three gave us 122, 129, 136, 124, 106, 95 and 130 miles – a total of 842. It also brought Colm's birthday. For this, naturally, we baked a cake. A degree of inventiveness was brought to bear on this.

Its base was the soda bread mix. To this were added raisins, a couple of Mars bars, seasoning and, to liven it up, *poitín*. This was baked in a circular biscuit tin, all done in secret, while Colm was kept on deck on various pretexts. After that night's dinner, the cabin rang to 'Happy Birthday' and other songs. Such a fine cake could not be taken dry, so an additional wine issue was taken from stock.

A further reason for celebrating was that we had finally done something about the leak. Our rate of pumping had been far too high, 150 strokes per hour plus, but because we were used to it we had done nothing about it. In a recent calm spell, we snorkelled under the hull and eventually found some loose caulking, in the last place we looked. This was at the sternpost, over about half a metre. After this was hammered back into place pumping was halved.

Progress towards Bermuda felt spasmodic, though in fact we exceeded 100 miles each day. Our erratic downwind track resulted largely from trying to get the best sailing speed out of the wind. We made full use of the engine in calms at this stage. This was partly out of desire to make progress and partly out of awareness that the hurricane season had begun. We had heard, during the previous week, that *The Pride of Baltimore* had gone down, with four crew lost.

Friday night of the fourth week out, the boat was, as Danny said, 'Like the last day at boarding school'. The wind had been good to us for the previous couple of days. Sights had been meticulously taken and even more carefully calculated and plotted. Bermuda is only 150 feet high, not much higher than the Saltees Islands off Wexford, 20 miles long, and the ocean currents hereabouts run up to three-quarters knot, variable in direction.

Just before dawn on Saturday, we saw the light flashing. Quiet relief and exultation. We timed the flashes, just to be sure. Yes, it was Gibbs Hill all right, one every 10 seconds.

The day broke over an empty sea. Here we were. All shampoo'd and ready for shore and no land in sight. Only the sound of Radio ZBM assured us that we had not been dreaming. By midday we had passed through Saint Georges Cut, smelling the scent of earth, grass and shrubbery. We tied alongside Somers Wharf; 26 days out for a passage of 2,900 miles.

Saint George is not unlike a smaller, colonial version of Kinsale, but American. Boutiquey shops, manicured grass, expensive restaurants and equally expensive beer. We found the rum concoction they call the 'dark and stormy' quite tasty. Three of our wives arrived a few days later and, through Irish connections, we moved into welcoming houses. For ten days we enjoyed doing the tourist thing, being very well taken care of.

In musical mood approaching land. Paddy, Colm Dubh, Johnny, Sean and Kevin (photo by Danny Sheehy).

There were boats, big and very big, on their way, as we were, to the Statue of Liberty celebration. From the US sail training ship *Eagle* we had got a new wire bobstay, measured and made up. We had met her helpful bosun Red Shannon – no marks for guessing where he was originally from. Off the Maxi racing yacht *Nirvana*, we met Niall O hUadhaigh from Blackrock. Later our wives were to have a day out sailing on that mammoth, unfortunately hitting one of the surrounding coral reefs. The 'best navigator in the world' was on board, but resting below. Both he and the skipper immediately offered their resignations to the owner.

Bermuda is a sailing paradise of clear waters, sandy coves, low-wooded islands and warm breezes. But we weren't sorry when it was time to leave. This, for us, was only a waypoint. We still had 700 miles to go to Boston, our intended landfall before going on to New York.

We left on June 19, an early start on an awful morning, under reefed sail. The last of a racing fleet from Newport were coming in. I mistook a buoy on the outer reef but we got away with it and settled back into our routine, almost forgotten. That first day was miserable. The wind, from astern, with heavy rain squalls every couple of hours, varied from nothing at all to 'drop all sail'. The following day saw the sun again and we dried out with a good warm sailing breeze blowing over the deck and through the cabin.

The sea temperature was 23 degrees, taken by putting a thermometer into a bucket of seawater. On Saturday afternoon, our third day out, a squall from the northeast had us reefed right down again and pushing us way westward of our course. In the early stages of this, a seawater temperature, taken on a hunch, showed a rise to 25 degrees. We were now in the Gulf Stream and the conditions showed all the signs of it. We were in a large scale 'wind over tide' situation, with the two and a half knot stream running directly into the near gale.

And there was no let up. Through the rest of Saturday and all of Sunday the seas grew higher. We close reached under jib, beam on or thereabouts, turning our quarter to meet any breaking wave that threatened us. The forecast, at time of leaving, had promised a shallow low pressure system to give us head winds, but not this. Gradually the boat, and much within, became saturated. By Monday conditions eased, but not to the extent that anyone felt like cooking or eating. It was soup, tea and goulash to keep body and soul together.

By Monday evening it had eased sufficiently for us to get the mainsail up again. We cooked a meal and all felt the better for it. We also got sights, which put us 90 miles westward of our intended course, which had been to go outside Nantucket shoals and Cape Cod. We decided to take the inside route.

On a lovely cool sunny Wednesday morning we tied alongside a timber jetty in Vineyard Haven on the island of Martha's Vineyard. 'They all look like Kennedys,' Kevin remarked. This was a lovely place, friendly people and great looking sailing boats. It felt like an area where it would be nice to live, even if the water was decidedly nippy. The next day we made passage, partly under motor,

Full sail into Boston
(photo by the Boston Globe)

through Woods Hole Oceanographic Center, Buzzard Bay and the Cape Cod Canal, to finish in Scituate, a town just south of Boston. We still hadn't cleared Customs or Immigration, but had phoned ahead. We were expected the following day in Boston Harbour at noon.

A police boat in Boston Harbour put the shudders on us as we came in – Danny had been deported from the States for overstaying a previous visit – until we saw that it was down to the gunwales with people, cameras, TV and flashing lights. Tugs hooted and Fire-boats sprayed. Old Connemara men on the shore, we were told, cried salt tears to see *Bád Conroi, Faoi Lán tSeoil* coming in under full sail.

Food, drink celebrations and music filled the next days. The hardest thing to come by was sleep. Now we had to get down to New York for July 4th. Leaving about midnight we went 90 miles to the southwest towards Newport, covering some of the same coast-line that we had sailed up a few days earlier. Time was tight so we used motor to make ground against the prevailing southwester-lies. A good time was had by all in Newport – the Mayor there was Irish – and some members of the Ancient Order of Hibernians came down. One discreetly shoved a 100 dollar bill in my pocket saying, 'Buy some new rope for that boat!'

The next afternoon we left on an overnight passage to Riverside, 105 miles, where ourselves and a Danish ship were being hosted. Now including several wives and friends, we were being put up by a local sailing doctor. Driving up his avenue we saw a huge lit-up building ahead. 'Oh, are we staying at the hospital?'

'Naw,' he said, 'that's mah house.'

Instructions were now coming in from Opsail. At 6.00 am on July 3, Long Island Sound in the early haze saw ships ghosting out under sailfrom coves, harbours and inlets, all pointing west for New York. The 250 boats in the Opsail fleet, bar twenty or so of the tallest that wouldn't fit, were to pass under Throgs Neck Bridge and informally sail down the East River through New York. We had a crowd on board and had a great time, under sail, tricolour flying high, enjoying the cheering and the banter with the people on the shore and the balconies of east Manhattan. 'Did you really come from Ireland in that? 'We stoked the fire to raise more smoke.

The parade on July 4th was everything it was hyped to be with an estimated 40,000 boats on the water 'spectating'. For most of the route, the wind blew Force 5 from astern; we tried to avoid gybing into some of the best known sailing ships afloat. Over the week we stayed in New York we berthed in South City Seaport, near Wall Street, then Morris Canal Basin on the New Jersey side, then back to Pier 83 on Manhattan's westside. We sailed the Hudson and lower New York Harbour with groups from Eamonn Doran's bar, who contributed handsomely to our now near empty pockets.

How were we to get the boat home? We all needed to get back to work. The boat needed a refit before she could be put to sea. To ship her needed serious funding. Into the breach stepped old friend Louis Hughes, now senior in Carrolls Tobacco Company, who said they'd pay the freight. In Kill Van Kull in Newark the Hooker was lifted ashore for shipment to Liverpool. In Liverpool, the six of us gathered a month later where she was put in the water and rigged. Sailing past the north coast of Wales, we saw in the distance the Isle of Man. We resisted the temptation to divert.

On Monday, August 4, we sailed by the Kish Light. *Saint Patrick* was home again.

16

Family and Faroe Islands

I still had a family, and they had got on fine in my three month absence.

Cathal was now seventeen, Caoimhe was sixteen, Muireann was eleven and Bairbre was nine. They were growing up to be fine youngsters, healthy and happy. Scoil Lorcáin, conveniently up the road from us, had given Cathal and Caoimhe good and wholesome primary school years, *as Gaeilge*, in a friendly and supportive atmosphere. Mary was on the parents' committee, so had a good handle on the general tenor of school matters. Both now had 'graduated' to secondary schooling in Coláiste Eoin/Iosagán in Stillorgan, three miles away, a manageable cycling distance. Muireann and Bairbre were in Scoil Lorcáin.

These schools were, for us, spot on in their ethos. They were Gaelic, without being overly zealous, academically good and had a positive life outlook. Equally, or more likely consequently, the kids all developed good friendships.

Cathal had been swimming with the Trojan Club and developed well competitively, taking 'top three' results in his races. This I knew as I did a fair amount of driving to the events, and watching. He had come to a crossroads however. He had to get totally serious about this, exclusively and with all the training required, or leave the competitive scene. To our considerable relief, he chose the latter. I could see that he would be very good, but not 'top gun' and all that training would just get him second and third places, albeit at a higher level. That decision, his own, allowed him the freedom and time to participate in the Dun Laoghaire Sea Scouts, the *Ochtú Calafort*, based by the Coal Harbour at the West Pier. Many of those with him were also school pals. There they did boating of all types, canoeing, rowing and sailing, together with hiking and camping; great all-round stuff, in a friendly, largely non-competitive, way.

Caoimhe, Muireann and Bairbre followed a similar path, enjoyed by all, though Muireann was perhaps less gung-ho in those departments (perhaps more like her Ma).

In bringing the kids to canoeing events, I occasionally did some myself, on the Liffey and the Inny – where nine times, in cold water, I capsized! I had never done the pool training in essential techniques, and paid the price.

Though it wasn't all fun and sport. A rat had taken up abode under the floorboards of our house, whose scratching could be heard and whose nightime visitations left a trail of depredations – and smell. Over these uncomfortable weeks, poison, traps and the efforts of the health board 'exterminator' were of no avail. I had gone to bed, 11.30 pm or so, when Cathal, downstairs with some pals, came upstairs and said, 'The rat is in the kitchen'. I had had a long day, with another due for the morrow, and was fed up with the rat and the domestic complaints. I hadn't invited him in.

A quick look confirmed what Cathal had said. There he was, on the far side of the kitchen, sitting on a yellow upturned plastic bucket in front of a radiator and some timber presses. Quietly and quickly I prepared. The noise of the bang near blew my ear, but the rat was no more as I ejected the empty cartridge from my shotgun. There he was – the bucket too – all over the wall, floor and ceiling. I'd been briefly worried about the radiator but there was no leak. The cordite smoke was clearing. Job done, I went back to bed.

The county council work scene at this stage had gone downhill. I had difficulty liking, much less admiring, my senior, Dullaghan. He had me transferred to the head office on O'Connell Street, colloquially known as 'grounding'. With little or no 'mileage', one was pinned down. I was put to doing a report, wide ranging in its terms of reference, on County Dublin's refuse disposal, which at the time was all by landfill.

Head down, I got stuck into this for a few months, meeting with the various parties involved in the State departments as well as the council's other depots. I was in fact quite enjoying it. With CIÉ I developed a proposal for rail transport of refuse from Connolly Station out to the council's tip in Rogerstown, commercially beneficial to all and reducing road traffic. On all of this I produced and delivered a report.

I'm unsure as to whether that report even made the 'dust-gathered shelf'; it may have reached the bin first. No one ever thanked me for it, discussed it or even 'rubbished' it.

I then was transferred to Drainage Design, a technical area of which I knew little. With college notes and textbooks resurrected, I got to grips with this, unenjoyably. A sole redeeming feature was that those twenty or so engineers, technicians and draftsmen around me were good company – which same could not be said of our then senior. Once, on being approached by one of the junior engineers about setting up of a small technical library, he was said to have responded, 'No need, if you want to know anything, just ask me.' Encouraging!

At least I had the active diversion of a busy time at home and in and around the boat. The mooring I had on the Liffey at Ringsend was the key to keeping such a big boat in the Dublin area. There always had been working boats moored on the Liffey's south bank, and by the early 1970s many were in increasing states of decrepitude. Simon Weafer's was one of the exceptions; he maintaining his in good order. It was he and Reggie Nolan who, around 1975, suggested I lay my own mooring. This I did and have had ever since, renewed several times over the years. This is located just upstream of steps down to the riverfront, reputed, according to Simon, to have been where Oliver Cromwell came ashore in Dublin. These steps still are there, but now largely covered. Poolbeg Boat Club was then in its infancy, operating from a disused ship's wheelhouse located near the top of a public slip. A masonry wall, some 15 feet high on the river side, ran from the river Dodder east to the Pigeon House Hotel, about a mile and a half long. This slip paralleling the masonry river wall was located upstream of the coastguard buildings and, with Cromwell's Steps, was the access to the river front. The drying gravel strand, muddy in places, was where I used to bring in the Hooker from the mooring to lie against the wall for maintenance and repairs – an altogether convenient arrangement, costing nothing.

And it was to there I again brought *Saint Patrick* after our return from America, and got her ready for the 1987 season, all the while crewing for Oliver Sheehy in his racing two-man 'Flying Fifteen'.

ଽ   ଽ   ଽ

It could hardly have been a more awful day, that Friday, June 5, as we loaded stores at Howth. The rain drove along the pier. However the wind was from the south and our destination was to the north. We pulled in all reefs and got going.

Until the Dinnéar na Bádóiri in Spiddal, this cruise had looked like being a non-starter. Later in the summer there would be the Hooker regattas in Connemara and relaxed coastal cruising. The idea now was for two weeks of fairly strenuous sea-going to the Faroe Islands and back. None of the lads who were with Saint Patrick last year were available – or thought that this was a good idea. However, out of Spiddal the nucleus of a new crew was formed. Paraic De Bhaldraithe and Ruaidhri Ó Tuairisg were both teachers and gleoiteog owners, the smaller version of the Hookers. I had known them on an occasional basis for a few years. Brendan Lennox, from Dublin, was a marine engineer I hadn't known previously. Later to enlist were Mike Fahy and Donncha Ó hÉallaithe, also new to Saint Patrick. Mike had no sailing experience, but had spent seven months motorbiking in Africa, including a crossing of the Sahara. I surmised (correctly) that he must be a fairly robust character. Donncha, outgoing, socially curious and entertaining, had sailed with Ruaidhri.

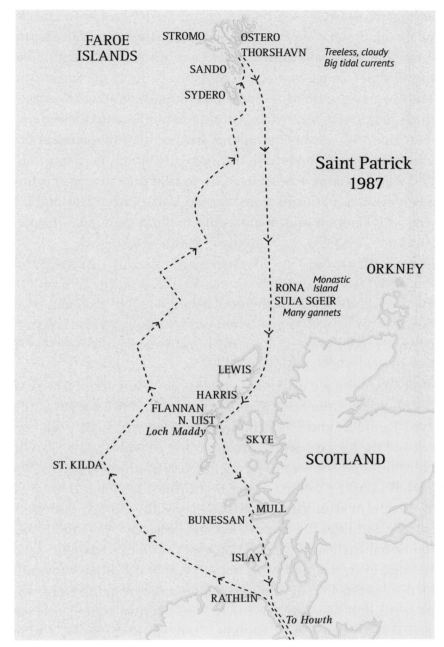

FAROE ISLANDS

STROMO OSTERO
THORSHAVN
*Treeless, cloudy
Big tidal currents*

SANDO

SYDERO

Saint Patrick
1987

ORKNEY

RONA *Monastic Island*
SULA SGEIR
Many gannets

LEWIS

HARRIS
FLANNAN
N. UIST
Loch Maddy

SKYE

SCOTLAND

ST. KILDA

MULL
BUNESSAN

ISLAY

RATHLIN
To Howth

Faroe Islands

Two hours out of Howth, we ran into Skerries for shelter, anchored for the night and at six in the morning got going again. The forecast was for gales on all coasts, but we enjoyed winds a little lighter, from astern, as we roared up the Irish Sea. Our borrowed Decca navigator showed our speed at a consistent seven knots plus. By dusk, late as it was at this time of year, we got into Larne, a satisfying 92 miles done.

The favourable northgoing tide had us again leaving at six in the morning. Unfortunately, the weatherman's predictions were spot-on. The low pressure system, which was to dominate our lives for the next week, had moved through, now bringing the wind to the north. When we spoke to Belfast Coastguard they gently enquired whether we had heard the gale warnings. We impressed on them our cowardly nature and our preparedness to turn back if necessary. With sails all well tied down we motored out.

Despite the favourable tide, headway was slow. In the partial shelter of the Antrim coast the spray was hard on the face and the sea foamed white. Carnlough and Cushendal were passed, unseen in the mist. We waited to be blasted out of it as Fair Head came up. Surprisingly, conditions in Rathlin Sound weren't too bad. The anchor went down in Rathlin Island, outside the old pier.

That afternoon we walked the high ground and looked out over the south-going tide, now foaming between Rathlin and Scottish Kintyre. Ruaidhri and Donncha went to Altacarry Lighthouse and met one of the keepers who turned out to be from Aran in Galway. The McFauls and some of their neighbours entertained us that evening. Neil's parting call to us was, 'May your big jib be always full'.

Early the next morning we caught the tide to the northwest, reefed sail and kept the engine running. The day appeared to be a more normal Irish summer one. At least the clouds had individual form; there even was a distant hint of blue. St. Kilda was 100 miles to the northwest, 40 miles out into the Atlantic from the Hebridean islands. All that Monday, and then Tuesday, we fought our way toward it. My watchmate, Brendan, took to sleeping in a white plastic bag which he referred to as 'my cabin'. On Tuesday night, the Decca, tired like ourselves, stopped working. Wednesday morning, 4.00 am, brought the reward of land in sight ahead. We cut the engine, shook out more sail and relished the silence. The islands

St. Kilda island. The old village, long deserted.

got higher, and starker, as we approached. It took a further two four-hour watches before we rounded into Village Bay. How had peopled lived there? This was no safe haven. Protected from the wind it may have been, but a semi-circle of surf, without a break, clearly identified where sea and shore met. The gravel beach at the head of the bay rasped, as the seas ran in and out.

At the foot of the great sweep of mountain facing the bay could be seen the stone houses of the old 'street' where its population had once lived. We landed in the dinghy and met a most welcoming sergeant from the army camp. The army had a set-up there tracking missiles from a Hebridean firing range. He warned us about the skuas on the high ground and the Scottish National Trust people on the low ground. Well, not quite, but it did seem that the Trust people hadn't thought much of the Army plans to demolish the old cottages for road-making material. The Trust folk, when we did meet them, were lovely people. They were volunteers, doing up the old houses. However progress was slow, not surprising from what we saw. They certainly didn't have the cut of a McAlpine concrete gang.

The sun shone on a blue, foam-flecked sea as we put out to sea the next day. Akraberg, the most southerly point of the Faroe Islands, was 220 miles distant. The wind still blew from the north, but it had moderated somewhat. We all were in great form, having visited this fabled and hard-to-get-at island. The lads played 'noughts and crosses', with licked fingers, on the dried salt on the black deck. In the distance we saw Saint Flannan's Isle and the hills of Hebridean Lewis. That night, Paraic and Donncha cooked a fine dinner, operating around the cooker like jugglers, as pots and plates bounced and slid. Outside it rained and the wind still headed us as we took long tacks, none in our desired direction. The log was filled with diagrams, square roots and trigonometry, calculating distances. A note by Paraic said, 'All this is purely for the amusement of the standby watch and has no navigational purpose whatsoever.'

All that Friday we lay into it, sometimes putting on the engine to help, until it wouldn't start due to flat batteries. In the next 24 hours, we found, courtesy of the Decca, now working again, that we had made good exactly 30 miles; still 100 miles to Akraberg. It now wasn't that the wind was so strong, but that the seas were still running high. The log notes: 'Topping lift off the boom', 'Masthead light is loose', 'Deck-beam smouldering at chimney'.

But Brendan had got the engine going again. On Sunday morning we saw the land ahead and through the day, now preoccupied with tides that run very strong through the Faroe Islands, we stood close by Sydero, Store Demon, Lille Demon and Sando, all green-cliffed in mist. That evening we got into the capital, Thorshavn, 700 miles from Dublin.

By Wednesday it was only three days later, but felt like a month, we had seen so much and met so many. Brendan had fitted a new regulator to the alternator and Mike had soldered the Decca antenna. The big find, for Donncha, was the TV station. Run on a shoestring with few staff, it was to prove a model, in which Donncha was a prime mover, for the setting up back in Ireland of Teilifís na Gaeilge, now TV4.

We said our goodbyes and for two days enjoyed the most pleasant sailing. The sea was gentle, the sun shone. We met a Dutchman trawling herring. Passing the small island of Sula Sgeir, Ruaidhri made a log entry: 'A wonderful sight. Millions and millions of gannets on rocks and overhead.' Paraic, the marine biologist, made a numerical correction: '10,000 pairs'. We passed inside Lewis and Harris. With Skye away in the distance we made in to Loch Maddy (one of the few Scottish names incorrectly translated; it should be Loch Madraí – Loch of Dogs).

We had a drink there with a Scottish charter boat skipper, who showed little regard for his *Sassanach* guests. When asked how he spent the winter he said, 'I hae this wee lorry, and I carry stones dún to Hadrian's Wall'.

Calling to Bunessan on Mull, we sailed delightfully by Iona and then throughthe Sound of Islay to go into Carnlough in Antrim. Then a light westerly breeze gave us an undemanding sail through the familiar waters of County Down, Louth, past Lambay and by Monday evening into Howth, the summer still before us.

Unloading, one of the lads remarked, 'Some day we'll have a cruise with no time limits, no alarm clock and the last man up will call the shots'.

It was indeed on such a leisurely occasion, later that summer, that I first 'ran into' Adrian Spence. His lovely classic yacht *Vilia* lay alongside the almost empty long pier in Teelin, Donegal. We in *Saint Patrick* came in, sails down, crew on deck, with shorelines coiled and ready. At slow speed, alongside we drifted onwards and onwards, until – crack. I, on the foredeck, saw it all happening in slow motion. We put our bowsprit straight into Adrian's mizzen mast, to bring it down in bits.

With embarrassed apologies – and checkbook in hand – I approached Adrian, this our first meeting. With humour and equanimity, Adrian made nothing of it, and said that that mizzen sail had always been of little use. No wonder I took to him and, I hope, at least bought him a pint that evening up the road in the Rusty Mackerel. Adrian, of course, will say that I didn't!

17

Rebuilding *Saint Patrick* in Connemara and Borrowing the *Cú Uladh*

My work fortunes changed. I was transferred into Drainage Planning, examining building planning applications from the perspective of their drainage, both the adequacy of their own drainage and any impact their plan might have on that of others, or the wider community.

And more particularly beneficial to me, I was to have as my senior John McDaid, who proved to be an enlightened man.

By the end of the 1987 season it had become apparent that *Saint Patrick* needed serious work. Her keel was hogged and her topstrakes were sagging. I got word that Colm Mulkerins would be prepared to take her on. Such matters are not mere commercial transactions. Impediments could be many and unspoken, personal and historical. It appeared that these, if any, were overcome. Through the good offices of Donal O'Brien, of construction firm John Paul, with whom I had worked ten years earlier, the boat was transported by road from Dublin to Colm's workyard in Carna, Connemara.

There a thorough examination revealed that the repair job I had in mind would be insufficient and something of a waste of effort and money. With timber workboats, however well built, the skin, that is, the planking, of larch is usually good for about 25 years; the frame and backbone, usually of oak, is good for about 50 years. She now was in her 76th year. Repairs had kept her going, and maybe more such would, but she really needed the full treatment, a total rebuild.

This was a huge commitment, physically and financially. I had seen it done, three or four times, by people or families who didn't have the steady income which I had. They were guardians, trustees, of inherited values, who did not let tight funding limit them. They could do so, and so would I. With Colm I agreed a lump sum price for all labour, £10,000, to be paid in stages and to take about one and a half to two years. *'As go brea leat, a Cholm.* Tear away.'

He made out a list of required timber: three-inch thick slabs of oak for the frames; five-inch timbers for the stem, keel, sternpost and futtocks; one and a half-inch larch for the planking – all to be clear of knots, shakes and waney edges. These I ordered from Jerry Byrne of Arklow, felled from the Wicklow woods and delivered in two truckloads. Later there would be more, plus iron fixings, boat-nails, oakum and red lead. I stood back and watched in awe as this shipwright, the best, took to the task, with me visiting once every three weeks or so.

Sadly, at the end of 1987 my dad died; in some ways a 'merciful release', as for the previous year a stroke had taken the enjoyment of life from him.

The following February, the 27-foot gleoiteog *Pamela* was bought by Roy McCullough of Larne, whom I had got to know through the Portaferry traditional regattas held in Strangford Lough. Roy was not a sailor, but just wished to have a part in the traditional scene. While *Saint Patrick* was being rebuilt I could have a loan of her.

She had been brought from Connemara to Dublin in 1943 and converted as a yacht. She had passed through several Dublin ownerships, notably that of Dalkey man Harry Knott and later naval officer Fergus Cahill. Now, in return for her use, I took on the work of re-sparring her, replacing a few frames, some planks here and there and putting sails on her to current Connemara size, in other words, big. In Connemara some said that 'I'd take a saw to another man's boat, but not my own'. She emerged in June as *Cú Uladh* – the Hound of Ulster – black and slender, much more like her form in the days when she carried post out to the islands. Of course, appearances were not everything; her deck concealed a Yanmar 16 HP engine, VHF radio, gas cooker and some lie-down arrangements. To sail this lady to Brittany, for it was there we were going to a traditional boat festival, I was joined by Austin Duke, a golfer really, Paraic De Bhaldraithe and currach man Brian Ó Carra.

We left Dun Laoghaire on August 5 in great fettle as, contrary to forecasts, the wind gave us a sailing slant to the south. However the wind did turn out to be 'on the nose', so after a lengthy viewing of Killiney Bay we put the engine on and began to make mileage. Somewhere south of Greystones the engine stopped, a foresail sheet wrapped around her propeller, bar taut. It was no fun cutting it free. My wetsuit had a hood, but my poor head took a lot of whacking off the underside of the boat while cutting the rope off the propeller, with the heavy chop pitching the boat about. I hadn't brought scuba bottles, no room; nor did we have a liferaft for the same reason.

Mobile again, we had a somewhat sick-making and wet night, clearing up the next day; we now were south of Tuskar. Dolphins appeared, 'bottlenose' Paraic said, and later a 'giant leatherback turtle', most unusual so far north. That evening brought a stew by Austin, drying out of clothes and 'will the diesel last?' Johnny Healion's Hooker *Morning Star* was somewhere astern, Con McCann's *Connacht* ahead. Watch after watch we passed the night, occasional fishing boats about. A container ship gave us a revised position – her watch officer had been at the traditional *Crinniú Na mBád* Kinvara festival.

With a light wind filling our sails – how is it that we always managed to have the red sails up for the picturesque entry! – we reached the Isles of Scilly on late Sunday afternoon. Hughtown, the capital, was not a place I particularly looked forward to as I found it too crowded, too prettified, paying money to the Duchy of Cornwall. However, this time things felt not bad at all.

We left the following evening and had a grand sail across the Western Approaches, as the entrance to the English Channel is called. (The French omit the 'English' part.) In a warm breeze, we did about twenty miles to the watch, crossing the shipping lanes and then getting in to the island of Ushant by Tuesday afternoon.

This was for us a first, having passed by half a dozen times but the conditions never had been favourable with big tides, heavy swell and poor visibility being the norm. As we had no dinghy with us, there being no room in the boat, we tied to the pier in Lampaul Bay, uncomfortably.

We found it an island of sheep and lighthouses, plain and un-varnished. From our conversations in the pub (Paraic had fluent French), we gathered that visitors were mostly locals and their fam-ilies, back from the mainland. They all seemed to know of Conne-mara, so we sang them 'The Queen of Connemara'. I hadn't known it, but Brian, as well as Paraic, was a whistle player. Truth to tell, our two whistles and skipper's guitar were limited enough and de-pended very heavily on foot-stamping, audience participation and the demon drink to make it sound good. In Breton, the island is called Ouessant, pronounced 'Wesson'.

We moved from the quay wall out to, more comfortably, an-chor and in the morning went swimming over the side. Later, tides obliging, we sailed onward to Camaret, past its marina and into the town quay wall. We drank a coffee across the road from the boat. Life felt good. For the next week it would be just socialising and short sailing. Douarnenez, where the festival was happening, was just 20 miles away.

At low water, when the tide had gone out, we took off the pro-peller for greater boat-speed in the racing ahead of us. We ate ashore and went quietly to our bunks as a soft warm mist fell – and leaked through the cabin roof. In the morning we breakfasted on croissons and baguettes, and moved out with six inches of water under our keel, and falling. From the Rade de Brest there were dozens of tradi-tional boats coming out, all under various ancient rigs and different nationalities and bound as we were, to the *fete*. A lugger of some description seemed to be making ground on us. We cut through the Tas-de-Pois, sniffing the barnacles, and as the day warmed set to composing again.

In the Channel, we had begun a song about *Cú Uladh*, in the heroic mould.

Eighty eight was the year for Douarnenez
The boats came from near and from far,
From Belfast came Con McCann on the *Connacht*
And from Howth came the bold *Morning Star*.
But what is that boat hauling wind there?
Her spars and her sails salt with spray.
Fág an bealach! Tá said ag dul timpeall,
Cú Uladh's into Douarnenez Bay.

To appreciate this doggerel, you'd want to be in the mood and, of course, to know the air – we selected a rousing marching tune. And then the *finale*:

'C'est magnifique magnifique,' roared the Frenchmen
As six hundred boats surged for the line.
The Dutchmen were soon out to weather,
Leaving Swedes, English, Germans behind.
But rounding the mark for the last time
There's two boats cutting through mighty fine,
'Twas the Russians, contagious to the Caspian
But *Cú Úladh* was first past the line.

Fantasy gone mad.

We swept into the old Rosmeur Harbour in Douarnenez and tied alongside *Connacht. Morning Star* arrived later. For the next five days you had everything (maritime) that you could want, except sleep. Music, eating, drinking, rowing and singing until the early hours, with sailing races starting much too early in the day. Two specific memories stand out.

A misty day, four boats and ourselves had sailed to anchor off. A blazing fire warmed the stony cove, sardines were grilling, three or four were playing music, wine to your hand.

Another day. About six in the evening, I had just dozed off, catching up on sleep. Heavy footsteps on the deck overhead barely pervaded my consciousness. And then, wow! The Douarnenez Brass Band Jazz ensemble had come to visit.

All morning on 16 August we made our goodbyes to Tom Cunliffe of *Hirta*, the oarsmen from Cadgwith, the Cadorets and festival people, chaloupe *La Concalaise* and indeed to Mary, who was driving home, as she had arrived, but now with Johnny Moynihan and his bike and many musical instruments.

With the racing done, our propeller was back on. Our passage back across the Channel was a windward one, assisted much of the time by engine. We sailed close by Land's End and its cliffside tourists and old mine workings and went in alongside the pier at St. Ives. Our diesel was topped up, 12 gallons for £5. We queried the low price. 'We like to see them boats comin' in.' We'll go back there.

For the next leg our log is bare of comment, eloquence in itself. Only the most frugal of entries was written with numb fingers as a towel sopped the drips from the chart. The wind rose. We got full reefs in. The engine which had been tried for the reefing wouldn't start. There was air in the system and little hope of bleeding it in those conditions. We didn't need it anyway, as we sped along at between five and seven knots.

During the night we passed close, too close, to a ferry. In the weather, I had taken it for a fishing boat, moving at between four and eight knots. How wrong I was. A blaze of lights went close astern, at more like twenty knots. It rained into the soup. Spray flew. No one could sleep in the wet noisy cabin. In the middle of our troubles, dolphins sported alongside, causing streaks of phosphorescence. 'Bio-luminescence,' Paraic corrected.

As we rounded Carnsore Point, the seas flattened, though the wind kept blowing hard. Our entry into Rosslare Harbour was nothing if not dramatic. Luckily for us the dockhands on the quay wall were used to taking lines.

A Rosslare Lifeboat mechanic sorted our engine and, a couple of uneventful days later, *Cú Úladh* was back in Dublin.

18

May Weeks and Sailing to Mountains

I came to mountains too old to be any good at climbing, but when I did I found that I thoroughly enjoyed both the high places and the company of the people who'd be there.

In the mid-1980s I bought my first mountain boots and hiked up the Glenmalure Zig-Zags for Lugnaquilla. It was with Brian Searson in Kerry that I first found myself in clouds on a high ridge. With little visibility, I initially was worried but took comfort from Brian's ease with map and compass. From Enniskerry on a monthly outing I would join the Saturday Walkers on the Wicklow mountains and the social pints which followed. It was at such, in spring 1987, that I suggested a 'spin' in *Saint Patrick* across the Irish Sea for a weekend trip to Snowdonia. *Saint Patrick* at that time had recently sailed to America, so there was probably both a curiosity and a confidence factor for the lads.

In Dun Laoghaire's Coal Harbour thirteen of us boarded on Friday evening, a very full load. Dick Morrissey, Liam Canavan and Rory Walsh I knew well, the others less so. We had a horrible overnight windward passage to Carnarvon. No one had slept. Nonetheless, boat tied to the wall in Victoria Dock, all emerged enthusiastically and knowledgably spoke of, and headed for, Pen-y-Pass and Grib Goch. A great mountain day was had, pints in the evening and a pleasant sail back on Sunday. It showed what could be packed into the combination of sailing and climbing.

And so, on the basis of getting the summer off to a good start, together with the notion that a missing week in early May might be construed domestically as 'last year', the May Weeks began and 1991 is probably typical.

On Friday evening, May 10, a westerly Force 3-4 took us under all sail up the Irish Sea, bound for the climbing areas of Scotland's west coast. On board we had a mixture of climbers and sailors. Gary MacMahon, from Limerick, David Walsh and Donal Ó Murchú, from the previous year's Arctic travels, were back for more. Pat Colleran, Paul Cooper and Pat Redmond were new to our ship and Malcome Hunt was new to any.

A pot of pre-cooked stew saw the Rockabill astern of us as evening darkened. The lights on shore marked the east coast as we laid off comfortably for the South Rock Light-vessel off County Down. We passed this at seven on Saturday morning as our course changed to northwestwards, and so did the head wind. But no complaints. We banged on the engine and had a fine breakfast of porridge and raisins. A good tide sped us through the North Channel to reach the Mull of Kintyre before the afternoon turn of the tide southwards.

Tucking in close to the shore, and into the bay of Machrihanish, we went northward to Gigha as the lights turned on in the Scottish twilight. As dusk fell the tide turned northwards again and the shore lights of the Sound of Jura started to move at a faster pace. At the top end of Jura we shot the anchor in Kinuachdrachd. There was one house, one caravan and an old stone jetty; deer grazed among the trees only a few boat lengths away. An hour before slack water we moved out past Corryvreckan to gather speed with the north-going tide through the Lynn of Lorne.

About 11.00 on Sunday morning we entered the broad water of the Firth of Lorne, as the long forecast southerly wind arrived. Up sail for a glorious thrash up the Sound of Mull, past Tobermory and Ardnamurchan to drop anchor by evening at our destination, Loch Scresort on the Isle of Rum.

Day 3, Monday. The rain teemed down. We lay abunk until 10.00 and rose slowly. Soon a break in the clouds brought urgency to our mood. We made for the hills. The so-called Ridge of Rum has five substantial peaks. In brightened weather we traversed them all, returning by a path five miles penitentially long – a hard but satisfying day.

Day 4. Sailed out of the anchorage at 7.30, with a good south-westerly wind taking us northwards to our primary objective, the Black Cuillin of Skye. Most of the crew had been here before and knew the weather for what it was:

> If you are a delicate man
> And of wetting your skin are shy,
> I'd have you know, before you go
> You'd better not think of Skye.

In Loch Scavaig we anchored. Paul volunteered to stay with the boat, as violent gusts off the mountains made it inadvisable to leave it unattended. By evening we had climbed the high gabbro of six peaks, regarded as being the finest climbing in these islands. And Paul had not been idle. Mussels gathered at the low water edge, baked and garnished to standards not at all normal on *Saint Patrick* presaged our evening eating. The Tilley lighted the cabin and smoke curled upwards from our chimney. The hillside, with its 'mad burn', turned through the open hatch as we swung to our anchor. All to bed – six in bunks, two on the floor, no problem.

Harry Connolly and Pat Redmond on Cuillin ridge.

Among the Scottish islands. Paul Cooper, Frank Nugent,
Pat Redmond and Jarlath Cunnane.

Day 5. 7.00. Anchor up and round the 12 miles westward to Loch Brittle, the idea being to get an approach to some of the other Cuillin. There are 22 peaks in all over 3,000 feet. We had promised ourselves a visit to a pub tonight, but where? The wind was from the northwest, so we sailed down to Coll, somewhat over-canvassed, but weren't we over-crewed too. We tore along east of Canna to round into the shelter of Coll's inner jetty. Our ship took the ground on a clean bottom and the hotel catered for our needs: 'eight pints o'heavy Jimmy'. Two other yacht crews, early season charterers, shared the bar with us. We had a few songs and left at closing time,

Day 6. Bound for Glencoe, with the northwest wind still blowing. A great sail over to Mull, again, and up Loch Linne, under the 18 metre bridge at Ballachulish to anchor off the village of Glencoe. 16.00 hours. Too late for climbing. This was an entirely different Scotland: inland wooded slopes, traffic on the coastal road, road signs. But it was for the mountains we were here, untouched by the doings below.

We walked the three miles to the Clacaig Inn, for old time's sake for some of the climbers, negatively reviewed the 'improvements' and taxied back to the boat for dinner. Those who went ashore for a further pint pronounced it a mistake.

Day 7. Three parties climbed. The sun shone, the wind was light, the rock was warm. Snow lay in the high gullies. Between us we took the view from eight 'Monroes', as the 3,000 footers are called. With rope and belays, David and I climbed the airy high rock buttress they call 'Agag's Groove' on Buachaille Étive Mór.

Well satisified all, we hauled our anchor at 16.00, homeward bound.

Days 8 and 9. We retraced our way southwards, working the tides, and considered where we might bestow our custom this Saturday night. Portpatrick, too soon; Peel, too far; Portaferry, wrong tides; Portavogie, never. Ballyhorn it was.

We left after midnight and were back in Dublin the next afternoon.

That trip was typical of the many over the years, though latterly we have slowed down. We've visited all the mountainy places. Jura, of course, Mull, Eigg, Knoydart, and one year up to Torridan and we've probably been in all of the Hebridean islands. Our shipmates have been in the dozens – Frank Nugent, Jarlath Cunnane, Pat Redmond, Paddy O'Brien, Peter Gargan and Ken Price being of particular note because these Scottish trips led to other things. We didn't always go to Scotland as we went sailing and hill-walking in Wales and West Cork or Kerry some years. A great way to begin any summer.

§   §   §

Pat Redmond, this being his first trip with me, was to become a very good friend and occasionally mentor or minder. His sailing background was in racing GP 14 dinghies, at which he had excelled. He had climbed in the Alps and, surprisingly it seemed to me, had also played cricket – a man for all seasons.

His energy was prodigious, whether in his work for Dublin County Council Water Division or at 'play'. One April morning, on a 6.00 am high tide, we put *Saint Patrick* onto Poolbeg slip to dry her out. Once she safely stood on the bottom, about 7.00, we left for a quick four-hour hike in the Dublin Mountains. We returned at about 12.00, the tide now fallen and exposing the underside of the boat. We set to an afternoon of scraping, scrubbing and then painting on her antifouling. At 6.00 pm she floated and we moved her to her Liffey mooring. All in a busy day!

I mentioned 'minder'. In Copenhagen, that *laissez faire* city, my bicycle was taken (on this *Saint Patrick* trip to the Baltic, we carried two). I thought to go 'find' another one. Pat said he'd come with me. In the event I didn't 'find' one. But Pat had in fact come with me to *prevent* my evil intent! Fair weather or foul, a good companion, sadly, since October 2007, no longer with us.

It wasn't all boats and mountains – Paddy and Frank.

19

The Rebuild Finished, and the Intel Years Begun

In June of 1989, at Crumpán Pier, the boatmen gathered approvingly and went aboard. *Saint Patrick* was back in the water. Colm Mulkerrins stood back, his work finished; it now was up to the boatmen. Pat Cheoinín Jennings took the helm, Johnny Peter Bailey, of *Capall*, the mainsheet, myself supernumerary. Others came aboard, including Tom Dairbe of *American Mór* and John Beag Ó Flahartaig of *MacDara*. If this maiden passage to Roundstone were to go wrong, many of the cream of the Galway Hookers would be left without their owners.

The rebuild had gone very well. Colm had a shed, but he liked to build in the open so that he could range the full boat with his eye. Indeed, most of the work was done by eye, an amazing gift. First he had loosened up the framework and planking by removing some pieces and undoing some of the key fixings. Then, with chain tackle, tying stem to stern at deck level, over several weeks he tightened, gradually pulling the old boat back into shape.

The old keel was taken out. Colm showed me the iron dumps, almost rusted to pencil thin – 'This is what you went to America on' – and the new one put in, 29 feet of oak, 18 by five. This was followed by stem, sternpost and futtocks. Cutting was by chainsaw, amazingly accurate – a razor blade wouldn't be fitted into the finished joints. Yes, he had electric tools, and an adze too, dangerously sharp. All this work he did, as far as I could see, on his own. He never was inclined to work while there were others around, myself included. Yet he got through an immense amount without ever seeming to hurry. I was there one Good Friday, a day when out of regard for the Crucifixion in those parts no nail is ever driven. But Colm needed a nail driven to hold a centreline. 'Will I chance it?' he said. 'No, you do it' – which I did.

The sole piece went in and the great curved frames, each with bevel to take the planking to follow. The old would be taken out, followed by the new piece going in. Gradually, the majesty of the rebuilt hull became apparent. She was now measuring two feet longer, stem to stern, than previously. In bringing her shape back, her stateliness had been restored, and extended.

On Sundays, when Colm wouldn't generally be there, but perhaps I was, old boatmen, of expert eye, would visit and judge the work approvingly. I was told that when I got Colm, I also got the accumulated expertise of Connemara. One remarked to me that a particular marking-out batten was one-half inch low, 'but the *saor* will know that himself' – *saor* being the shipwright. And this comment would of course find its way, as intended, to be accepted or not.

In all this, I had no function, other than to keep the necessary materials coming in, at this stage mostly bolts and square iron for 'dumps' to be dipped in tar and sledge-driven into round holes, thus binding the timbers together. No additional timber was needed, Colm's original list being complete. The larch planking went on quickly, only a little steaming was required at the bent ends. Where the timber had knots, he put these planks in locations without any bending. Lesser men might have rejected them.

The cost of all this was racking up. I had initially borrowed £5,000 to get the job going, but now with the end in sight and new sails on order, the outcome was looking like £23,000. To say that I was stretched …. Years later I was asked had the boat cost me much over the years? 'About the cost of a small bungalow,' I replied. Maybe a small bungalow on Aylesbury Road!

Priming the hull with red lead I did myself during Easter of 1989, while Colm worked on the spars. The mast was of Douglas Fir, 44 feet, square at the base. The several coats of black paint followed, undercoats and gloss, her 'bend' being white. The rudder was hung, she was craned into the water and spars stepped. Pat Ceoinín and John Dairbe measured for the sails and cut them for sewing by Downer in Dublin. Rigging went on, some of the old, some new. Ballast went in. She was ready to sail.

That summer we sailed the regattas, the boat going well, being open and light, with her new bigger sails. Not quite well enough though to win; she still needed tuning, and the standard of the other Hookers had risen.

At Roundstone Pier, on a wet weekend in August, Jarlath Cunnane and myself put the engine back in. We had met a couple of years earlier, he having sailed back from Boston in James Cahill's *Ricjac*. A carpenter by trade, I thought him an engineer. He now was a construction manager but could in fact do anything, a man

Now under mighty sail, the Burren of County Clare behind
(photo by Joe St. Leger).

of extraordinary skill and the best of company. He was quietly spoken, but always worth listening to. From Knock in County Mayo, but working mostly in Dublin, there he had built a steel, 34-foot yacht named *Lir*. I had enjoyed helping on some of the unskilled grinding of welds and melting of lead ballast. He, too, for this project, needed additional funds, so together we did some 'nixers', he providing the skill and me the help.

Arising from our experience in working with lead for boat keels, we developed an expertise in making lead sash-weights for 'up and down' windows. In Dublin, old buildings were being restored with many requiring new or replacement sash weights. These needed to be of an exact weight to counterbalance the weight of the window. These we manufactured in my shed in Monkstown. As our lead-melting boiler raised its pungent, and toxic, smoke the neighbours must have wondered what it was that we were barbecuing.

Meanwhile, back in Dublin County Council I continued working along on the Drainage Planning, not too inspiring but at least a necessary job, and it did get me out of the office on site inspections – Friday afternoons being my speciality, as my senior, John McDaid, had observed. No problem there, I was doing the work. As he later said, 'When you get Paddy, you get product'.

By August of 1989, the recession was showing signs of improvement. From Jacobs Engineering, an American firm with an Irish branch, I got a work offer. They had a substantial project coming on stream, client as yet confidential, for which they would need staff for three to five years. The money would be good, paid on hourly rates. The risks would be project abandonment or just plain 'the client taking a dislike to you'. I decided to go for it, to take a five-year career break from the Council. This should have been straightforward. The Council system allowed for it, in fact encouraged it in order to get its wage bill down. It did however require the agreement of one's department boss who, in my case, refused, unwilling to concede any reduction in his staff numbers. Stalemate, it looked like.

I still cringe at what followed. Through my friend Eugene Magee, my predicament was conveyed to the Minister of Local

Government. Two days later, what was described by my boss as 'a big breeze' blew down his corridor, and I had my career break approved. That minister, whom I never had met before or since, was Pee Flynn merely exercising his power, a minor political favour.

My only real regret at the time was that John McDaid felt that, in leaving, I had been disloyal to the council.

Arlan Emmert was the American running Jacobs in Dublin. He introduced me to the client, Intel, who were about to set up in Europe, using Leixlip in County Kildare as their base. They were first going to set up a 'medium-tech' assembly facility, ESSM, followed by a full state-of-the-art Wafer Fab making silicone chips for the latest in computer technology.

My function on ESSM would initially be to organise the various engineering contracts and later to drive the construction to completion, all in nine months. Jerry Loughrey, Jacobs lead architect, Gerry Fogarty, estimator and myself went to Intel's Portland, Oregon facility, accompanied by Arlan. There, jet-lagged, we were briefed by Intel's people. Jerry Loughrey must have worked all night because the next morning he had for them full and detailed architectural proposals, with drawings. On the trot, Gerry Fogarty did the pricing and I did the building and schedule outline. The client, we think, was impressed. Before returning to Dublin, we were sent to Albuquerque, New Mexico, for a few days in Intel's Wafer Fab facility there.

The pace never let up. It was great. Decisions would be made on Friday and work would start on Monday. By February of 1990, the roof was going on; by June the ESSM building was finished. There was a 'however'. Arlan had accepted that I would be gone for the summer of 1990 for three months. He waited for a good time to tell the Intel people but a good time never came. With just a week or so to go, as we finished a meeting, he told Intel that 'Paddy's goin' to be gone for ninety days'.

'What?' said Intel. 'Nine days?'

'No, ninety,' said Arlan.

20

Arctic Voyage to Spitsbergen
and Murmansk, 1990

A hurried visit to the Faroe Islands in 1987 had given a tanta-lising glimpse of the northern world as seen from its lower edge. I thought no more about it. But as work on the rebuild of *Saint Patrick* advanced, I began to feel that such a fine boat should have a substantial outing.

Over the winter of 1989/90, back in Dublin, the open boat was decked and her fittings reinstalled. In deference to our intended travels she was fitted with weather-fax, Sat Nav and an all-band radio transceiver.

My early plan had been to go to Novaya Zemlya to the northeast of Murmansk. However the Russian authorities showed no enthu-siasm for this, so we changed our focus to Spitsbergen, in the Nor-wegian Arctic. The Russians did give us permits to visit Murmansk.

School pal, and now civil engineer, Johnny Rooney and Gearóid Ó Riain, student friend of my son, would be with us for the three months. Mick Brogan, doctor and Hooker sailor, would be with us for two months; Neil Rooney and his friend Joe May from Skerries, until Iceland.

Blessed we were initially, as on Friday, June 1, an easy sailing breeze carried us up the Irish Sea. As personal gear was stowed Johnny announced that both his money and his sleeping bag were not to be found, an unhappy prospect indeed. Happily, both items emerged, as things found their proper place.

**Arctic Voyage
Saint Patrick 1990**

80°N

Polar Pack-Ice

FRANZ JOSEPH
LAND

80°N

GREENLAND

SPITSBERGEN

Barents Sea

Polar Pack-Ice

BEAR ISLAND

SCORESBYSUND

JAN MAYEN

HAMMERFEST

TROMSO

MURMANSK

*Norwegian
Sea*

SEYDISFJORDUR

NORWAY

SWEDEN

FINLAND

FAROE

SHETLAND

ST PETERSBORG

HEBRIDES
ISLANDS

Voyage to Spitsbergen

That passage northwards to Iceland was dogged with bad weather. Mick wrote:

The journey up to Iceland, is worth a verse or two,
Strong winds blew from the Arctic, a tester for our crew.
But *Saint Patrick* shouldered all the waves, and through the
  seas did run,
'Twas a lovely sight comin' up the fjord, we had reached the
  midnight sun.

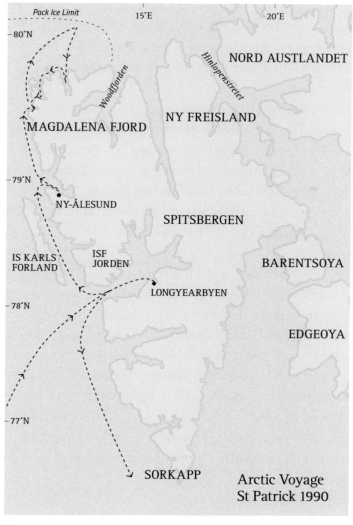

Spitsbergen

We dropped sail and motored up the eight mile cleft in the mountains, called Seydisfjordur.

During the following days we walked the mountains, stepped through the snow and wondered at the constant sound of waterfalls cascading to the sea. We approached the people as we would in any unfamiliar place in the west of Ireland and were well rewarded. These people, with a reputation for being dour and unwelcoming, we found to be open and friendly. We responded. Mick 'resined' up his bow, my guitar was tuned, and like Aladdin's Lamp the music opened doors for us. We played every reel and slide we could and sang songs we had forgotten we knew. At a village concert the 'Saint Patrick Céili Band' had their first onstage gig, and probably their last.

Seydisfjordur, a village of 900 people whose main occupation is fishing, was the ferry destination for connections with Faroe and Denmark. The fleet was a mixture of big trawlers, who went out for a month at a time, and small inshore boats. Iceland is very regulated; nothing moves without a licence. Rescue is a constant theme, whether on snowbound roads or offshore waters. These people have carved out a good life by dint of hard work and systematic arrangement.

There was, however, a dark side; there had been four suicides in the area in the last six months. And for us, it was very expensive.

We had now been joined by Gary MacMahon of Limerick and Cathal Ó Méalóid, son of Colm Dubh, who had been across the Atlantic with us. They replaced Neil and Joe.

We looked forward, with some trepidation, to our next passage, a thousand miles northeastwards to Spitsbergen. In a hundred miles we would be crossing the Arctic Circle, and then would be north of it for the next two months. Three or four days onward lay the island of Jan Mayen. If the weather proved suitable, we planned to anchor and visit.

On Sunday, June 24, I wrote:

Walrus Bay, Jan Mayen. 71 degreees north, 8 degrees west. We are lying to 2 anchors in a small bay on the northside of this island. Outside the thermometer shows 4 degrees. The sea is whipped by gusts off the mountains. Overhead, the clouds fly by. About four hundred yards away, where the protection of the mountain ends, the sea is whipped into white.

We are torn between wanting to be on our way to Spitsbergen, 600 miles on, and caution. Caution wins, hands down. Three hours ago I had written in the log, 'The weather prospect is bleak. There is no improvement in sight. This so-called Force 7 hopefully is local only to this mountainy desolate place. Warm memories of Jan Mayen will now pale as the reality of wet quarters, cold watches and slow progress in rough seas becomes our world.

We sit round the cabin, reasonably well rested. Johnny and Mick are picking out our next 5-day food supply. Cathal and Gary wash up after dinner. Gearóid lies in his bunk. Our Perkins 70 HP engine has stood up manfully, sails up sometimes, but mostly serving to steady the boat rather than to provide driving force. Visibility has been poor. Thankfully also, the Satellite Navigator has never faltered.

Across the bay stands a lonely cross, commemorating seven Dutchmen left to overwinter here in 1633, to mind the Dutch whale fishery. They died that winter of scurvy. Many more crosses and plaques are here. There is one for the Norwegian weatherman who lost his way back to his hut after taking weather observations in 1950. There is one for five British scientists drowned in 1961. A sixth survived, enduring an epic climb up and round glaciered Mount Beerenberg, to reach the safety of the Norwegian Camp.

But the good side? We have been lucky ashore. We approached this island intending to anchor on the south side, then protected from the northerly wind. About five miles off, we first saw the mountain as the fog and cloud lifted and Beerenberg, 8,000 feet, showed in all its majesty. The splendid magnificence of that mountain made the privation of the passage from Iceland worthwhile – almost.

Jan Mayen Radio spoke to us – a woman! The bad news was that the wind was forecast to go easterly. We eased sail and ran off, 10 miles round the south cape to find better shelter on the northwest coast. The weather closed in, with visibility down to about a quarter of a mile. By dead reckoning, we felt our way round to this place, Kvalros Bukta or Walrus Bay. We found flat water and laid out one anchor, and then another; satisfied and tired.

On the shore, near a hut, was a Land Rover and two people. We prepared our inflatable dinghy and Mick and I went ashore. It was about midnight – broad daylight of course. Dressed in army fatigues, a man and a woman introduced themselves as Eden and Thorarnfin from the Norwegian station. They had heard us on the radio. They would collect us next morning at seven.

They were glad to see us, visitors being rare. There were 25 people on the island manning the weather station, the Loran Navigation station and Jan Mayen Radio. There are supply ships every three months. The monthly air-drop had been missed for the last two times running. The plane had come all right, but in the fog couldn't find the runway to drop the cargo. And today was Saint John's Day, the day the Norwegians celebrate mid-summer. There would be a barbeque that evening. Of course we would come. There are twenty men and five women. There's a nurse, four in the kitchen, four on the Met., eight on the Loran/Radio. The others run the machinery, the generators and the workshops of this well regulated world out here on the edge.

The commander made us very welcome, stamped our passports and gave his blessing to the warmth of the hospitality now being shown in practical ways, the showers and the canteen. My letter of some months ago to the commander had been posted on their noticeboard – no wonder they knew we were due. They were somewhat relieved that we were not pursuing the possibility of climbing Beerenberg. Having no rescue arrangements, they would have had to refuse.

During the afternoon we marvelled at the trappers' huts, still intact in the cold, where men had endured in search of the skin of the fox and the polar bear. The Norwegians carry a gun at all times while outdoors. Bears had not been seen since last May, but any still about would be getting aggressively hungry by now. During that afternoon, word came by radio that the supply plane was coming.

Bulldozers, lorries and jeeps converged on the landing strip. All machines have VHF radios. A speck appeared in the ski to the east. It grew, circled the landing strip once, twice and on the third round, about 30 feet up, dropped a bundle, then did a circle dropping twice again. It turned and flew back eastwards.

Half an hour later the post had been distributed. There wasn't a soul in sight. All had retired to their rooms with the long awaited post from home.

As if the day wasn't already sufficiently full, word came that two fishing boats would be coming in to allow crew, a month out from Norway, to take a break for Saint John's Day. The camp dory, a 32-foot steel boat, was launched by bulldozer. I went out in it, like the others clad in a survival suit. We brought the outgoing post, including our own freshly scripted postcards, and brought in twenty men, a wild but competent-looking bunch, and thirsty, as we soon saw.

There was no scarcity of bonfire material. The shore was covered with driftwood logs, swept down, they said, from Siberian rivers in the spring thaw through ice drifts and the sea, finding their way to the shores of Novaya Zemlya, Svalbard and Jan Mayen. This driftwood has provided an unending supply of building material and firing over the centuries, possibly serving even Irish monks. The *Norsk Polarinstitutt* publication on 'Historical Remains on Jan Mayen' refers to visits by Irish monks in the sixth century.

That evening the mountains looked down on almost double the usual population, gathered around the outdoor fire on that rare fine evening. Mick played fiddle, I played the guitar. Later in the bar I listened to men who spent months at a time at sea fishing. They enquired about the rate of pay on our ship, shaking their heads with incredulity that we should be doing this for 'fun'. I spoke to a man, aged hardly over 35, who had been six years on the west Greenland whale fishery, three years in Antarctica and four years in Spitsbergen – and we amateurs think we know the sea. These men are the direct descendants of those who travelled tothe Poles with Nansen and Amundsen. Our own Tom Crean from Annascaul and Ernest Shackleton could take it too, but weren't bred to it like these hardy sons of northern Norway.

We gathered to go. Two four-wheel drives were used now, as there were a few coming to see us off. We assured the chief that we

*Gary MacMahon, on passage north of Jan Mayen. He used to say,
'It's the bits between the harbours that I don't like!'*

would not be leaving until morning – the Norwegians were not the only ones who had been celebrating. The two Land Rovers pulled slowly up the inclined road. We were now alone in Walrus Bay, with that lone cross.

For three further days we lay there, a third anchor out. The wind rose, whipping spume off the sea. Our hands suffered as we adjusted twisted anchor chain and rope while we moved into better shelter. Within the boat a warm fire burned, but it heated only the immediate area. The rest of the cabin was cold, but dry. The radio operator, from the other side of the island, said that it now was blowing a mean speed of 50 knots at the airstrip. We kept full sea-watches, sometimes running the engine to relieve tension on the ground tackle.

The wind eased and, glory be, went round to the northwest. We were off. With the wind on our beam we drove hard, sometimes reefed, sometimes headsails only, but consistently making more than 25 miles a watch.

On the fourth day, the white peaks of Nordenskold Land in Spitsbergen appeared ahead. Eastward up Isfjorden we raced, the high glaciered mountains of its south side close to starboard, while off to the north the sun caught the whiteness of that vast mountainous land, here and there lighting a sparkling river of glacier ice.

We rounded into Adventfjord, on which is the settlement capital of Longyearbyen. The 600 miles we did in four days out of Jan Mayen compensated for a lot. We tied at the jetty to meet our climbers, David Walsh and Donal Ó Murchú. They had flown out a couple of days earlier and had been camped by the airport. They were glad to settle in to the warmer, if somewhat mankier, cabin of *Saint Patrick*.

Mick left and was replaced by Jimmy Conlon, a school friend of Gearóid.

The ice reports showed that a circumnavigation of Spitsbergen would not be possible. In many ways this was good, because instead of rushing around trying to knock off mileage and steal a few mountains on the way, we would be able to take our time, select our mountains and dally if we chose.

Passing out of Isfjorden, we turned north up Prins Karlandsundet and a couple of days later made into the settlement of Ny Alesund. This is the most northerly village in the world, now a scientific research station of about twenty people. Formerly it had a population of about 300 coalminers, defunct since 1963. Earlier Amundsen had set off from here, with the Italian Nobile, on their transpolar flight on an airship to Nome, Alaska. The mooring mast for the airship still remained. Reindeer grazed. Arctic terns would take the head off you with their pecking if you didn't wave a stick over your head.

We set off to climb, and were defeated. Slogging up the *arête* in fog, on rock with the consistency of loose sugar, we could have gone on but didn't. As David said, 'When in doubt, count your children'. We did, and retreated. Roped together, downward, pitch by pitch, we went and then had the long walk back to the village across icy moraine.

Overnight the whaler *Globe* came in, now converted for carrying tourists. Her master, Captain Einar Abramson, had been aboard since 1946. Between the Arctic and Antarctic oceans she had killed

Magdalena Fjord, west Spitsbergen. Glacier behind, French kayakers aboard.

over 6,000 whales, of which he had fired the harpoon on 4,000. In this situation you pass no remarks, whatever you might think. Whaling was a living for these people when there was little else for them.

We untied our lines and pointed our bowsprit to the north, our steering compass now increasingly lazy. All day we sailed about two miles off the shore until that evening we laid our 'hook' in a corner of Magdalena Fjord, formerly favoured by whalers of all nationalities. A graveyard is the sole reminder of those who never made it home.

There we climbed, very satisfyingly, on good snow and in good visibility. Coming down, we spied tents – an Austrian climbing party who had been dropped off and would be collected two weeks hence. We envied their skis, great for getting down mountains quickly. They envied our boat, and our mobility.

Next day, as we lay at anchor, we were surprised to hear voices outside and to see four sea-kayaks. They were a French party who had been dropped off north and were taking a month kayaking/

camping southwards. We invited them for coffee, to which they added cognac all round. Pleasantly the day passed.

The next day it was goodbye to the French and off to the north for us, and perhaps the magic 80 degree line. We passed outside of Amsterdam Oya and Dansk Oya and onwards, in thickening fog. The Sat Nav might not be as picturesque as the sextant, but it does a great job without all the hassle. We counted down the seconds of latitude and cheered as '80 degrees north' flashed on the screen.

For a few miles we kept going. The pack ice had to be soon. The sky showed 'ice blink' ahead, a white upward reflection in the sky. The fog, at a temperature of four degrees, felt clammy. Our heaviest clothing, hats and gloves, was now being worn. Shortly we met a solid field of ice, the polar pack. We turned to the southeast.

That night our anchor lay in Raudfjorden on the north coast of Spitsbergen. True isolation and majesty surrounded us. David and myself, in the dinghy, spent a couple of hours doing a reconnoitre of the various climbing prospects. He selected an inland peak being more likely than a coastal one not to have been climbed, the price being a daunting walk-in.

Climbing Party. Johnny Rooney, Paddy, David Walsh,
Gary MacMahon, Donal Ó Murchú.

At 11.00 am we started and thirteen hours later we finished, all in, but happy. Lead climbers David and Donal, Gary, Johnny and myself had climbed a mountain where no foot had ever stood before. The peak, reached after eight hours of cold struggle, over crevassed glaciers, unstable snow slopes, gaunt rock ridges and finally 100 metres of corniced terror, was sweet indeed. No cairn adorned it. We were first up. Roped, cramponed, ice-axes in heavily gloved hands, our downward five hours compared with Caesar's triumphant return to Rome.

Time pressed now. We had to get south.

In light wind conditions we engined – and sailed by opportunity – in the high Arctic, winds in summer generally being slack. At Prins Carls Foreland, we anchored and did an eight hour sortie to climb Mount Monaco. Approaching Longyearbyen, nostalgia reigned. David and Donal were leaving by air. We were setting sail, 700 miles to the southeast for Murmansk. Jimmy, fresh from his final engineering exams, must have been apprehensive. For the rest of us, it seemed like just another week ahead at sea.

The southwest coast of Spitsbergen is deeply indented by bays and fiords for the eighty odd miles south to Sorkap. But we saw little of it, as fog reduced visibility to a half mile or so. A freshening wind from the southeast forced us to use engine power to make useful headway into the rising sea. We had a thoroughly miserable 20 hours or so as the tidal stream, which had helped us make such good time from Jan Mayen, was now against us.

The wind direction forced us out from the land, one problem less, but we were reluctant to stray far off the rhumb line course as we only had a week to sail the 700 odd miles, past the north coast of Norway and into Soviet waters in time for the first ever Arctic Regatta in Murmansk, to which we had been invited.

Sorkap was left astern. The wind backed to the east, which allowed us to sail our coursewhich was just as well. The engine, which had been backfiring, now ceased to work at all. Unperturbed, we sailed on. We had fixed various engine problems before, mostly to do with fuel supply, but this one we failed to remedy. We bled the system, changed the filters, the fuel pump, the fuel lines, even the fuel tank, all to no avail. We were now truly a sailing vessel, a long way from anywhere.

Close hauled still, we spoke to the radio operator on Bear Island. It would have been nice to call in but we pressed on into the Barents Sea. Sometimes we could lay our course for Murmansk, but too often we were being set south. We kept at it, hoping that a wind shift would favour us. If we had to tack back to the north, our chances of being in time would be slim indeed. Johnny sailed like a man with a mission. There was no way we were going to miss this regatta, even if we had to swim and tow the old Hooker.

Sad to say, our enthusiasm was not enough. With still 200 miles to go, the wind fell away. Eventually, the coast of Norway became visible. We were not going to make Murmansk, in time at any rate. Dejected, we altered towards land and, slowly, got into Hammerfest.

I'd like to say that we got a crew to work all night and get the engine fixed, or that the wind blew and we sailed a record passage, but that did not happen. But what did was that Johnny 'sussed up' a local plane, which took us to the Norwegian border town of Kirkenes. There we 'bivvied', that is, slept out without a tent, and the next morning got a ferry across the Soviet border, around Kap Nemetski and up the mighty Murmansk Fjord, home of the Northern Fleet. Now we could see why our visas were so hard to get. Right and left rode the grey vessels of the mightiest collection of naval power in the world. Floating docks and workshops lay on both sides of the fairway. In the midst of this high-tech hardware, some of it nuclear, lay derelict hulls along the shore in various stages of decay – an amazing contrast. We shortly were to discover this running through all of what Russians call 'the system'.

Let me describe the Arctic Hotel, finest in town. This showpiece of 17 stories and 700 rooms had been built only six years previously in the city's prime location. The main door was approached by magnificent steps. On closer approach, the door itself appeared to have been cobbled together from scrapyard metal, and definitely by men who 'took a drink'. They also must have left the job in a hurry – and the painters never turned up!

This extraordinary door was typical of the standards we saw. But the system did seem to grind along, just about.

In the midst of this were the people, and they were truly wonderful – warm, fun-loving and generous. I could write about the crew from the White Sea, who had sailed 400 miles to be here – in tracksuits. They fed us for three days, despite our protests, and wined us – or should I say 'vodka'd' us – daily to oblivion. *Nas Darovia* was the cry every five minutes, it seemed, as the toasts were drunk.

For the big race, about 20 boats lined up. The organisation of the Regatta and associated eventshad been distinctly ragged, but the enthusiasm of the organisers, the Murmansk Shipping Company, compensated. The Norwegian boats, heavily built cruisers, had no chance against the 'stripped out' Russian boats – because the Russians had so little to put into them. The crew of *Saint Patrick* were spread through the fleet, so we couldn't lose!

Five days in this 'other world' came to an end as, exhausted, we retraced our steps to Hammerfest. Gary had left, to be replaced by Adrian Spence. The engine had needed parts from Oslo. In Norway things were never cheap; I'll spare you details of the cost of a fuel injection pump, flown up and fitted. It transpired that the diesel we had been given in Jan Mayen, old stock from old tanks, had been contaminated.

From Hammerfest southwards, now joined for a week by Mary Barry, we passed through fjords, broad and narrow, mostly sheltered, on the Hurtigruten route. There were magnificent mountain backdrops, deep water and the nights getting darker; a welcome trend, as we never had quite got the hang of sleeping with the sun still in the northern sky. The stone and rock gave way to a greener hue, as grass, stunted willow and birch trees grew on the slopes. Isolated houses gave way to clusters of houses.

Tromsø had been described to us as the 'Paris of the North'. It was not, yet was attractive.

In Gratangan, we enjoyed the hospitality of a traditional boat museum group before winding our way through sheltered channels to Svolvaer, capital of Lofoten. From there, having greatly enjoyed the sheltered passages through the magnificentwaters of northwest Norway, Mary flew home. We prepared for the open sea, 700 miles to Shetland.

We made it, but with difficulty much of the time against head-winds and with the engine requiring nursing both of fuel supply and fading batteries. Under sail we arrived at Mid Yell, thence to Lerwick, capital of Shetland. This was followed by a good 200 miles sail, with wind on the beam, to Stornoway, from whence we had departed almost 11 weeks earlier. David rejoined us and we went to Loch Scavaig to climb the most magnificent Cuillin. Poor weather sent us inside the Mull of Kintyre, through the Crinan Canal, to climb Goat Fell on the island of Arran. A couple of days later, September 1, we were back in Dublin.

ໆ   ໆ   ໆ

The generosity and encouragement of John Gore-Grimes of Howth during this period, and long after, was most welcome and helpful. He, in his yacht *Shardana*, had sailed several seasons in these Arctic waters. He loaned me many charts, which I never could have afforded. Many times he hosted our crew (and wives) at table with wines of the best.

And, most generous of all, at that time an international doyen of high latitude sailing, he pulled me up onto his sporting platform to share the honours which came our way.

I also have to 'thank' him for the painful aftermaths of some great nights out 'pinting'! My recollection of these is hazy, but I do recall him saying that I shared with his neighbour, the notorious C. J. Haughey, the characteristic of being 'well used to adversity'!

21

Brendan Caffrey – Are You Still Running?

We met in Sean JD's pub in Ballybunion when I was working in Tarbert. Soon he had me running the long beach with him. In 1968 I had given up rugby and running but in short order he had me at it again. On summer weekends he would be down from Limerick, singing 'The Captains and the Kings', and running.

Brendan, entrepreneurial, was dabbling in shares, with some success it seemed. And he convinced me of the merits of seeking that path to easier living. I put a thousand pounds – yes, a thousand – into Broken Hill Proprietary. He did too, calling it 'The ICI of Australia'. Their share price immediately started to go down, and down. When it reached 600, he said we should 'get out' and onto a 'faster moving share for the quicker recovery'. We each bought Timor Oil; about a week later there was a military coup in Timor and our shares were worthless.

Going our separate ways, we lost touch.

About 15 years later an envelope came in my lettterbox in Monkstown containing a thousand pounds – no address, just a 'Best Regards, Brendan'. Wherever you are now Brendan, thank you – you didn't have to do that.

I kept on running. I did a Dublin Marathon in 1983; Mary saw you there too, at Westland Row, with about a mile to go.

I started jogging again about 20 years ago around whatever park would be nearest my work. In sailing, it's a great thing to get off the boat and stretch the legs, escape the cabin fever. Forest tracks are particularly nice, though sometimes easy to get lost on. I had some memorable forest runs on a White Sea trip in Solovetski Island, in Karelia, and later in Sweden. The clifftop runs too can be bracing, such as Vestmann in Iceland or Faroe. But the very best of those is home here on the Great Blasket Island.

When I'm in Connemara, I like to do the Mannin Run, on the sandy machair grass of the seashore and, back in Dublin, for me it's Blackrock's Rockfield Park. Three rounds used to take me 30 minutes; now it's more like 40, but it doesn't matter.

PS. You don't stop running because you get old – you get old because you stop running!

22

Intel 'Highs' and Greenland, 1993

In September 1990, after Spitsbergen, it was straight back to work for Jacobs on the Intel 'Wafer Fab 10' project. Initially, in Jacob's Merrion Road Office, the various construction packages were put together, about twenty; each big enough to attract substantial contractors, but not so big as to eliminate smaller firms whose resources could usefully be brought to bear on the project.

The specialist engineering designers, American and Irish, would assemble the technical material. I, and others, would 'package' these, together with contract documents, for bidding, and then construction by the preferred contractor, generally the lowest compliant one. As with ESSM, I had no trouble dealing with the building and civil contracts, but on mechanical, electrical and process work I was on unfamiliar ground, not to mention the very specialist 'clean room' construction coming down the line. John McGowan was Jacob's 'main man' and I, reporting to John, was contracts manager.

Then it was out to the Leixlip site again, my old firm Ascon doing the early civil and building work. There was possibly some concern on their part that I might be carrying 'baggage' in relation to having been 'let go' by them some years earlier. I didn't in fact have any such misgivings, realising that firms are 'organic' and people move on. Leo Harmon, Ascon's engineer-in-charge at Intel, had once, long ago in Platin, asked me for a rise. As he describes it, my reply then was, 'Leo, do you have any idea how keenly we priced this job?'

The work was intense, as necessary engineering design kept just ahead of the 'field' requirements. To again borrow the phrase, 'This was no place for old men'. Jacobs had about 25 on site, Intel about eight, with the contractors' men numbering maybe 600; it was a busy place. The work was getting done, the 'milestones' were met. Yes, there were some money issues, but no bad feeling – it was just business. And that too was Intel's aim. They were in Ireland for the long haul and wanted their people, which included us, to be physically and mentally able, and adequately paid – but without any 'fat'.

Intel's programme required a finish in early summer of 1993. Little did they know that the most motivated man on the site was myself – because on June 18 I was heading for Greenland.

Aboard with me on *Saint Patrick* as we left Dublin were veterans of 20 years on the boat, Sean and Kevin. Gearóid and Jimmy, who had been youths on the Spitsbergen trip, now took their berths as men. Davy McBride, from Waterford, latterly Howth, whom I had known on and off for years, joined us in Baltimore. Our 'radio base-man', back in Dublin, would be veteran climber/sailor Pat Colleran.

From Mizen Head to Cape Farewell, on Greenland's south tip, is 1,300 miles. The early days of our passage were delightfully easy, allowing a comfortable settling down into sea-going routine. High pressure in mid-June gave fine weather to Ireland and the eastern Atlantic, warm and sunny. We spoke to Valentia Radio until we were out of their 300 mile range. On our fourth day, we left behind the Porcupine Bank and the trawlers we met there. Sean wrote in the log, 'Dolphins disporting themselves around the boat, joining us in celebration of a beautiful night'. The sea even turned that turquoise colour that the sun, south of Madeira, gives it. What sort of Arctic voyage was this?

We soon were to find out. On the sixth day, a falling barometer and a heaving swell presaged a change. The wind rose from the southwest. We travelled fast and wet. This was the real thing. The party was over. Full reefs in the mainsail and our two headsails flying, we lifted and soared, plunged and flew. The rigging was

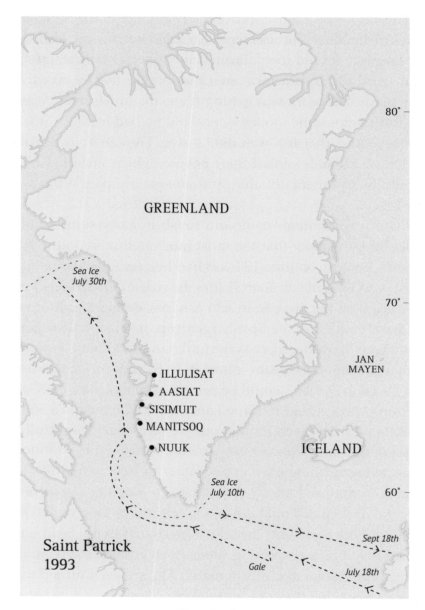

Greenland

bar taut, the sails tight, like the skin of a *bodhrán*, except when the helmsman would lose concentration, or in the sheltered trough of a wave when almighty flapping and clattering would rattle the boat until she was again forced into trim.

We had lightened the bow of the boat by drawing off stores and diesel from there first and were glad now. The seas were big and breaking, all was wet, with pumping necessary every half hour or so. A sail seam tore and was re-stitched. Davy managed to do us a 'Fray Bentos' dinner in the oven. We changed to the Greenland side of our Atlantic chart.

The following days we made good progress, but in conditions of little cheer. There was rain and cloud, wind on the nose mostly, sails up and down, engine on and off. The log had succinct notes such as 'unpleasant watch, wet, cold and miserable. 16 miles'. On our tenth day a full gale blew from the northwest. All sail was taken down and we lay ahull, the tiller lashed to leeward and us all below. The sea was littered with fulmars come down from the sky to shelter from the cold howling wind. In the cabin the coal stove burned, as we lay for 36 hours, being blown backwards. Occasionally a wave would break right over, and partially into, the boat. Then we pumped.

Nothing lasts forever. The wind fell to a moderate level, though the seas remained high. We pointed again for Greenland, set small sail and engine. Miserable. Our compass had been washed from its bracket during the gale – we should have taken it in, I suppose. We rigged a jury Silva mountain compass. Our spare diesel, in drums on the foredeck, had been carried away also. There was nothing we could do about that now.

During the period we were hove-to we lay quarter to the seas. We had considered whether we would be better with her shoulder to the seas, which could probably have been done by streaming our tyre fenders, on long warps, from the foredeck. We decided to leave well enough alone. Our ship had looked after us.

Then the engine oil pressure fell from 60 psi to 20. Big trouble? On our fourteenth day I wrote:

> How the problems ebb and flow. It was (and still is) the diesel quantity. It was (and maybe still is) the engine oil pressure. Now it is the identification of the limit of sea-ice off Cape Farewell. We're about 250 miles to the east of it. Two weeks ago it extended 30 miles out. Now, on the radio, Narsarsuaq

Ice Central told us that it is gone much further south. They will be flying their Twin-Otter Ice Reconisance tomorrow and will advise us.

We altered course to the south/southwest. Apprehensively sailing and motoring in alternating fog and drizzle, we put back the ship's clock a further hour.

The fifteenth day, a Saturday, dawned cold and clear to the northeast. A brightness, low on the horizon, clearly was ice – how far or how near was difficult to tell. We checked our position – ninety miles south of land. Height of mountains, 2,000 metres. Yes it was possible. That land disappeared in cloud, cold grey and damp. Helmsman spells were reduced to half hour. But we had seen Greenland.

At 9.30 am the ice was two miles off our starboard bow. Small growlers and bergy bits were in the water around us. There was exhilaration and a rush for cameras. As we got closer, we could see dirty glacial ice mixed with it. We came to within 50 metres of it. 'Careful now, this stuff is floating rock as far as the boat is concerned.' We held our course, in clear water, and considered the prospect.

Our information now was that the ice in this wide band, coming down Greenland's east coast and, clockwise, rounding Cape Farewell, ran all the way up to Nuuk, at 64 degrees north. This was 400 miles distant. Our notion of making a purposeful, two-week passage were gone. There would be another week at sea, maybe two weeks if the wind turned northerly, as we were too low on diesel to run the engine for more than another thirty hours or so.

Following the bad luck came the good. Through Qaqortoq Radio we made contact with a tanker 60 miles to the east of us, *Oregreen* of Copenhagen. Her function was to re-bunker fishing ships at sea. She agreed to refuel us.

We had to hand it to those Danes on the tanker. They loaded us with 500 litres of diesel, sent us down tee-shirts, hats, the bill, delivery docket (three copies), a sealed sample of the diesel provided and its test certificate. We returned, in the same plastic bag, payment in

Paddy on the tiller approcahing Greenland.

kroner and the signed dockets. By midnight we had cast off and, with much waving and thanking, separated into the mist.

For two days we had good sailing and then, the wind falling, went to start the engine, only to hear a loud clanking within. No engine. For two days then we tacked in light headwinds, making little enough ground. Then the wind blasted out of the southeast. Great, but hard going. With fully reefed sails we ran northwards before it, making great progress, but being very much on edge and forced over to the Canadian side of the Davis Strait. We could have run under headsails only but, without engine, wanted to optimise this good wind. For almost three days we ran northward, in pretty awful conditions. On the Friday night, the clew of the mainsail blew out. We fixed it the next morning with a new boltrope forming an eye. Then the wind fell away to nothing. For two days we drifted, the sails slatting about. We were about 60 miles from Nuuk, and in any decent breeze or with a working engine could have been there in 12 hours.

We met two trawlers and then the Danish Navy fishery protection vessel *Agpa*, bound for Nuuk. We took their offer of a tow and at 3.00 am, 21 days out, were tied alongside the harbour in Nuuk.

A neighbourly nightcap with our new Danish navy friends – the skipper and ourselves now being on first name terms – turned into quite a session. They had been at sea for several weeks and too were glad to be in.

The engine repairs kicked off the next day. Through the friendly intervention of the local Danish, Greenlandic shipyard mechanics went to work immediately. The engine was stripped down by these quietly spoken, competent men and taken away. The crankshaft was found to be broken. Parts would need to be ordered from Copenhagen and payment in kroner equivalent to £3,000 was required before ordering. While we organised this in the bank, they went ahead and ordered anyway.

It would be 11 days before we had that engine fixed, back into the boat and tested. During this period we got to know Nuuk and

Happy to have reached Greenland. Gearóid Ó Riain, Sean Mullan, Paddy, Jimmy Conlon and Kevin Cronin.

its surrounds pretty well. We hiked the mountains and went sailing into the fjords for a few days on a visiting American yacht, *Blue Northern*. Her skipper/owner had paid for the boat from earnings as a welder on the Alaskan pipeline – and 'blue northern' was the name of a particularly vicious wind which sometimes blew there. Up town we drank a lot of coffee and Tuborg beer, favourite of Greenlanders. We visited the museum and various houses, including an awful-looking block of apartments, housing 5,000 people, 10 per cent of the population of Greenland. Eric Muller, harbourmaster and agent for the Royal Arctic Line, took us out on *Kivioq*, his pride and joy, the vessel that had been used by Knud Rasmussen in his 1920s exploration of the north.

For all this conviviality, there were occasional reminders of the harshness of this unforgiving country. Three Greenlanders had died of exposure on the hill across from town last September while hunting caribou. That had been put down to inexperience. But a seasoned Inuit hunter had also gone missing last year, without explanation. We took salutary note. Mobile VHF radio and overnight gear always accompanied any shore party of ours.

Kevin left and Adrian, Terry Irvine and Harry Connolly arrived. Terry, a hill farmer from Antrim, needed a big berth to take his substantial frame. Harry, a climber friend from Dublin now working in Luxembourg, was lighter and more agile so he went to a confined forward berth.

On Friday, July 23, we were mobile again and away to the north, bound 200 miles to Sisimuit. The length of the populated west Greenland coast is about 1,000 miles, and on this coast there are seven towns, their average spacing being something under 200 miles. In between, at about 50 miles spacing, there are some small villages, called settlements.

The total population is about 55,000, half of whom live in Nuuk, the capital. Most are of mixed Inuit/European blood, Danish in particular. About 10 per cent are pure Inuit, the hunters, largely living in the old way though less and less so. Another 10 per cent are Danish – engineers, medical and administration people and those on

*Greenland does have some 'green' in the sheltered south,
for a few weeks in summer.*

short-term contracts such asconstruction workers. The Greenland-ers and Inuit do not like to be referred to as 'Eskimos', an out of date and somewhat pejorative term. Their religion is Lutheran.

Greenlandic is the spoken language, with Danish being the sec-ond tongue and English very much following. For many hundreds of years, Denmark ruled it as a closed colony, paternalistically, and at some cost to themselves. In the 1960s, following outside criticism and their own awareness of the poor condition of the people, Den-mark introduced modern health, schools and housing (hence the block of flats in Nuuk, already mentioned). However in so doing, many of those people in outlying areas were brought into an urban environment to which they were unsuited – a dilemma of which the Danish were aware, but felt that there was little alternative if their lot was to be improved.

And so, in too short a period, one generation, a major change in the life of Greenlanders was brought about; similar changes in

Davy McBride on pier. Note the protective metal sheathing on the boat waterline—put on for ice protection.

others countries, including Ireland, typically had taken place over many years.

In recent years Greenlanders sought, and got, Home Rule. Though not unlike the more advanced Faroese, they want independence, but to the Danish they say 'keep sending us the money'.

What's in this for Denmark? The benefits are two-fold. The first is that by reason of its dominance of the vast area of Greenland, and its associated Arctic segment extending to the North Pole, Denmark has a significant place at the 'world table'. The second is the prospect of mineral wealth to be found there.

None of this greatly concerned us. We were there to visit Greenland as an interesting, wild and mostly untamed place, and to meet some of its people overcoming such challenges as might present themselves.

Sisimuit town itself was somewhat of a dump, with much dog-shit and general debris. Greenlanders are not tidy, by nature, and in any event the place was snow-covered for 10 months of the year, hiding all. Harry and I had a good mountain outing, which is what we were here for and so later felt justified in having an extra beer or two as the band struck up in the Hotel Sisimuit. Greenlanders are hugely musical and love to dance.

Next passage was to Qeqertaarsuaq, formerly Godhavn, on Disco Island. We were getting the hang of some Greenlandic and using the older Greenlandic names in lieu of the Danish ones. For example, *suaq* means 'big' and *siaq* means 'small'. In pronunciation, accentuate the 'q' as a throaty 'chk'.

The weather was settled and pleasant, with long days and no nights. Icebergs were plentiful but not a threat. We met occasional boats either fishing for halibut or hunting seal. Going further north, around the west side of Disco, we pulled in daily, meeting fewer people. We cooked on the shore, practised with our gun (for polar bear protection) and hiked mountains and old sledging routes. The last town, going north, was Upernavik. Then it was more or less into the wild. The mapping of a village might not have assured its continued existence.

Pleasantly under sail, about ten miles north of Upernavic, we met two guys fishing, Peter Aronson and his cousin Matthias, who led us into their Tugsaaq island home. We met their families and their sledge dogs, chained up for the summer and not to be trifled with – these were not pets. Peter assured us that getting to Thule, our intent, would be no problem and sketched for us the movement of the sea-ice, all in sign language. He agreed to come with us for two weeks, fee agreed. His kit was simplicity itself: *kamik* (sealskin) boots, fur trousers (polar bear), anorak and hunting rifle.

First we would go north to Nugsuaq, where from his cousins we would get local advice on the sea-ice. This we did and then onward to Kuvlordsuaq, with its mountain called the Devil's Thumb by the old whalers. Jimmy, Harry and I tried to climb its easiest looking rock face but had to admit defeat. Far out to the northwest, Melville Bay looked ice-covered. Our ice-pilot and guide, Peter, was unperturbed.

Adrian Spence, Greenlander Peter Aronson and Harry Connolly.
Peter came aboard for a couple of weeks as 'ice-pilot'.

Two days later we were on our way back. We had gone into it, following open water leads, zig sagging under Peter's instructions, deeper and deeper. This was only first-year ice, relatively soft, like timber, not the rock hard multi-year older ice or equally dangerous glacier ice. It was, however, enough to stop us. We could go no further. Looking at the current ice-charts, Pat Colleran, our baseman back in Dublin and an experienced arctic sailor, had been surprised that we got as far as we did.

A week later, the little brown man in the sealskin boots, Peter, waved us goodbye. We had dropped him back to his island home. It was time for us to be getting back south.

We travelled at a comfortable pace, sailing slowly, motoring more often, shore walking, bivvying overnight beside driftwood fires. Occasionally some of us would go for the snowy high ground. A couple of times a walking group traversed a 'sledge route' across a peninsula shown on the map, while the boat went the long way round. These routes are not in the least flat; the dogs, pulling sledges in winter, did not have an easy time. Greeenlanders love the snow and the dogs. 'Give me winter, give me dogs,' said Rasmussen, 'and you can have the rest.' These people, Danes and Inuit alike, love the winter and the sledging. The Danes do it for sport, the Inuit Greenlanders for hunting. The kids start practising with a short whip and one dog, gradually working up to a six metre whip and a full 12-dog team. They crack the whip behind the dog, or beside the lead dog, to turn him. They don't actually hit the dog, unless they need to. When the dog becomes too old to work, it is shot. 'Goodbye dog – I can't be feeding you if you can't work.'

On August 8, bound for the settlement of Nugatsiaq in Karatfjord, our trim-tab failed. This trim-tab is our 'secret weapon' for taking the weather helm, the pressure, off the rudder and so making it much easier to steer. So we used Davy's 'handy-billy' on the tiller, a multiple pulley. Gearóid used to call it his 'silly-billy', but not now. Later, the boat tied in a rocky cleft, I dived down to the rudder in a wet suit and did a lashed repair.

Going south, we visited villages and climbed on Upernivic Island and Umanaq. That picture on the front cover of the boat through the ice arch was taken from the dinghy shortly after leaving Umanaq. It being early in the day, late night before, there had been a reluctance to be bothered launching the dinghy. Harry and Adrian went in it, Gearóid helming. Both had cameras and there still is some contention as to who took this picture.

By August 22 we were in Illulisat, back on the more populated coast, with two weeks to get down the west coast and then two more to get home. Harry and Sean flew out, Johnny Rooney arrived bearing rashers from Ireland and, more importantly, replacement ball-joints for the trim-tab linkage. Icebergs abounded from the great Illulisat glacier.

In the last month and a half, we had reefed only twice but the weather now was turning livelier. Harnesses, gloves, full gear were necessary once again. In Aasiat, Bjorn the Chief showed us around the town, including the jail. 'Always full,' he said. They are let out by day to go to work and are back in at night in enforced sobriety.

Going south we visited Manitsoq, crossed the Arctic Circle, skipped Sisimuit and called to Nuuk again, of course. The days now were autumnal, geese gone south, contract workers packing up, nights longer. On August 28 we left for Paamuit, previously inaccessible behind the offshore ice. There we met a Breton, Christian Gallot, one of those French single-handed sailors who, unsung, roam the ocean. His 28-foot plywood boat had been damaged by an ice 'growler'. Now repaired with a half sheet of ply, he had painted on it *Putain de Growler*.

Qaqortoq was the next stop, a thirsty place, in fact all of south Greenland appeared to be in party mood thanks to a 'tax rebate'. Then Hvalsey, with its Viking remains, and the hot springs at Unartoq and Nanortalik where Jimmy and myself had our last Greenland walk.

On September 4 we entered Prins Cristian Sund, that magnificent cut through the mountains north of Cape Farewell, overnighted at the village of Augpilotoq and called to the weather station at its eastern end. There five isolated but well paid Danes welcomed us and we took our departure for Ireland.

Our passage home was uneventful, apart from one wonderful viewing of the *aurora borealis*. Ten days later we saw the mountains of Donegal, pretty inconsequential looking.

Both Gearóid and Jimmy had developed into fine reliable shipmates who could be trusted to look after our ship, as indeed they did.

Gearóid, an all-rounder, was particularly good mechanically. Back in Spitsbergen, while we were on the mountains at Magdalena Fjord, it was he who copped that the prop-shaft had disconnected from the gearbox (low temperature contraction) and fixed it. In Nuuk when the engine re-installation by the local mecanics was slowing down, it was he who worked all night to move things along. Never complaining, 'sound as a pound'.

Jimmy, his classmate from Coláiste Eoin (as was my son Cathal), was more reserved. He would tend to stay in the background, smiling and enjoying himself, but he had quietly put me in my box when, ahead of this Greenland trip, I had taken him on the Connemara Bens on a 'test'. He had, without effort, stretched his legs and walked upwards and away from me!

Without such men, and the others who sailed with me, none of what we did together would have happened.

Collecting the Blue Water Medal in New York. (front) Johnny, Paddy, David, Adrian, Austin (back) Gary, Kevin, Mick.

23

Wexford 'Lows', Back to the Council and Baltic, 1996

While I was in Greenland, the Sherriff had come calling.

There had been a knock on our door at home, the Sherriff's man. Mary answered, at a busy time for her. She'd just got word of a flood in my brother Fred's apartment, on foot of which the door had been broken to get emergency access – he was away and hers was the contact number. She was also right then due to meet a friend coming in on the Dun Laoghaire ferry.

'Thanks, thanks,' she said to the little man in black, stuffing the letter away.

'No, no,' said yer man, 'this is a Revenue Warrant, sign for it, and pay the money or we'll be here in days to take possession of goods-to-the-value …'– about three grand it was!

Before I left for Greenland, I had said that when this cheque arrived from Jacobs to then post to the Revenue the cheque I had left for VAT payment due to them. This hadn't happened and the very on-the ball Revenue had now got the Sherriff moving in. There was quite a flurry, financially speaking, and then it was sorted.

What happened was that Muireann had tidied the hall, putting the post, mostly junk mail, in a drawer where it lay, incoming cheque and all. So no post went to the VAT-man.

There now was a further financial problem. Contrary to my expectations, neither Intel nor Jacobs had work for me. I was unemployed, and thus so remained for another two months, five months in total since I had been working with only rental from an apartment coming in. With Muireann in college, Bairbre in school and both Cathal and Caoimhe qualified, but not yet 'gone', there were six mouths to be fed.

Johnny Rooney made the vital connection for me. Wallace's of Wellingtonbridge was the contractor for Wexford Main Drainage, and they needed a contract manager. Well, they certainly did. Good guys, energetic and practical, but building was their thing, not civil engineering, and this scheme was not going well. Additionally, Wallace had underpriced it.

Paddy Hannon, their CEO, made me welcome, agreed good money, and I got to work, back into the trenches so to speak. I moved to Wexford and managed to put some order and organisation into the work – no need for me to push, the Wallaces and Hannons did the pushing. However, digging trenches and laying pipes through the narrow winding streets of Wexford, 'Wexford Lows', was a far cry from the spacious, well funded, fields of Intel.

In 1994 my five year career break from Dublin County Council was up. I could go back to them or choose to stay in the commercial world. Reluctantly, I chose the council, the persuading factor being that I now would be Dun Laoghaire-based. I introduced my old-friend and Ascon work colleague Liam Bohane to the Wallaces and left for Dun Laoghaire.

In the Dun Laoghaire-Rathdown County Council I was put onto the supervision of road and bridge construction as a resident engineer, overseeing contractors. And thus I spent the next thirteen years.

My senior was, once again, John McDaid. How lucky I was – good engineer, great guy. He recognised I was a poor fit in the council's scheme of things, but ensured that I was placed to the advantage of both the council and myself.

Conventional sailing and hill-walking continued. In 1994, it was to the Hebrides and around Ireland with old friends and new. Earle Bloomfield, Australian, could quote Greenlandic and Coledridge in equal measure:

And then there came both mist and snow
And it grew wondrous cold
And ice, mast high, came floating by
As green as emerald.

Similarly, in 1995 it was Scotland again and around Ireland, though this year nearly had a bad ending. At summer's end we were returning to Dublin overnight about ten miles south of Hook Head in Wexford. The wind was blowing fresh on our beam and we were sailing towards the Coningbeg Lightship, the lights along the shore shining brightly.

From astern, we were hit by a merchant vessel striking us on our bow. I still have nightmares of that overhead wall of steel scraping us as she pulled along, and then the rumbling of her propeller and foaming water. We were lucky not to have been sunk. I believe that the vessel never knew she hit us.

We were carrying the usual navigation lights, but being timber, *Saint Patrick* wouldn't have shown well on their radar. We hadn't

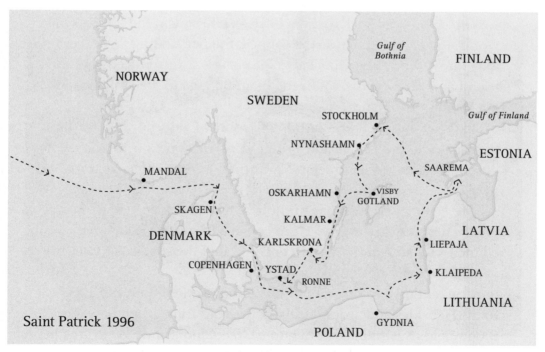

Saint Patrick 1996

Baltic

seen her lights among the many shore lights. We limped into Dunmore East, and some days later onward to Dublin.

In 1996 we did two things. One was to begin building 'a handy lugger' for a forthcoming plan. The other was to sail to the Baltic.

Jarlath Cunnane left his own fine yacht in Clew Bay to join Austin, Sean, Kevin, Pat Colleran and myself. We went through the Caledonian Canal, across the North Sea to southern Norway and then south to Copenhagen. For the last couple of days, down the coast of Denmark, we were joined by Gregors, he who in 1993 had towed us into Nuuk in Greenland.

For the next fortnight we had aboard Sean, Kevin, Fionán de Barra (no relation), Ruairc and Darrach Ó Tuairisg, Pat Redmond and Paddy O'Brien. We sailed to Gydnia in Poland where the vodka flows free. Kevin and I went ashore there, to meet Mary and Suzanne for rail travel. Pat then skippered for the next ten days, calling to Lithuania and Latvia, countries then in post-Russian decay, before continuing to the Estonian island of Saareema, where Kevin

Alongside in Stockholm. Donncha, Sean, Raphael and Ruaidhri.

and I rejoined, as did Raphael McIlhone, Donncha Ó hÉallaithe and Ruaidhri Ó Tuairisg for the next fortnight.

We crossed to Stockholm – what a change from the broken down south side of the Baltic – and travelled southward along the east coast of Sweden, altogether pleasant and civilised, rounded its southern side and returned to Copenhagen. There I recovered my bike which I thought had been stolen. It had been left six weeks earlier outside a pub – what honest people.

Jimmy Conlon then skippered *Saint Patrick* home, in the good company of Gearóid, Cathal and friends. They sailed across the North Sea to Inverness and then through Scotland to Dublin. I'd say they had quite a party, though their lowlight was a night-time engine failure in Loch Ness, leaving them under sail in this very tight place. They did it, and fixed the engine problem. Well done, the 'next generation'.

24

The Antarctic Adventure on Shackleton's Trail

Mountaineer Frank Nugent and I had met in September of 1993 on a group hill walk of Mount Leinster, he back from Everest and myself from Greenland. In the chit-chat, Shackleton's name came up. In early 1995 we met again. 'Any plans?' Frank mentioned Shackleton and joined our Scottish climbing cruise that summer. In December we decided, together with Jarlath, that we'd try to put a scheme together. Kerry climber Mike Barry (no relation) and all-rounder Jamie Young of Killary Adventure Centre joined us. Mick O'Rourke would be cameraman and John Bourke would be manager, finance and communications. To get going, we each put in £2,000. I would be skipper and Frank would be lead climber and joint expedition leader.

Ernest Shackleton's life was one of glorious failure. Scott had him invalided home from the Antarctic in 1904. In 1909 his own attempt to reach the South Pole failed, though he got within 97 miles of it before wisely turning back. His 1914 expedition to cross Antarctica never even got started because his big ship *Endurance* was crushed in the ice. His fourth expedition on *Quest* also never got going as he died before it began. But his escape from the *Endurance* shipwreck has assured his place in the history of survival.

To repeat some of this survival journey, by sea and over mountains, was what we now planned – an 800 mile sea journey, followed by a 30 mile climb, never repeated since done by Shackleton in 1916.

'In sight of our goal'. Shackleton's inspiring – or frightening – arrival off South Georgia (Marsden, Shackleton Expedition Artist).

Shackleton's boat, called *James Caird* after one of his sponsors, was no more than a rowboat of 23 feet length. She is preserved in Dulwich College, London. There Jarlath and myself inspected her hull and rig closely, checking the measurements.We would call our replica *Tom Crean*, after the Kerryman who had been such a significant participant in both Scott and Shackleton's expeditions. The building was done on a FÁS training scheme by boatbuilder Micheal Kennedy in Tipperary under Jarlath's close direction. Ours would be identical to Shackleton's, only stronger and more water-tight using double diagonal planking and epoxy glues. Our friend Liam Canavan did the metalwork for rudder hangings and water-tight hatch closure. The sails were of brown Duradon, a modern version of old sailcloth.

In parallel with the building, we began fundraising – and boy, would we need funds. The support vessel we engaged, *Pelagic*, a 53-foot yacht run by Skip Novak, would cost us £54,000. We would, on October 5, be shipping *Tom Crean*, together withour kit and rations, in a 40-foot container to Ushuaia in Tierra del Fuego. From there

Our sea trials in Dublin Bay, before shipping out (photo Mick O'Rourke).

our boat would be transported by a Russian cruise ship south past Cape Horn to Antarctica.

Sea trials were done from Jamie's base in Killary and then continued during September of 1996 in Dublin Bay. More ballast was added and sealed in, a ton in all, and sail area reduced. With great relief, we made the despatch date, all within the container and gone on its way.

There should then have been little for us to do, other than training, until our own post-Christmas departure. In fact, things got busier, fundraising mainly, doing talks and passing round the 'hat'. Digicel came on board as did Kerry Foods, as also did some sailing and climbing clubs. We formed an 'Iceberg Club', €100 per member, got a Government grant and did some further digging into our own pockets.

On December 29 we flew from Dublin, bound for Ushuaia, by way of Madrid and Buenos Aires. Three days later we passed over the Straits of Magellan. Below we saw Tierra del Fuego's bare windswept crags, down between two of which our plane swooped into

Ushuaia on the Beagle Channel. This was it all right, 'the uttermost part of the earth', as missionary/farmer Lucas Bridges had written of his time there. (It's not – we'll come to Siberia later!)

Even our new Chilean navy friends were powerless to protect us from the Machiavellian machinery of the Ushuaian Customs which cost us an additional $1,800 in 'fees'. *Tom Crean* was loaded onto the deck of *Molchonov*. Jamie would accompany her, while we travelled on *Pelagic*, all bound for King George Island, lying off the Antarctic Peninsula.

Southward of Cape Horn, the Cape Petrels were ever-present for a couple of hundred miles, busily flapping their black and white wings, but it was to the Great Wandering Albatross we looked, giants of the bird kingdom. 'Logbook for Grace' gives an appropriate comment: 'I have joined a band of upper mortals, for I have seen the albatross.'

Four days after clearing Cape Horn, the white of King George Island showed through the cloud and mist. Penguins, like small dolphins, rose and fell through the water in playful fashion. Two whales, species unidentified, blew. Penguin Island sent its stink in our direction, even though we were a mile off. We turned into Maxwell Bay and then into its subsidiary, Potter Cove, to anchor off the Argentinean base.

We dined, compliments of the enthusiastic hospitality of Base Commander Adolfo, together with their full team of fifty scientists and workers. We had a few days until *Molchonov* would be arriving; time to assimilate the splendour of this gateway to Antarctica, reminiscent of Spitzbergen, but wilder in its winds. At 62 degrees south, the summer nights were short. Temperatures were an acceptable minus five degrees at worst, though it was the wind and its associated chill that gives the bite. We practised our overland ski technique and tested our cold-weather clothing.

Molchonov arrived and her Russian deckhands made short work of unloading *Tom Crean*. By dusk she lay at the stern of *Pelagic*. Quickly, *Molchonov* sailed away into the midnight gloom. From Potter Cove to Elephant Island, our intended start, was 150 miles. We had met

Molchonov in Potter Cove because of the shelter to be had there. At Elephant Island there is no shelter and unloading *Tom Crean* might not have been possible. We considered going under sail to Elephant Island (named after the 'elephant seals', once numerous there), but as Shackleton's start was from there, so too would be ours.

For the tow, the five of us were aboard, together with all rations, equipment and clothing. I had one change of underclothes for the month ahead. Gibbs Island and O'Briens Island came abeam, high, sharp and snow-covered. Then we rounded Cape Plenty (names in the polar areas are often so descriptive, but usually of the unhappier kind such as Cape Desolation or Doubtful Bay). Our spirits were high as Elephant Island came into sight. To the east, Clarence Island showed only its 6,000-foot peaks above the haze. We prepared our anchor and sweeps as we approached Cape Valentine. This was where Shackleton had made landfall with his 27 men in three boats when they came in from the ice of the Weddel Sea, after his ship *Endurance* had been crushed and sunk. This was for us hallowed ground. But we could see why Shackleton and his men had moved on. The sea reached to within feet of the cliff base. Our primary objective was to reach Point Wild, ten miles further on. This we did by late afternoon, anchored and went ashore.

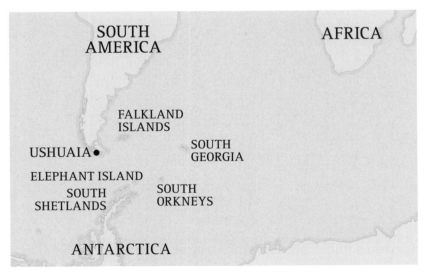

On Shackleton's trail, 1997

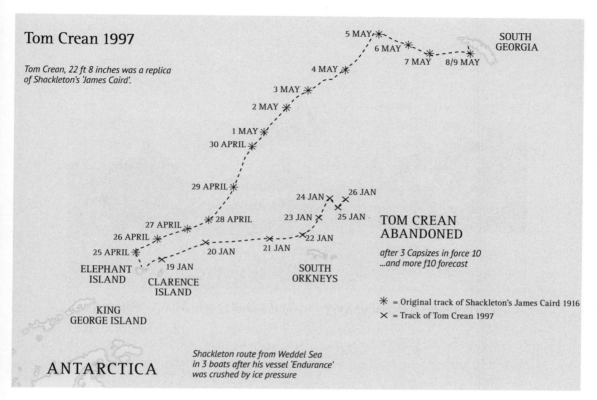

Tom Crean 1997

Tom Crean, 22 ft 8 inches was a replica of Shackleton's 'James Caird'.

5 MAY
6 MAY
7 MAY   8/9 MAY
SOUTH GEORGIA
4 MAY
3 MAY
2 MAY
1 MAY
30 APRIL
29 APRIL
24 JAN   26 JAN
23 JAN   25 JAN
TOM CREAN ABANDONED
27 APRIL   28 APRIL
26 APRIL
22 JAN
after 3 Capsizes in force 10 ...and more f10 forecast
25 APRIL   20 JAN   21 JAN
ELEPHANT ISLAND   19 JAN
CLARENCE ISLAND
SOUTH ORKNEYS

✳ = Original track of Shackleton's James Caird 1916
✕ = Track of Tom Crean 1997

KING GEORGE ISLAND

ANTARCTICA   *Shackleton route from Weddel Sea in 3 boats after his vessel 'Endurance' was crushed by ice pressure*

On Shackleton's trail, 1997

The fur seals, the colour of grey rocks, were snarlers and biters. A bite from one of those would do your leg no good. The hair stood on my neck in wonder and awe at this terrible place where 22 men had endured for three and a half months through the Antarctic winter of 1916. The metal detector which I had brought to seek remains of these men, perhaps the blubber stove, was a joke. The rock, often swept bare by gales and storms, was now covered in guano. Here, under one of the two upturned boats in which the 22 had lived, the boy Blackborrow had had his frostbitten toes amputated. Here Frank Wild, left in charge by Shackleton, had kept the 22 from despair, as each morning he had urged them to 'roll up your sleeping bags, the boss may come today'. The sea ice, it being winter, would have given some protection and provided drinking water. They ate penguin and seal.

187

The penguins watched us leave Elephant Island (photo Mick O'Rourke).

It had been Easter Monday, April 24, 1916 when Shackleton and his five companions had begun what was to be the greatest ever small boat voyage – a journey to rescue the 22 who remained.

It was 22.00, on Saturday, January 18, as we pulled away under oar from Point Wild. Light brash ice, from calving glaciers nearby, tinkled against our 23-foot hull. In cool, but near perfect conditions, we raised our lugsails with relief and jubilation that at last we were on our way. The planning, the fundraising, the boat-building, the complexities of getting to our start were all behind us. Now it was just the immediate reality that we were too big for this cramped little boat. The simplest movements required a choreographed re-arrangement of limbs, gear and bodies; just five of us in the boat, sailing to South Georgia, 800 miles to the northeast.

The single-burner gas stove was an abiding hazard to nearby sleeping bags and sleepersboth. This was such a danger and commanded such respectful caution that it gave us no trouble whatsoever. We ate potato mash, tinned meat and on alternate days kippers. We also had muesli, ryvita, porridge, jam and tea, with maybe a dollop of cold sea-water splashing in for good measure. Food was but fuel for the body. If we couldn't sleep much, at least we could eat, on the good days anyhow.

Our first couple of days were great – 76 miles on the first day and nearly as much on the second. But then the wind 'veered' round from the north (or was it 'backed', everything turns the opposite way south of the equator) so that, although we were going well, we were being pushed off our course. This little boat, a faithful copy of Shackleton's, little more than a rowing boat, had no windward performance.

The third day was difficult. All day we close-hauled to the east, with a fresh northerly wind. The boat would go only 90 degrees to the wind. The South Orkney Islands grew ever closer, a dangerous lee-shore, eventually being only 25 miles away. By afternoon, it was blowing 25 knots and that evening we put the boat about on the other tack, steering northwest. The wind rose to a full gale. With backed jib and helm lashed alee, we lay to for the night and were glad not to be blowing down on the Orkneys.

This was the first bad weather we had met and the boat rode the seas very well, however the cockpit pump was inclined to airlock until Jamie fixed it, using an offcut from the top of a used can of beans.

That blow lasted about 12 hours. We tacked and were away again to the east. We now were happy and confident, though bloody cold all the time, even in the sleeping bag. Inside our boat, the hull ran with condensation, sweat and spillage – a mixed brew indeed. Outside you could at least stretch yourself in the biting wind, swing your arms and stamp your feet until a shout from below: 'Stop the football match.' For a toilet we used the bucket.

Day 4 was the grandest you ever did see with a clear sky, sunny, and a cool light breeze off the beam, a flattish sea and us steering our direct course, 040 degrees. We had all our gear out drying and were hanging around the cockpit chatting. We ran a 'book' on our day of arrival at King Haakon Bay. The stake for each was one day's Ushuaia wages, twenty dollars a man. I went for 13 days, although

Tom Crean *at sea (photo Mick O'Rourke).*

I thought it would be less. We had been making 60 miles a day on average.

Later, with cold fingers, I scribbled:

> My back is stiff with the cold and damp. I took a couple of Brufen, which help. God, it has been cold, wet and miserable, even in the good weather. The cabin is so confined. Watch change is a major hassle, getting out of 'oilies', putting them somewhere, getting off gloves and boots, putting them somewhere where you'd hope to find them, best under your head for a pillow; contorting into the damp sleeping bag, inside its waterproof cover. I pull my socks, 2 pair, and gloves into the bag with me.

> Then at the end of your off-watch, having maybe got some sleep, mostly not, you'd do the opposite. Your feet would barely have warmed up the bag, but it's time to get out again – head first, onto your knees, sideways, turn around, sitting in your dry gear on someone else's wet gear. We try and get the 'oily' trousers on while inside the cabin, and then, quick as we can in the cockpit, get on jacket, gloves, harness and hood-up. Handling the boat is the easy bit.

On our fifth night a gale blew from the north and we had to heave to. Not a bad night at all. In the morning, the wind fell and went westerly. We then had a rollicking four-knot sail for a while, and in the right direction. On the GPS our TTG (time to go) even showed 95 hours for a brief spell. Alas, for most of the time, even with a light following wind, we sailed along, adjusting sails and just doing the best we could. But in the last 30 hours we had made good another 66 miles.

On Friday, January 24, at 05.35:

> Mike and Paddy on watch. The wind is from the north-east, Force 2/3. We are sailing to the northwest, at 2 ½ knots. It's a cold morning, misty and generally miserable. But all are in good heart, awaiting a change of wind for the better. 393 miles to go – of which we made good only 6 miles in the last 10 hours.

Later I wrote:

> Hove-to in Gale No 3 (in 6 days), northerly – as usual.

The deck-log finished here. What followed was written about four days later.

The wind and sea rose to a greater extent than in the previous two gales, and kept on rising and rising. By nightfall the wind was lifting water, not just off the wave-tops but off the flattened sea. The seas grew, first into regular big even crests, 30-foot maybe, but then became steep walls of water, the crests tumbling down, being wind-carried off in flying spume.

We put the sea-anchor out from the bow; it seemed to make no difference. To look directly into the wind wasn't possible as the flying spume would cut into your face and eyes. The boat was lying beam on, try as we did to keep her head to windward, with all other sail lashed down and the tiller lashed alee. We raised a triangular piece of mizzen sail. This brought the head around about 20 degrees, thus bringing the seas ahead of the beam.

But the seas became irregular and now were coming from all directions. We were pointing upwind, downwind, lying, running, being tossed and battered about like in a washing machine. We all now were wedged in below, waves belting the boat, first on one side, then the other, then the deck. Going out to check the lashings of spars and sails required a dash through the hatch with the harness already clipped on, then out, slam and lock the hatch and clip on a second harness.

About 4.00 am on Saturday morning, this being after our seventh night, we all were below, battered, cold and eating the odd Mars bar with water, when a great hissing sound rose above the now familiar racket. I was in a sleeping bag and stiffened at this new sound. Then I felt us being carried sideways, swept, and then the silence. We were upside down.

Blood from a cut in my head blinded me. Jamie later said that he looked through the hatch (it was see-through polycarbonate) and saw only green sea. Forever it seemed there was nothing we could do. She lay upside down, before rolling slightly on. We all scrambled to the side of the cabin to help her back up.

There was no solid water inside – good hatch – but the pressure of water on it, from the full cockpit outside, wouldn't let us open it. So we had to open a bulkhead valve, letting the water into the cabin, then pump it away using the inside pump. Ten minutes of this and the outside water level was low enough to let us get the hatch open and finish pumping from the outside.

Amazingly, all spars and sails were in place. No damage had been done, except to burgees, antenna, radar reflector and so on. Twice in the next 12 hours we capsized again with the same result. We radioed *Pelagic,* now some 15 miles distant, for weather information.

They had been registering wind speeds of 50 to 60 knots, sustained, and had been knocked on her beam by a 'Shackleton Wave'. The wind now is south-west 40 to 50 knots, sea completely white, air temperature 4 degrees. Three cyclonic depressions are following in from Cape Horn. If we do not get above them, we'll get hit by all of them.

They sat-phoned a U.S. specialist weather service and, an hour later, gave us the bad news:

For the next 10 days a deepening low pressure system, going down to 965 mb., would give northerlies all over this area, with another 60 knot session in about 3 days time.

We were not quitters, but the risk was too high. Sooner or later when capsized again one of us would be swept away or the mast would pull the deck out – bye-bye boat, and us. At best, that wouldn't happen but we would be carried hundreds of miles southward of South Georgia. The wind eased but I made the heartbreaking radio call to *Pelagic*. 'We want to abandon.'

It was the following day before the seas went down to a manageable state and *Pelagic* made her way up to us. Veering down their inflatable dinghy and three times winching it back with ourselves and our gear in it, we left our hopes and our dreams behind having scuttled our *Tom Crean*, lest she survive and be washed up God-knows-where and cause alarm.

Our position when we abandoned was 59 degrees 46 south, 44 degrees 57 west; half way between Elephant Island Island and King Haakon Bay, South Georgia.

For the next two days *Pelagic* raced the 270 miles using engine, sails, any which-way, to get to the shelter of the nearest part of South Georgia before the weather broke. Our bodies recovered quickly, our spirits less so; but we were unshaken in our determination that we would continue and do the mountain crossing, as Shackleton had done. We called to Larsen Harbour, briefly, and were anchored in Cooper Bay when the forecast weather struck. With keel in the mud, anchor and chain out and four warps tied to steel slings around surrounding rocks, we were happy to be here and not at sea.

We determined that to ensure success in the mountain traverse, we would work hard at getting ourselves and our gear up to snuff, getting familiar, if not comfortable, with South Georgia's mountains, snow, ice and, most of all, weather. During the next two weeks we sailed northwards on the east coast of South Georgia calling to Ocean Harbour, Grytviken, Leith, Stromness and Antarctic Bay. We saw the wildlife, the abandoned whaling stations, Shackleton's grave, Prince Edward Military Base (17 men) and got into shape for the mountains.

The weather was so changeable, maybe fine in the morning, but snow, wind and blizzard four hours later. On February 5, within Leith Harbour, we had gusts of 38 metres/second (about 90 mph), with snow.

To enter King Haakon Bay on board *Pelagic* was bittersweet. The sea was flat anda light breeze blew from the west. *Tom Crean* would have had no bother. Setting these thoughts aside, we dinghied into the narrow Cave Cove, that cleft in the rock, about 200 metres east of Cape Rosa, where Shackleton had landed. There we bolted a bronze

Before the traverse of South Georgia. Paddy, Frank, Jarlath (went round by sea), Mike Barry and Jamie Young (kneeling) (photo Mick O'Rourke).

plaque, cast in Dublin, to the rock face commemorating his landing and the words of Amundsen: 'In the history of Antarctic exploration, the name of Shackleton will be forever written in letters of fire.'

That night we anchored further up the bay and at 10.00 am our traverse began. Frank was the leader with Mike, Jamie and myself. It was only 30 miles, but those miles included three mountain ranges, heavily crevassed glaciers, snow fields and the crossing of a near freezing river. Plus the weather.

It largely was horrendous weather that had defeated any previous attempts to make the crossing, by British military specialists in particular. We considered whether we would go 'Alpine', that is, attempt to travel light and fast, or go 'loaded', prepared to hunker down if necessary because of weather, and then continue. We went for the latter option, carrying a three-man tent, sleeping bags and rations for four days – which could be stretched to a week on 'short rations' – with mountaineering skis, crampons, rope and ice-axes.

Glacier crossing, now called the Crean Glacier.
We camped overnight on this (photo Mick O'Rourke).

Fifty hours later, with aching bodies, blistered feet, striped shoulders but light hearts, we four descended exultant into the ruined Stromness Whaling Station. We were the first, since Shackleton had done it with companions Tom Crean and Frank Worsley, to complete that crossing of South Georgia.

Later, Frank and I had a go at the then unclimbed Mount Roots. Loose snow, friable rock, nearby avalanches and doubtful weather beat us on that one.

On February 26, we departed South Georgia on *Pelagic* and sailed 1,000 miles westward, leaving the Falkland Islands 60 miles to our starboard, Staten Island to our south, through the Straights of Le Maire, up the Beagle Channel and, on March 8, into Ushuaia.

We might borrow a line, this time from Addison.

'Tis not in mortals to command success,
But we'll do more Sempronios, we'll deserve it.

And to finish with a verse I added to 'The Ballad of Boss Shackleton':

They set out in a whaleboat, to save the twenty two
But the winter ice was on them and that boat could not get
    through.
But *Yelcho* made a fourth attempt, from Chile's friendly land
And on her bow was Shackleton, he greeted every hand.

25

Ilen *returns from the Falkland Islands, 1998*

We nearly drove her right up the slip in Baltimore, County Cork, the day we brought her home. Luckily, we got our stern line around a pier bollard as we passed. Steam and smoke rose from the wet rope as it stretched and the sails came tumbling down. *Ilen* slowed and stopped, and the crowd cheered.

Conor O'Brien, scion of the O'Briens of Inchiquin, latterly of Foynes Island, had sailed around the world in a boat built in Baltimore which he called *Saoirse*. Calling into the Falkland Islands, they were impressed with his boat and later commissioned him to build and deliver to them a similar but bigger boat, 56-foot and suitable for carrying cargo and sheep around the Falkland Islands, under engine and sail – and the vessel *Ilen* (pronounced eye-len) resulted, named after the river that runs through Skibbereen and into the sea at Sherkin.

She was timber-built in the Fishery School at Baltimore in 1926 and sailed down to the Falkland Islands by Conor O'Brien, Con and Denis Cadogan from Oileán Cléire. For fifty odd years she served her purpose, based in Stanley, 'capital' of that bleak and windswept place. Then, laid up and replaced by a modern vessel, she lay at anchor, unused and forlorn. About 1994, out of curiosity, I had written to the Stanley Harbour Master, who replied that she was indeed for sale, but some Chileans had an option on her. I thought no more of her until in the autumn of 1997 Gary MacMahon of Limerick had not only bought her but arranged to have her shipped to Dublin as deck cargo. I offered to help.

In the Grand Canal Basin, myself and the lads who sailed *Saint Patrick* worked that winter and spring on her. We hosed out the sheepshit – she once, reputedly had carried up to 200 sheep at a time – and Liam Canavan and Louis Purton worked on her ancient Kelvin engine, grinding out better teeth on her huge flywheel. We got her two masts back in and a 33-foot hooker boom as a topmast. With lines and blocks from Beaulieu Boat Jumble, we rigged her. There were seven sails – foresail, jib and flying-jib, mainsail and mizzen, staysail and aloft a topsail, being another Hooker sail, a jib, turned upside down. Peter Gargan repaired some of the metalwork; Paddy O'Brien and Pat Redmond felted the deck. We were ready to go.

She sailed sweetly south to Glandore in West Cork.

On Sunday, May 31, we gathered, two crews on board. Gary had with him a crew from Limerick, I had a selection of *Saint Patrick's* best. Ed Walsh of the University of Limerick, who with Tony Ryan had helped, was on board, with a big hamper of 'nicies'. A fresh and cool northerly wind gave us a fast and enjoyable sail the 15 miles westward to outside of Baltimore Harbour. We were early, and so jilled about, now tucking into the hamper and tasting the wine. Local boats joined. Pat, acting on my suggestion, went round all on board *Ilen*, one by one, ensuring that each knew what they were doing.

Baltimore Lifeboat came out, the big one that in 1979 had played such an active role following the Fastnet disaster. Kieran Cotter, a cousin of the Cadogans, was her coxswain. 'Let's go' came the cry. Helm up and sheeting sails, no topsail or flying-jib – it was too fresh for that – we close hauled in, through the narrow gap at Barrack Point and then over towards Wallis Rock. 'We'll have to tack,' and we did, but found that we'd now have to go through the moorings before tacking again in towards the pier. I thought I could hear a band playing.

Ilen *sails back into Baltimore.*

'Start the engine,' I said. As we tore through those moorings, Pat was ready to give the shout when I nodded. About fifty yards out he did, and all sails together were hauled down. Too late. On the wheel, I realised that we were going in too fast. 'Engine hard astern,' I roared. Great noise came from the exhaust but no slowing of the boat – the gearbox wasn't connecting! The crowd cheered and the band played. I paled. This was not going to be good but at least the slip ahead was empty. We could just run her up and let her fall over on her side. Impressive it would not be.

Thankfully, that stern rope held.

A week later we sailed her over to Crookhaven and let her dry against the wall outside 'the dock' and on June 14 took her in to North Harbour, Oileán Cléire, to another great welcome.

Later she was taken up the Ilen River to Hegarty's Boatyard. There for some years she languished. Now she is at an advanced stage of a very high quality rebuild, organised by Gary MacMahon and being carried out by Liam and John Hegarty, with much being done by Fachtna O'Sullivan and voluntary help. That boatyard is probably unique in its capacity to build and repair wooden vessels, both commercial and leisure, and is a pleasure to be around, though you'd sometimes have to tune your ear to the accent and the wit. Liam once spoke to me of a man 'who never saw a bad day, or a good night'.

Her new spars and rigging are ready in Limerick. Before long, we'd hope to see her afloat and flying.

26

The Northwest Passage, 2001

Jarlath Cunnane was skipper and I was expedition leader – the distinction was undefined but broadly I dealt with overall management and navigation while Jarlath built and ran the boat. It was in essence a partnership, in conjunction with some good friends. While this was primarily planned as adventure sailing, some climbing was intended as well. We also would be taking an interest in nineteenth century Arctic explorers, particularly Irish ones.

We had discussed this over 'pints'. Jarlath, Frank and myself, with our Antarctic Shackleton trip almost three years behind us, considered that it was time for another worthwhile outing – the Northwest Passage. Mick Brogan, doctor, and Gearóid Ó Riain, communications, joined. We'll meet the others as we go. Twelve boats had succeeded in making this passage since Norwegian Roald Amundsen first did over three years from 1903 to 1906.

Jarlath's boat *Lir* being too small and *Saint Patrick* being unsuitable, we decided to build a 47-foot aluminium vessel, purpose-designed for polar expeditions. In February of 2000 we received the plans from her French designer, Gilbert Carroff. We each kicked in €3,500 and building of the inverted hull began at Easter in Jarlath's Mayo workshop. Aluminium was chosen, in preference to steel, for ease of building, durability and low maintenance. The heaviest of the plates, the 12mm thick, 1.25 metre wide keel plate, was lifted into place by the local football team one evening after training! *Northabout*, as she would be called (my wife Mary's inspiration), was pulled out from the workshop and turned in September.

Amundsen's Gjoa. *This inspirational painting is in Tromsø Museum, Norway.*

Her hull was then finished, and the inside sprayed with 75 mm of insulation by February of 2001. Jarlath's formidable boatbuilding skill and energy were supplemented by the help of good friends in Mayo and Dublin both. I kept material and fittings 'flowing' to the workshop and did fundraising, one donation of €30,000 being particularly helpful.

Passage preparation, which I did, was the collecting of charts, pilot books, weather and sea-ice information, together with establishing good communications with various Canadian authorities, Customs, Ice-Service and the Coast Guard in particular.

Northabout was launched on June 1 at Westport Quay, her mast stepped and then motored around to quieter Rosmoney Pier for rigging, final fitting and the loading of stores.

Midsummer bonfires blazed on the coast of Achill on St. John's Eve, June 23, as six of us sailed for Greenland. Aboard were Gearóid and myself, on board for the long haul, while Pat, Harry, Cathal and youngster Eoin Coyle would be on board for the first month. Aboard were stores for eight months, being planned for two to three Arctic seasons. Diesel tanks took 1,800 litres to run her 90 HP Perkins engine and Dickenson stove. We were charted through to Vancouver on the Pacific side of Canada.

Northabout *departing from Westport.*

The departure date was dictated by backwards arithmetic from the time of normal ice break up in Melville Bay, West Greenland, which was usually the last week of July. Therefore some finishing work on the boat remained and sea trials would take place on the passage to Cape Farewell, south Greenland, 1,300 miles to the west/northwest.

Low pressure to the south gave us the delightful benefit of a northeasterly wind, mostly on our quarter, making for a terrific passage. We drove her hard and she stood up well. On Sunday, July 1, seven and a half days out, we saw ahead the coast northeast of Cape Farewell, magnificently stark with black mountains streaked with snow and ice. The *storis* sea-ice, driven down the east coast of Greenland and northwards up the west coast, prevented our making a landing until three days later when we reached Paamuit, 250 miles further on.

During those thre days we passed along outside the ice-edge, and sometimes a little inside it, in unsuccessful attempts to break through its 10 mile band into shore. For a while it blew 40 knots from the east. Once clear of the iceband, we attempted to get into shelter in Arsuk Fjord, but making little headway stood back to sea and hove-to. Though clear of the *storis*, the icebergs, at about two mile centres, still seemed all too close.

Well fendered, we tied up in the busy harbour of Paamuit. We stretched our legs in the surrounding hills, and undid the good in Peterson's Bar.

Over the next two and a half weeks we cruised northward 500 miles, calling of course to Nuuk, where we lay alongside a friendly La Rochelle yacht, 10 years out with skipper Michelle. Sailing up the fjord to Sadelo Island, three humpback whales with their white tails practically splashed us. Sermitsioq mountain gave us a good climb, but denied us her summit. At Manitsoq, a lovely harbour, we had a beer in the Ajo Bar and climbed the mountain marked on the map as '1,325' metres. Harry summitted.

Greenland is putting a big effort into tourism, and one by-product for us was the availability of many good hiking maps. We called to Sisimuit, where Michelle had overwintered her boat, and then sailed on to Qeqertassuaq (formerly Godhavn) on Disco Island. Our hero, Captain McClintock from Dundalk, on a Franklin search in the 1850s, wrote: 'I do not know a more enticing spot in Greenland for a week's shooting, fishing and yachting than Disco.' We hiked.

Sailing east to Illulisat, we met the many icebergs calved off its huge glacier, its bergy water much covered with small brash ice. Here we crew-changed. Arriving to join Gearóid and myself were Terry, filmmaker John Murray, Frank, Kevin, Mick and of course Jarlath. We were eight in all.

Cathal De Barra and Eoin Coyle, youngest of the 'delivery crew'.
2,000 miles to Illulisat, west Greenland.

The NWP Team. Paddy, Kevin, Frank, Gearóid, Mick, Jarlath and Terry (kneeling). Not shown is John Murray, who took this photo.

On July 22 we left and at Upernavic purchased final available stores and took stock. The sea-ice in Lancaster Sound, the entrance to the Northwest Passage, normally cleared by mid-July, still remained ice-bound. But the nearer Melville Bay was open. (We were getting, on our boat's email system, the daily Canadian Ice Service charts). We met Bob Shepton and his crew, who were sailing northwards to do a crossing of Bylot Island, following in Bill Tilman's many footsteps. Northwards we went along Greenland's increasingly icy coast. At Tugsaaq Island we visited the hunter Peter Aronson who had been with us aboard *Saint Patrick* in 1993. We passed Kap Shackleton, called to Kraulshavn and thence to Kuvlordsuaq. There Frank and I climbed the Devil's Thumb, so-called by the whalers of old. Mick, with his fiddle, entertained the villagers. It was now July 29 and Melville Bay, before us, was completely clear of ice. This seemed incredible after all the stories and, indeed, our own 1993 experience when, several weeks later in the season, the sea-ice had stopped us.

A couple of days later we were off Cape York, but not before the excitement of spotting our first polar bear, a young one, first seen asleep on a floe. And a more unlikely sighting was *Dodo's Delight*, Shepton's boat, he bound for Bylot and us for Thule. The ice still was clogging Lancaster Sound. Rather than sail over and just be looking at it, we decided to go the 'scenic' route and so detoured north. At Thule US Airforce base the welcome was frigid. Happily at Quaanaq, 75 miles onward, the opposite was so.

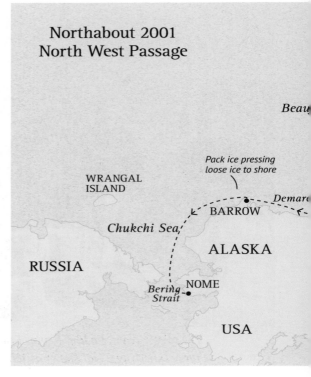

Northabout 2001
North West Passage

This village is where the Inuit Greenlanders, displaced by the Americans, were sent. It has no natural harbour, the only village in Greenland to be so disadvantaged, but the anchorage is good. This is where Peary based himself in the 1900s in his attempts to reach the North Pole. Here we met the Greenpeace ship *Arctic Sunrise* and her crew, a most varied and interesting lot. They said the same about us!

Meanwhile, ice had improved in Lancaster Sound. More improbably, Peel Sound, beyond it, was showing signs of clear water. Leaving Smith Sound, gateway to the North Pole, to our starboard, we left Greenlandic waters and raised the Canadian red maple leaf flag of its new province, Nunavut. The fog hid all. The compass had gone from being lazy to useless; we were approaching the 'magnetic north pole'. But our GPS worked a charm, as did our radar and echo sounder for depth. Coburg Island, off Jones Sound, has a shallow bay on its south side which gave us a good anchorage,

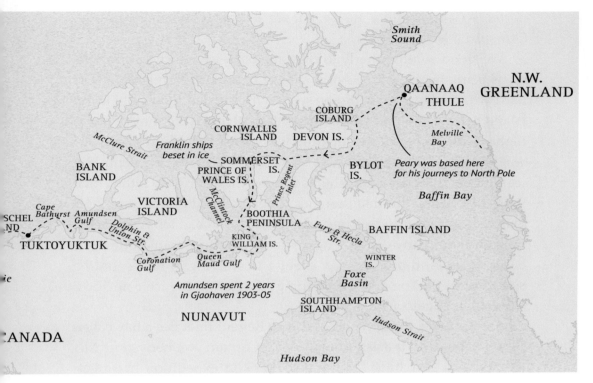

Northwest Passage

ice-free, once we got in. Our shore party came across a disused hut, more scientific than hunting, and French, to judge by the remnants.

Going southwards towards the entrance to Lancaster Sound, few of our four-hour watches passed without working through bands of 3/10 to 4/10 ice, generally being one-half mile wide or so. These never seem so daunting when open water is visible beyond. The sea-ice nomenclature denotes the proportion of sea covered by ice. Thus 10/10 is 100 per cent. A strong small boat cannot 'break ice' but can get along in 3/10 or 4/10, albeit slowly as one zig-zags through the ice floes. Sometimes to pass through, if they are not too big, one pushes them with the hull, the crew on the foredeck also poling it out of the way. It is largely for this work that a strong crew is requird, as well as keeping going twenty-four/seven, when conditions allow.

On August 7 we rounded Cape Sherard and were into Lancaster Sound. The Northwest Passage proper had begun. Conditions were perfect – clear visibility, no ice, flat sea and a light northerly breeze. Our spirits were high.

We stood southwesterly to clear the pack-ice which was reported as being heavy on the north side of Lancaster. Sure enough, its hard white edge soon could be seen, with the mountains of Devon Island behind. We met an icebreaker later that day, or maybe it was night. With no darkness our time was measured in our four-hour watches. She had come eastward out of Resolute settlement. Her ice-officer advised us that she had come through 7/10, rather than the 9/10 charted, but that there was ahead a band of first-year 7/10. She gave us the latitude/longitude of where she had left it. We tried, by going south, to avoid it. Fog descended and we found ourselves beset in ice. And thus we lay, silent and still, for 24 hours, until a slight lift in the fog and the opening of a gap in the ice coincided. We were off again.

On the northwestern end of Prince Regent Inlet lies a bay called Port Leopold. Our Irish antecedents, Captain Kennedy and Mc-Clintock, in searching for the lost Franklin expedition had over-

Inuit kayaker

Into Lancaster Sound. Terry on a floe, with gun in case of bear.
We had met some.

wintered here. Ice prevented our entry, but 10 miles onward we anchored in Rodd Bay which was ice-free. Some of us hiked back. Our reward was to see a school of white beluga whales disporting themselves inside the ice of Port Leopold. There also was a cairn with a bottled note, erected by some worthies in 1974, emulating the old style of message-leaving.

More interesting was the stone inscribed 'E.I. 1849', surely chiselled by some men of the search ships *Enterprise* and *Investigator*. Beechey Island, with its remains of Franklin's three crewmen, was inaccessible to us, but Peel Sound awaited, largely ice-free and marvellous. This is the great icy door on the Northwest Passage, normally remaining closed until the end of August if it should open at all.

Joyous, with all sail set, a 'one-hat day', we ran towards it and then southwards. Onwards we sailed, through the shallow, sometimes narrow, channels which for so many years had been hidden in this elusive passage. In by the western end of Bellot Strait, the name a reminder reminder of that plucky French officer, and then we landed on Cape Victoria. A caribou tossed his head and took off, Terry with his gun behind but too far away. Empty shells of the modern Inuit hunters lay among the stone rings of their summer tents. Surprisingly, there were no cairns, so we built one, leaving within a message of our passing – our note in a whiskey bottle, empty of course.

James Ross Strait is shallow and narrow. In near perfect conditions, we wound our way through. An island, shown on our chart as PA, position approximate, certainly was as it was about one-half mile out of position, a bunch of rocky fangs, barely peeping out of the water. With relief we continued and next day entered the village of Gjoa Haven, named by Amundsen in 1903. It was eight days since we had left Quaanaq.

Months of preparation and communication had gone into the details of our planned entry into Canada. The Canadians had even raised the spectre of our carrying Foot and Mouth Disease. These problems melted away in the welcome by RCMP constables Todd and Christine, first names all the way from the very beginning. They told us that we had been 'spied' coming and that in two hours' time there would be a Drum Dance in the hall for us as a welcome from the Elders of the village. We responded with a medley, our 'act' by now getting almost polished.

Gjoa Haven was dusty, and scattered, with 1,000 inhabitants. It has a large school, a sports complex/pool, two shops and many ATVs (all terrain vehicles), little four-wheel-drive quads. These quads are like mosquitos buzzing. Mothers use them shopping and collecting the kids from school, teenagers 'cruise' in them, hunters go to 'the land' in them. We met Paulus Amundsen, a grandson of the man himself, with a likeness plain to see (contrary to Amundsen's official account, a certain 'fraternising' had taken place). Driven around in the RCMP pickup, we saw the village and went out to 'the land', a wilderness where that hardy race of Inuit Netsiliks managed to thrive on an abundance of beluga, caribou, seal and bear, living in igloos in winter and travelling with tents in summer. In winter dog-pulled sledges and skidoos are now used in about equal number. In summer it's the ATVs.

Moving on westward, we landed on Todd Island and saw skeletal remains, thought to be some of Franklin's men. Through twisting Simpson Strait we had the benefit of many transit beacons before fog closed in. A northwest headwind blew in from Queen Maud Gulf and rose to gale force. We dodged shorewards to anchor in shelter, 'feeling' our way in, the GPS and chart position differing by about a mile. Next day, the wind gone down, we passed Jenny Lind Island. Distant Early Warning stations, relics of the Cold War, now unmanned and automatic, stood like lighthouses every 100 miles or so. Seas were ice-free.

On August 3 we entered Cambridge Bay, with its population of about 1,500. It's a government centre, busy and brash; well, relative to the last couple of months, it seemed so to us. Notwithstand-

In borrowed caribou skin; hunters' winter outer clothing, Gjoa Haven.

ing, we met some great people, individuals all. The town is a 'dry' one, but apparently not at weekends. Our intended single-day stop was delayed by weather. We had leave the exposed jetty and go to anchor in a bay three miles distant. Both anchors and all our chain were well-tested as a gale blew.

At anchor, the Arctic char were running well. Fisherman Kevin was active and the helpings were generous. The days were dark and cold, with a wind that would cut you – 'two-hat' and gloves for sure. It didn't snow, but could have, the halcyon days of Greenland now long gone. Impatient to be off, we left on August 19, bound for Tuktoyuktuk, 650 miles westward. The first two days went well, going through Coronation Gulf, then Dolphin and Union Strait as though turning through pages of history, until in Amundsen Gulf we again met sea-ice. Progress slowed as we shimmied and banged our way through it.

With accumulated confidence in the strength of our vessel, we now felt capable of dealing with up to 5/10 ice, depending on ice-type. At Franklin Bay we detoured about 60 miles. An ice-breaker had assured us that they had found only 1/10 ice some hours earlier. How quickly it had changed, wind- and current-blown. We rounded Cape Bathurst and had a clear run to Tuk with the north coast of Alaska on our minds.

The Ice Service now was saying that, 'lower than normal temperatures are forecast in the Beaufort Sea for the second half of August. Northerly winds are forecast during the fourth week of August.'

This would tend to push the ice in towards the land from west of Herschel Island to Point Barrow. This was not good for us; our route could be closed off.

Life on *Northabout* was generally fairly comfortable, the big heater in the saloon good for clothes drying and cooking. Sometimes it would even be too warm, making for a difficult temperature contrast when going outside. The underlying mental state was not so much one of dealing with hardship and work in the cold, but one of anxiety – if things should go wrong, the 'what ifs'. So the crew for journeys such as this have to be somewhat inured to worry, while at the same time not being too cavalier.

Tuk, near the mouth of the great Mackenzie River, had once been a busy commercial harbour. Now it was desolate. Nonetheless, it could serve as an escape place for us if we were trapped for the winter. We were on the one hand optimistic and pushy about getting through, on the other watching our backs.

We sailed across MacKenzie Bay, 120 miles, to Herschel, island of American whalers, in darkness. Radar, sounder and GPS took us into anchor. Next morning two Inuvik Park Rangers gave us a tour, including the history:

> My grandfather said that when the white man came, they brought the 'book', the bible. Twenty years later, we had the 'book' – and they had The Land.

All too quickly we left. Mick stood on the foredeck, binoculars in hand, as often he did, feeling 'caribou in his bones'. What he saw, we all did, was a magnificent male polar bear, first on a floe nearby, then ashore and lightening fast, four legs spread, up a cliff. And I would have felt safe on top of that cliff!

From Herschel to Point Barrow is 400 miles. The band of clear water was narrowing. We pushed on with all speed, mostly in ice-free water, but the white of the pack ice was visible out to sea. We used engine, sails, sometimes both, whatever would work best for speed. On the US border, we had a little flag-changing ceremony; nearest humans were some 200 miles distant. Immediately after-wards we ran into serious ice. In the twisting, turning and back-tracking to get out of it, Kevin reckoned that we had the wrong flag up many times over.

About 10.00 pm local time, dark coming on, ice now all about but loose, and fog reducing visibility to about 200 yards, we were going into anchor in Demarcation Bay. Its eastern end was clogged with ice and impassable. Its wider western end, a mile further on, was clear, as far as we could see. Then the engine gave a queer rat-tling noise. Oh, Lord! With headsail drawing lightly, we ghosted into the bay, now dark, and ran our anchor out. And dark were our thoughts too as Frank and Gearóid set to work on the gearbox. Thoughts flashed before my mind so quickly – of having to lay-up the boat here for the winter, radio for a bush plane, flying out with gearbox, bankruptcy! With relief, the lads soon had all to rights and we slept soundly.

At dawn, four hours later, still in fog, we 'felt' our way out of the bay, our position not exact because the chart is about one-quarter mile out in this area. Our log for most of that day tells of our strug-gle to get through the ice. We tried to go along the shore where it was lightest and there was a relatively free strip of about 20 yards wide. But even with our centreboard up, and then drawing only four feet, we still went aground again and again. In one instance we went aground and couldn't get afloat – we were stuck. Using our dinghy, we ran out an anchor and took a line from it back to our biggest winch. With this line bar-taut, and most of us in the dinghy to lighten the boat, the engine going flat out, full revs, she pulled off. By nightfall we were going goodand kept going through the dark, there being just about enough light to make out the floes. We weaved through them. Twenty miles east of Prudoe we took the inside 'lagoon route', 10 feet of water generally and clear of ice. On the VHF radio we could hear the chat of the oilfield, workboat men of few words, laconic. We spoke to a few, unseen, and rattled on in freezing fog with ice in our rigging.

The next day was better for us. We blasted on, through light ice, but with solid ice never far away to seaward. Now we weaved through ice at six knots, which only weeks before would have had us slowing to a crawl. The weather forecast, Cape Lisburn to Cape Halkett, gave a Small Craft Advisory (we were now in the USA), 25 knots northeasterly – great.

Our log reads:

> 09.10 – Ice floes frequent. Reduced from Yankee to Staysail. Running rigging frozen.
>
> 10.40 – Cold wind blowing. Light ice all over deck.

We rounded Point Barrow at 6.00 am the next day. The village was 10 miles on. We had hoped to anchor and go ashore, however there was too much surf to land the dinghy. We shook hands, had a celebratory tot, raised twin headsails and were on our way.

The wind backed northerly and blew 30 knots, most likely bringing the ice on to the coast we had passed only the day before. For three days we were pushed, roughly but effectively, 500 miles southwest through the Chuckchi Sea, through the Bering Strait, and on Sunday, September 2, entered Nome Harbour, Alaska.

We were the fourteenth boat ever to have sailed through the Northwest Passage. There in Nome *Northabout* was lifted ashore for the winter.

§   §   §

In the last fifteen years global warming has led to a significant diminution of the Arctic sea-ice. Many small boats have being getting through, though not every year. The ice regression, while inexorable, is not doing so in a linear manner. There still are some 'bad' ice years. However, we like to think that we were the last, or among the last, to do the Northwest Passage when it was still the 'real thing'.

Journey's end, Alaska.

27

The Loss of Saint Patrick, *2002*

*S*aint Patrick had two lives. Her first was that for which she was intended. Pat and Joe Casey built her in 1911 on Mweenish Island, Connemara, as a cargo carrier.

Most of her working life was spent in the ownership of the Conroys of Rosmuc. They had a shop and *Saint Patrick* did a weekly run to Galway to collect and bring out goods – ironmongery, paraffin, calico and all that an isolated rural area required. Her general load was 12 tons, carried in her open hold, with a tarpaulin cover, although I once met a man who told me that he had loaded 16 tons of potatoes into her, measured and bagged.

In the 1950s improved roads and lorries came into Connemara, displacing the Galway Hookers. For 10 or 15 years, until about 1970, they continued to bring turf out to the Aran Islands. The availability of bottled gas and electricity largely killed off that trade and *Saint Patrick*, like the other Hookers, was laid up. It was later said that if the outboard engine and bottled gas had come ten years earlier, communities on the likes of the Blasket Island might have been saved.

Saint Patrick was sold to Galway first and then to Goleen in County Cork. In September 1973 I bought her and her second life began. After extensive repairs and with new sails and engine she was sailed back from Dublin to Connemara in 1979. Happily, this coincided with a general revival of these Connemara boats.

In the following ten years *Saint Patrick* sailed progressively further to France, Spain, the Canary Islands and the USA; for my youngsters she was a playground. In 1987 she went to the Faroe Islands and it was time for a proper rebuild.

Within sight of where she was first built, Colm Mulkerrins, master shipwright, rebuilt her in her entirety keeping only two ribs for continuity. She emerged two feet longer.

Decked out again, in 1990 she went to Spitsbergen and in 1993 to Northwest Greenland, cruising all the while between Scottish and Irish waters.

The sailing year of 2002 began as usual with a 'May Week', this time to Barmouth in Wales, 'In Search of the Major' – Bill Tilman. There we sailed to where he had lived between adventures in his Bristol Pilot Cutters *Mischief*, *Sea-Breeze* and *Baroque*. We visited his house and walked his Welsh Mountains, then sailed overnight to Glandore in County Cork.

On Sunday, May 19, we put her on a Cork County Council visitor mooring and left her. These moorings are rated at 15 ton and have a substantial top eye. Our 11mm chain was taken through this eye, to the starboard mullard, double shackled and moused. We were in no hurry as there was plenty of time to catch the bus from Leap into Cork city. While I shackled the chain, I remarked to Peter Gargan, 'Always tie as if you won't see her for a year'. We returned to work in Dublin.

Two days later a southeast gale sent a big swell into Glandore Bay. In mid-morning, after top of the tide, she was seen on the rocks underneath the Rectory. I got the bad phone call. Wind and sea did not allow any boats going to help.

By dusk I was there and conditions now allowed the putting aboard a towline from a 600 HP vessel. The hull and spars appeared intact, though she was awash and still rolling and pounding. Her own mooring chain was seen to be intact at the mullard, but to have parted lower down, presumably where it had gone through the mooring eye.

No amount of pulling took her off the rocks, though in the process her shore side was seen to have been stove-in. By morning she was in bits, broken. On the following Saturday her pieces were

The wreck of **Saint Patrick** *off Glandore.*

towed ashore to the beach at Glandore Pier. Using heavy excavating machinery, she was taken away to be put in a hole and buried.

I was devastated, for months, years and, occasionally, still am. Fortunately, she was insured and payment was made expeditiously.

PS: I recovered her tiller, my guitar floating about, undamaged, and a couple of bronze 'medallions' attached to a piece of timber bulkhead.

28

The Bering Sea and Alaska

We flew into Nome on June 1, 2002. The sea ice had cleared ten days previously. Summer had come and, like the shear-waters, we had arrived with it. The plan was to retrieve *Northabout* from her winter quarters and get south to more temperate waters for the next couple of months.

In the yard beside us stood a fishing vessel on which the owner had last year put a sign – 'For Sale, $130,000'. Now the sign read '$75,000 – Pick-up truck included'. The fishing had indeed gone down.

Sue Wagner, electrician and formerly a crab-fisher, had done a good job in minding our electronics in warm storage over the winter. Now she gave us the loan of a big pick-up truck, just the job for running around the town and getting *Northabout* back in the water and into sailing commission. No worries about insurances, driving licences or any of that nonsense up here! The Board of Trade Saloon and other pubs, which last year seemed so hospitable, still were but now seemed a little tatty. Where you've come from, and one's per-ception, conditions all. Nome is a town of mixed-race population, natives from the north and whites from the 'Lower 48' states, some of whom had dubious personal histories. English is the language.

On June 7 Jarlath, myself and, new to the boat, Ben McDonogh, Micheal McGarry and youngster Richard Brown slipped out of the harbour The autopilot, broken since we had passed near the Mag-netic North Pole, still was not working. Our intended first call was to Savoonga, 140 miles to the southwest on St. Lawrence Island. It

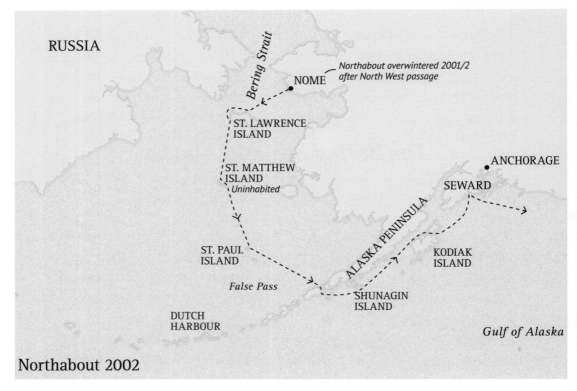

Bering Sea and Alaska

was daylight all night, as we alternately sailed and motored in a calm sea. A patch of 3/10 ice was passed through without incident. I slept through it, so there can't have been much hull-banging or engine-revving.

Next morning we sighted Cape Kookoolik and got the weather forecast. In the Kodiak area, a thousand miles away, 50 knots of wind were due. Our area expected a mere 25 knots, to become 30 knots. The Bering Sea is a breezy place. By mid-morning we had anchored amongst loose ice off Savoonga village and when ashore walked a few miles out. Some locals, all here were native, spoke to us about a permit for walking? Always the money thing. The white man has much to answer for. I pleaded ignorance.

The anchorage was poor, the village unwelcoming and unattractive. It had looked better from a distance on our approach, with the white-on-black of snow against the hills.

On the northwest side of St. Lawrence Island lies Gambel, its other village. As we approached at 1.00 in the morning, a line of ATVs, 20 or 30, were silhouetted Apache-like on the high gravel shoreline. We sought anchorage. It took two anchors and all our chain to get bite on the gravel bottom. Here, in contrast, the villagers made us welcome and gave us the 'tour', riding on the back of ATVs. I was taken to 'tea', very special, and listened to stories of Inukpaq life on this outpost. On the one hand, the local government, heavily supported with State oil revenue, gives access to 'mod cons', including free third level education down in Anchorage or Fairbanks. On the other hand, the 'old ways' are ever present. Six umiaks in skin-boats stood ready for sea. Under sail or paddle they are quiet, and so are preferred to the noisy, high horsepower outboards for hunting the migratory whale.

As it happened a California grey whale was taken the next morning, just off the shore, shot, lassoed by his tailfin and hauled up the beach by bulldozer, before being flensed and the meat divided among the villagers.

Thirty-seven miles to the east, the Siberian Chutosk peninsula became visible as the day lightened. Over 10,000 years ago, with lower sea levels, man had walked across the Bering Land Bridge. Now, visits between the two continents are occasional only, discouraged by both Russian and US authorities.

We left, sailing gently southward, bound for Glory of Russia Cape on St. Matthew Island, 200 miles distant. The forecast was for 25 to 30 knots from the north. Great.

Next day at 2.00 am a log entry records: 'Nice sailing, wing and wing, whale blowing, baked bread. Engine had fuel starvation, now fixed.' Hopefully not by the hands which baked the bread!

We passed by Cape Hall island, barely visible in grey mist. A day later we coasted the north side of St. Matthew Island which was mountainous and bleak, not even a hut visible to tempt the curiosity of a shore party. Cape Upright on its southeastern end had guillemots by the huge number as we left it astern, pointing now for the inhabited island of St. Paul, 200 miles southward.

We were a grey boat in a grey sea. The nights now were darkening. St. Paul doesn't have much going for it. Its weather, its history, its people reflect the lack of sunshine. It once did have a lot of fur-seals. The book *Slaves of the Harvest* tells of the oppression of the native Aluetian people, first by Russians and then by Americans, in pursuit of the valuable fur. During World War II, under threat of a Japanese invasion, the whole population was forcibly cleared out by the US Army. They were taken to disused canneries on the Alaskan mainland and detained there for the duration of the war.

In St. Paul we found a depressed fishing industry, hungry foxes, crab-pots lying idle and stacked high, and empty fish-processing plants – the visible misery went on, together with the worst pub in the world. Here we were stuck for four days while a gale blew.

The Russian Orthodox Mass was interesting, but had marginally less attendance than the near empty monthly dance in the hall. A sign outside the school said that it was 'gun-free, drug-free'. This was, after all, the United States. A Fish and Game research group had us to dinner, reindeer and halibut, and still the wind blew. On the beach, big male fur seals were ashore, minding their patches, before the arrival of the breeding females.

When we left, it was not as we had intended for Dutch Harbour, but for False Pass, 120 miles to the east of it on the Aleutian Peninsula. Our time was running a little tight; we now had two weeks to get to Seward. With this dodgy weather we couldn't chance taking the longer and more interesting route.

The next day:

> Good sailing, foggy, noisy sea-birds, grey and desolate. One Orca. No ships.

On the following day at 5.00 am in a dull dawn, Unimak Island was visible through the mist on our starboard bow. An hour and a half later we entered the wide but very shallow and treacherous Bechevin Bay. There were buoys marking the channel every three-quarter mile or so, but barely visible. The channel wound tighter and tighter with no room for error. On our starboard, an unnamed mountain showed on our chart as being 9,372 feet high. It was covered in soft-looking, un-climbable snow. As we approached the narrows of Ivanotski Strait, two vessels appeared coming against us, they with the tide, us plugging against it. North of the Aleutian Peninsula and Islands, working boats don't travel alone.

By midday we were through False Pass and into a different world. We now were on the south side of the Peninsula and into the Gulf of Alaska, North Pacific Ocean. We carried sail, going eastward through the islands, in a flat sea, even with some sun, to get into King Cove by evening and tie up in the workboat marina (the 'king' was King Salmon).

I was stretching my legs, stepping it out from the edge of the town, when this old-timer with dungarees and beard says to me: 'Watch for the barrs that come down in the evenin' – and the wolves.' I quickly about-turned. Yup, brown and black bears are a serious feature around here. The houses in the town all have a big dog chained near the door for warning and protection.

The bar was loud. Three Harley-Davidson gringos outshouted each other. An unsmiling woman shuffled cards with an off-putting dexterity. We remarked, to ourselves, that she looked like Robert Service's Malamute Saloon 'lady that's known as Lou'. The cannery ran all night. We were told that the price for salmon was very low, only 70 cents a pound. Farmed salmon, imported to the USA from Chile, had hit the price paid to fishermen here. In St. Paul we had met guys from a freighter going to the 'date-line' to pick up fish from a Russian vessel for this same cannery.

The next morning, leisurely, we left. In the sun now, we were bound for Sand Point, 80 miles onward. Snow lay on the mountain ridges and peaks, greenery below. The breeze blew from astern. We all were in the cockpit, lunching and chatting – how quickly the bleakness of the Bering Sea was forgotten. Russian names on the islands were a reminder of who it was opened this country in the service of the Tsar, the native Aleutians aside of course. At 9.00 pm there was a log entry: 'Now at Yunga Spit, 16 miles to Sand Point – we'll hardly make it to the pub tonight.'

But we did, with guitar we climbed into a pick-up and whooped it up for about twenty fishermen, all of whom insisted on buying us a drink.

The next day 'last night's fun' was dearly paid for, going 13 miles into a headwind for Gormon Strait and then for Foggy Cape, 147 miles, banging into a lively sea. The following day, the wind moderating, we went through Semidi Islands, by Cape Trinity and north of Kodiak Island, then by Tombstone Rock. A gale now was forecast, low pressure deepening in the Gulf of Alaska. Through Whale Narrows we went and into the town of Kodiak. The sign on the jetty said: 'What to do in an emergency, if the sun shines.' It doesn't much.

The next day we left for Seward and with rock and snow peaks in the mist to our port, motored through the islands, 170 miles to 'vacationland, end of the road Alaska'.

There, on June 27, we left Jarlath, welcoming his new crew, to sail *Northabout* on south to Westport, Oregon.

29

A New Boat, the Yacht **Ar Seachrán**

To build or buy a new Galway Hooker to replace the lost *Saint Patrick* and put her into good cruising condition would have cost about double the insurance money. In any event, I didn't want to begin another 'project' which such would entail. Additionally, the physical work in running and sailing such a heavy timber boat was getting too much for my sailing friends too. So, in August of 2002, I began searching for a timber 'classic' yacht. Soon I realised that such a delicate vessel would not fare well in my hands, so instead I searched for a 40-foot metal boat, steel or aluminium. Glass-reinforced plastic (GRP) never entered my head.

With our excellent experience of aluminium as a boat material on *Northabout*, I soon confined the search to aluminium of which there were on sale half a dozen. I inspected a 40-footer in the south of France and made an offer, without response. In the Adriatic was an elegant-looking 45-footer – too elegant. But two events coincided: a drop in the asking price and my discovering that Ryanair flew close by. I could see that she was well-built, a thoroughbred. She was a racer, now converted for Mediterranean cruising, but with over-complex instrumentation, piping and wiring. Her engine was a diesel Mercedes – solid.

In November I bought her and arranged new standing rigging, including removal of the hydraulics on the forestay and backstay. In March, with a full team of technical sailing friends we went out for a 'commissioning week'. It was done in a day and a half so we went cruising, first to Venice and then to Trieste. She was a delight

225

*Ar Seachrán under full sail
(photo by Paraic De Bhaldraithe).*

and her new name, given by my kids, would be *Ar Seachrán* –'on the wander'.

I considered whether to leave her in the Mediterranean for a year, but the desire to move her along to home waters was stronger. Eight of us went out in May. Danny, Paul, Paddy and Peter, all well used to each other, and to myself, and we also had Maurice Wilson, Tony Reilly and Pat Gilmour, all of whom knew how to make a boat go fast.

It was 400 miles southeastward to the 'heel' of Italy, then a further couple of hundred miles westward to Syracuse in Sicily. Going south, the sea warmed, just about okay for swimming. The islands and red roofs of Croatia were left behind. We had blue sky and fresh wind, good for sailing but tricky when getting the boat stern-to into quay walls to tie up in the Mediterranean way. We'd arrive somewhere in the afternoon, visit whatever monastery or castle there was, eat well ashore for very little money and be on our way around midnight. In Mola di Bari we saw on the Cathedral floor a mosaic of our Saint Brendan, holding a sinner by the legs over the side of his boat, while a shark-like fish swallowed his head – little compromise about this triumph of good over evil.

In the Golfo di Squillace we got pasted by a 30-knot headwind, the boat not going at all well. 'Nothing that €10,000 for new sails won't fix,' said Paul helpfully. In better weather, in fact brilliant, we tied up in Syracuse, the boat to be left there for a month. The lads flew home. Mary and her cousin Kay Conway came onboard with me for a week of hedonistic idleness.

On June 25 we returned – Danny again, Sean Mullan, Donncha Ó hÉallaithe, Raphael McIlhone, Ruaidhri Ó Tuairisg and Rory Walsh; a crew fit to sail any Galway Hooker. The plan for the next fortnight was to sail the 1,100 miles to Malaga in Spain, which we did, our daily routine being much as previously. There were two differences. One was that both Donncha and Ruaidhri loved to cook, and would have the dinner ready as we would tie up, though Sean and most others preferred to try out the eating on shore. The other was that heat during the day was overpowering. How we would look forward to the cooling swim, stopping the boat every now and then. Even in the bunk at night you'd need a bottle of water to hand, and sip it slowly lest you run out before your off-watch was over. We called to Agrigento and Favignano in Sicily, Cagliari and Calaforte in Sardinia, Mahon and Soller in the Balearic Islands. It was in Mahon that Raphael, emptying the teapot over our side, splashed the big gleaming white topsides of the motorboat alongside us causing consternation among her paid crew. To clean it off, Raphael went at it with our scrubbing brush causing even more apoplexy.

Ibiza was awful; it pains me to write about it so I won't. Much better was Cartagena on the Spanish coast, and similarly San Jose and Puerto Madril. Benalmadena, outside of Malaga, was not bad at all, as big marinas go.

For the next leg, a fortnight to Ireland, Ruaidhri, Raphael and myself were joined by my brother Fred, Cathal, Harry and Al Lennon from Killyleagh. Fred and Cathal would be getting out somewhere in northwest Spain.

On July 12 we left, getting into Gibraltar for three and a half hours, about three too many for me. At the convenient fuel berth, the attendant had been reluctant to let us lie for a few hours. Fred had a quiet word with him and advised us that 'his reluctance had been overcome – by a tenner'.

Against a still strong headwind we, under motor mostly, got to Vilamoura on the south coast of Portugal, upmarket and artificial; thence to anchor off Sagres, hallowed ground from where Henry the Navigator had gathered the best of mathematicians, astronomers,

This was an elegant boat, if complicated.

cartographers, navigators and seamen to this centre of learning on the very edge of the then European civilised world. It wasn't by accident that from here Magellan, da Gama and Bartholomew Diaz sailed to discover so much of the then unknown, world. Northwards we went along the coast of Portugal and to Galicia in Spain. Fred and Cathal left for Santiago de Compostella and home.

We sailed 520 miles across the Bay of Biscay towards Dursey Head. For three days, with great wind, we flew, though rough at times. About 100 miles south of the Mizen we began to see gannets; it was great to be back in Irish waters. Three and a half days out we sailed into Dingle. Ruaidhri was found to have several broken ribs.

⅋   ⅋   ⅋

Ruaidhri Ó Tuairisg and Harry Connolly were very different. Ruaidhri is Connemara, *Indreabhán*, to the core, Irish-speaking of course. I had known him as crew on our good friend Con McCann's Galway Hooker *Connacht*. With Con he had sailed in the Portaferry Regattas and the traditional boat festivals in Brittany – all the while sailing his own gleoiteog back home, mostly with his good friend Donncha. Ruaidhri was teaching in Galway, a livelihood which gave him time for planting and tilling the vegetables in his garden and cutting and saving the turf on his bog. That done by early summer, he would then be a free man. Politically, he was never mainstream. He once told me that he had never voted for anyone who had got elected. That didn't change until socialist academic Michael D. Higgins became President of Ireland.

When the *Connacht* was lost, with Con, off County Down in 1989, I sort of 'inherited' her crew – to my great benefit. This primarily was Ruaidhri, together with Raphael McIlhone. Raphael deserves a chapter to himself. Small in stature, with flat cap, handy out with a net or in a boat, whistle player, Gaeilic enthusiast and knowledgeable in the ways of everything that flies, swims or grows. Lovely man.

Harry Connolly is from Walkinstown, Dublin and has been living and working for the EU in Luxembourg since 1993, for as long as I've known him. His willingness to lie under *Saint Patrick* on a sheet of plywood on the mud of Pigeon House harbour, applying the antifouling paint to her bottom, impressed me greatly! He is is principally a climber and skier, but a fine sailor too. Wiry and careful, he is the most unlikely of us to fall out of the boat. I've watched him 'levitate' on some fairly dodgy mountain ground. Once in particular, on the slippery 'back' side of Skellig, possibly unclimbed since the monks' time, I watched him skip lightly upwards where 'angels would fear to tread', and was myself glad to be below on the deck of a boat.

When banging through the ice of Melville Bay, he used to go to his bunk in his full outdoor arctic rig. Terry Irivine had remarked, 'no way that Harry was going to be caught on the ice in his Y-fronts'.

30

Siberia and the Northeast Passage

In Anadyr, Chukotka we had barely tied *Northabout* to the broken down quay when I was arrested.

Four weeks earlier, we had left Prince Rupert in Canada, sailed across the Gulf of Alaska and enjoyed some pleasant and interesting days around Dutch Harbour. We then were well on our way up the Bering Sea when we got an emailed message from the Irish Embassy in Moscow. 'The FPS have conveyed to us that you will not be welcome in the Russian Federation.'

'What?' For a year and a half we had been to-ing and fro-ing to Moscow and Murmansk in arranging to get our necessary permit to sail the Northeast Passage. We had organised a Russian Partner, met the many individuals responsible in the various departments including the KGB (now FSB), Pogranichnik (FPS, Border Guards), Northern Sea Route Administration and the Navy. We had the permit, we thought. Jarlath and myself were sailing the boat to Anadyr, our Russian port of entry. The others of the team were flying to meet us there, bringing the permit from Moscow. With us for the 2,000 mile passage to Anadyr were Brendan Minish, Tom Moran, Joan Burke and Eoin McAllister, who would be flying home from there.

Two days after that first embassy message, we were still continuing northwards, the embassy having advised that all was now in good order. All of this I explained to the arresting officer. As we drove through various gates, there was a lot of heel-clicking and saluting. At least he was a major, if I correctly understood the sign on his office door. With a senior officer there is some chance of being understood. In preparation I had done a year's night classes in Russian and so had some language basics – just about.

'*Bolshoi problema*', he said, a phrase we had got to know well and would continue to hear. *Bolshoi*, as in the Moscow theatre, means 'big'. Was this a problem of the nine-hour time difference between here and Moscow, or something more serious? A couple of hours later I was released. There was much handshaking and smiles as I was driven back into town in the major's Jeep, even stopping at the bank to allow me change dollars into roubles.

Next day the lads flew in, Mick, doctor and Kevin, money manager, cameraman Gary Finnegan, Rory Casey, IT man to run our communications, Colm Brogan, our real Russian speaker (he had worked in Moscow for 10 years) and Slava, about whom more later – eight in all. As before for the Northwest Passage, Jarlath was skipper and I was expedition leader, although in essence it was a very 'horizontal' organisation, each with his own speciality.

This Northeast Passage was more difficult by far than the Northwest Passage. It was longer, it was more isolated, the language(s) were unfamiliar, and the bureaucracy was worse – as we already well knew. And we had Vladimir Samovich (Slava) thrust upon us as a condition of our permit, supposedly as an 'ice pilot' though more likely as commissar/spy we speculated.

But some things in the high Arctic are a constant. For small boats intending to travel in ice-strewn waters, the possible navigation season runs from the first week of August until the middle of September. Too early, and you're waiting for ice breakup; too late, and you'll be frozen in. We were not the first small boat to traverse this passage. The German Arved Fuchs had done it, as had Frenchman Eric Brossier, both going west to east. So had Russians Nicolau Latau in *Apostle Andrew* and Serbei Cherbakov in *Sibir*. If we succeeded, we would be the fifth.

We took on diesel, no problem, pumped from the fuel tank of a tug in the harbour. Cash to the Man. Getting clean water was more of a problem. We were directed a mile out and upstream into

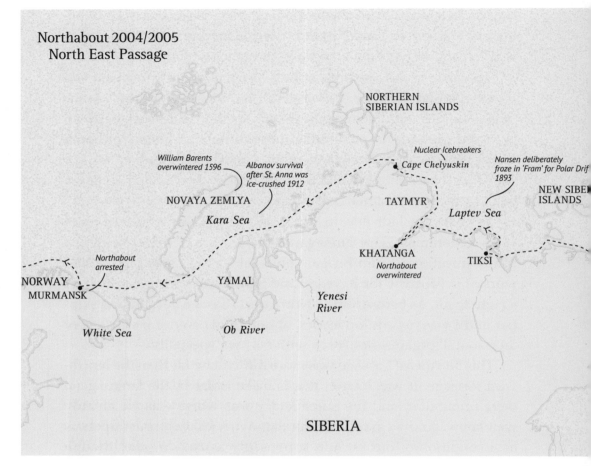

Northabout 2004/2005
North East Passage

NORTHERN
SIBERIAN ISLANDS

Nuclear Icebreakers

William Barents overwintered 1596

Albanov survival after St. Anna was ice-crushed 1912

Cape Chelyuskin

Nansen deliberately froze in 'Fram' for Polar Drift 1893

NOVAYA ZEMLYA

Kara Sea

TAYMYR

NEW SIBE
ISLANDS

Laptev Sea

Northabout arrested

KHATANGA

TIKSI

NORWAY
MURMANSK

Northabout overwintered

YAMAL

Yenesi River

White Sea

Ob River

SIBERIA

Northeast Passage, Siberia.

the Anadyr River and there, where its colour was grey rather than brown, a water supply vessel pumped it into our tank. And for this, we paid more, per litre, than the diesel had cost us.

On July 30 we left, well stocked, well charted, our ship and men in good spirits. We went past the town Provideniya (meaning 'providence'), through the Bering Strait and turning northeast entered the Chukchi Sea. No sea-ice as yet. On the radio, we called a ship inshore of us but no reply. As we moved closer, it became apparent that it was a wreck on the shore. Later we heard that pack-ice had forced it ashore.

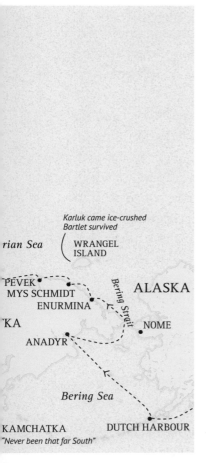

Karluk came ice-crushed
Bartlet survived

WRANGEL
ISLAND

rian Sea

PEVEK
MYS SCHMIDT
ENURMINA

KA

ANADYR

ALASKA

Bering Strait

NOME

Bering Sea

KAMCHATKA   DUTCH HARBOUR
"Never been that far South"

Further on, 100 miles or so, our Pilot Book said that 'there was reported to be a polar station and trading station in this area'. Indeed there was, the Chukchi village of Enurmina. We anchored off and went ashore to a most welcoming people. They live, fairly basically, on fishing and hunting. No ATVs here. Their permitted annual 'take' is three whales, 30 walruses and unlimited seals. They have a twice monthly helicopter service from 'outside'.

Further up the coast we met a fisherman. He came aboard and we towed his boat. He turned out to be an atmospheric physicist, Sascha, not fishing but taking samples. For two days he was with us. One place where we anchored he showed us around the derelict buildings of a landing place for the former Dolstroi Gulag. In Stalin's time, 12,000 men had died there.

At Cape Vankarem, with its small village, Newfoundlander Captain Bob Bartlett had come ashore over the ice from Wrangel Island in April 1913, after *Karluk* was shipwrecked. His escape stands with that of Shackleton and Valerian Albanov.

And then we met the ice which was to be our constant companion from now on, sometimes out to sea, sometimes around us. It sometimes stopped us, sometimes allowed us to shimmy through it, sometimes it forced us backwards, sometimes it opened into long leads. Gary called one a 'Long Mile Road' lead. But all the time Slava would be telling us we should be doing other than what we were. He thought that he was in charge. 'I have been 23 years ice-pilot'. Yes he was, but on big ships. We were different, a small sturdy boat which could weave through narrow leads, lift our centre-board and go in along the shore. He didn't understand that and constantly harangued us, myself in particular, as I would try to explain it to him.

Mys Schmidt (not Miss Smith, as some of us quipped) was our first town, pretty broken down, the military having gone when the cold war ended leaving a town in decay.

Pevek, a few hundred miles on, had once been a busy city. It had cranes on its extensive quayside, all now derelict. I walked into the hills behind, meeting some families gathering berries and mushrooms, altogether friendly. Later, down the town, it wasn't as empty as it first appeared. Outside Café Romashka, three guys stood hunched; inside, the joint was jumpin'. It was someone's birthday. Vodka, flowers, music, dancing and, as always in Russia, the toasts. We 'brought greetings from the people of Ireland'. All had a great time, Slava too.

We got diesel and continued westward, out of the East Siberian Sea and into the Laptev Sea, the New Siberian Islands to our north.

Above, two Chukotka men – hunter/fishermen. Below, their village,
Enurmina. Note the old Soviet watchtower, still standing
(photos by Jarlath Cunnane).

It now was easier to measure our progress in degrees of longitude as the mileage meant little. It was 800 miles to our next destination, Tiksi, nothing ashore in between except for the endless, flat tundra. We were now at 164 degrees east, a number we had to keep reducing. We all were learning some basic Russian:

Ostrov = Island
Guba = Bay
Mys = Cape or Headland
   (remember Mys Schmidt)
Proliv = Strait
Severnay = North
Novi = New.

This, of course, was in the Cyrillic alphabet on the Russian maps and charts we had.

Our food, on which I was not at all the expert, was *kasha* in the morning – porridge to you – snacks during the day of omelettes, cheese ortinned sardines on biscuits and dinner later of rice, pasta, with salmon or char. Kevin baked bread daily and Mick cooked the dinners.

Our day was split into three-hour watches. So if you're next on at 4.00 am, you'd get a shake or shoutabout 15 minutes ahead of time, crawl out of your bag, pull on your thermals (if you haven't slept in them), pull on your next layer of cosy 'mid-layer' stuff and a couple of pairs of socks, then come up, look out and see what sort of a day was it. Fog? Ice? Wind? Then you'd pull on the heavy outer oilskin, boots, gloves, a hat and, if a very cold day, goggles.

By August 14 we were at longitude 133 east. Tiksi was only 80 miles away, but proving elusive. During the previous 24 hours we had travelled over 100 miles through ice, but made good only 20. On August 16 and 17, ice surrounded, we lay at anchor in a bay south of Buor Khaya (Yacutian translation is Cape Big Nose). On the radio we heard of an ice breaker-led convoy. 'Going which way?' We asked Slava. 'Nobody knows,' said he. Russians are like that, 'say nothing'. In fact it was coming our way and going our direction. Didn't we

Ice all round – up the mast looking for a way out (photo by Gary Finnegan).

hustle, anchor up and push out into the ice to meet it. In the fog, it nearly ran us down, but we got in behind the last of the convoy, the tanker *Lena Nef* (Lena Oil), not believing our luck.

Much as we were glad to reach Tiksi, we were even more pleased to leave it and be on our way again. There we had met Dutchman Henk de Velde, in *Campina*, also doing the Northeast Passage. He had started last year, but got stuck and had overwintered in Tiksi. We agreed to keep in radio contact. The next leg, 1,200 miles around the Taymyr Peninsula, had at its northern tip Cape Chelyuskin, the Cape Horn of the Russian north.

We cast a wreath outside the delta of the huge River Lena, where Corkman Jerome Collins had died, frozen and starved in 1879, from the wrecked American vessel *Jeannette*.We followed for 18 hours a vessel bound up the Khatanga River, which threw ice lumps from her stern that bashed us. We continued north.

August 25th, made 68 miles.

August 26, made 12 miles, ice and light snow. Polar Bear on the shore, thin and hungry lookin.

August 27, stuck, solid ice ahead. Forecast for the next 5 days is wind from northeast; which will pin this ice to the shore. But we're only 150 miles from Cape Chelyuskin.

In a lagoon, we dried out the boat. There we fixed a bad leak, through a transducer in the hull, which had been damaged by bashing ice.

For 11 days we were stuck at 76 degrees north, forward progress not possible. We moved locally for the best protection from changing ice and wind. There was an occasional bear about, sometimes too close. Nights were getting longer, birds gone south. This *was* the 'Uttermost Place on Earth', not a living person on shore within many hundreds of miles.

This monument marks the 180 degree line of longitude, formerly of navigational importance.

On September 6 grease ice covered the sea around us. There were four inches of ice around our anchor chain. Waiting time was over. We had to get south. On our sat-phone we spoke to Nicolai Babich in Murmansk to whom Slava had daily given our position, in return getting the forecast and ice-report. Babich recommended that we go to the town of Khatanga, 350 miles to our south, 100 miles up the river. For there we turned.

On our way south, we met *Campina* which was disabled, her rudder ice-damaged. She was in water too shallow for access by a salvage vessel. We were asked, and readily agreed, to tow her into deeper water, which we did with great difficulty and no little danger to ourselves. Mick and Kevin went aboard her to help manage the tow line. Through increasingly heavy ice we pulled her 30 miles, eventually in darkness getting her alongside a 30,000-ton freighter, *Archenesky*. Bound for Tiksi, they lifted her aboard.

On Tuesday September 14, we left Khatanga. *Northabout* had been placed within the hold of a big river barge about to be frozen in for the winter, as were all vessels in Khatanga. This storage was costing us $8,000, 'cash to the man', Valodia, he of status unknown. But didn't he make things happen. A big floating crane took our mast out and then lifted *Northabout*. Hatch covers were placed over the cargo well of the barge and welded into place! Security looked first class, and assuredly was needed, we were told.

The Tupelov 154 flight to Moscow lifted slowly. The tundra, reddish grass, yellow birch and willow, shimmering land of lakes and waterways, spread below us.

ε   ε   ε

The following year on August 7, 2005 we left Dublin for Moscow. The last three months had been another exercise in heroics as we went through the process of getting our permit renewed. Colm did well, as did Rory in recovering all our electronic charts. These had been stolen from the boot of my car the night before we left Dublin. Now, in a gargantuan all-night technical exercise on a very slow system, a copy was emailed by Brendan Minish out to us in Moscow.

Three time zones east of Moscow, in the Siberian Republic of Krasnoyarsk, the tundra rose to meet us, green among the lakes, as we flew in low under the cloud. As we touched down, so did some of the aircraft's ceiling. Khatanga was scruffy and broken-down as ever, but *Northabout* was looking well, tied to the quay wall. Our friend from the town, Vladimir Yurshenko, had minded her since Jarlath and Tom Moran had been out in June to get her out of the barge and ready, which in itself was an achievement.

Vladimir headed a parachute rescue team, funded by a Japanese airline, on standby in case of aircraft mishap in this area.

Migrating reindeer crossing the River Khatanga (photo by Mick Brogan).

In Khatanga we waited. To travel in the Arctic is to wait. For two weeks the wind had been blowing from the northeast, pulling the sea ice down from the Laptev Sea onto the coast of the Taymyr Peninsula, exactly where we needed to go. There was no point in leaving the relative comfort of Khatanga until there was the prospect of at least some clear water. A tanker, overdue in from Tiksi, was making slow going of it, even with an ice-breaker leading.

On August 17 we left. We had seen migrating reindeer crossing the river and, in an ice-cave, the remains of a 23,000-year-old mammoth. We had full tanks of diesel and water, which being from the river was brown – 'we'll boil it well'. The Russian Orthodox priest blessed us and the boat. Half a dozen people waved us off. The fire station siren wailed and a ship on the river hooted – well might it 'toot' as we had left a lot of money in Khatanga.

A three-knot current carried us out, the shallows and blind channels in wait for the non-vigilant. That night we saw more reindeer and the river ferry *Taymyr* going upriver, old friends. She flashed her lights in salute. We waved our thanks. Out of the river and into the sea, we carried all sail as the wind blew from the northwest. Would it blow the ice away from the land and let us through? We

Working through the ice was hard going, anxious and wearing.

made great progress for the next several days, with only the occasional band of ice requiring our fighting through.

At 75 degrees 50 north, 30 miles short of last year's 'furthest north', Nicolay Babich, our Murmansk 'controller', told us that there was heavy ice inshore ahead. 'Atomic I/B (Ice-breaker) is stationed 70 miles from us, offshore, outside the ice. We should make for it.'

We fought all we could for about two miles, sparing neither boat nor ourselves, until we came to a full stop. We could go no further. We were faced with the prospect of sitting tight in the ice, waiting for a change, or going backwards, if we could, to shelter. We chose a third option. We radioed *Sovietski Soyuz*. 'Any chance of a dig-out'? Not a hope, they had no instructions, never heard of us. We then sat-phoned Murmansk, got hold of Mr. Babich and Slava turned on the charm, and how. 'Stand by,' said Babich.

Over the next hour, tension filled our cabin. Outside, the ice filled in around us in light fog. Silence. Then, at midnight, came the word. The I/B was on its way, going through the ice at 18 knots. Four hours later it appeared. What a machine, 75,000 HP, filling the horizon.

This mammoth blew us a channel 40 metres wide, through which we followed at 7 knots. Ten hours later we were out into clear water, ice-free all the way, we were told, now only 110 miles to Cape Chelyuskin. Exultant, posing for our cameras, whiskey glasses out, even as snow fell, we rounded. Two miles away, over on the shore, we could see the disused Polar Station, with its half a dozen buildings, antennas and oil tanks. Access was possible, but dodgy. We stayed out but later in the day once again met ice being blown in from the Kara Sea ahead of us. Additionally, there now was a forecast of a northwest gale, which would blow even more ice in on top of us.

With great difficulty, over the next eight hours, we struggled towards Bolshevik Island, southernmost of the Northern Siberian Islands group. The prospect of being swept back into the Laptev Sea lent urgency to our efforts. We got to shelter and anchored in Sun Bay, so called. There for four days we lay, snow thickening, paw prints of a polar bear about 30 metres away onshore – as long as there were none on deck!

Slava was comfortable and confident about us, and on the radio chatted with his contacts on the ice-breakers. As they say in Russian, *bceo kharasho*, everything's good. We could hear the chat on the radio of a west-going convoy being assembled. On August 27 a call came: 'Let's go.'

We were last in a line of ships being led by nuclear I/B *Vaigach*, pushing and breaking the ice, followed by I/B *Sovietski Soyuz*, blowing it out with her beam jets to form a channel. Two nuclear ice-breakers! We passed a mammy bear and her two cubs on the ice. Once clear, the ships of the convoy went in various directions, we for Dikson, port town on the mouth of the great Yenesi River.

There we got a *banya*, Russian for sauna, diesel and not much else from that unfortunate place and 24 hours later, in the fog, we were at sea again, watching on our radar for any vessel which might be coming down from the big mines upriver at Norilsk.

It was ice-free now in the Kara Sea as we lashed south-westward towards Novaya Zemlya (new land). It hadn't been so for Valerian Albanov, first officer in 1912 on *Saint Anna*. His story of a one and a half year survival epic is told in *In the Land of White Death*.

*Under guard in Dikson, at the mouth of the Ob River.
'We'll be glad to get out of here'. (photo by Rory Casey)*

We went ashore for a few hours on White Island at the tip of the Yamal Peninsula. There, in the distance, we saw reindeer and muskox. The local Nenet people, further south, live by the reindeer. That night, the Aurora showed its splendour, a moving curtain of colour filling the northern sky. It now was 800 miles to Murmansk. We were at longitude 71 degrees east.

We would have liked to land on Novaya Zemlya but couldn't; it is military-run and radioactive on its northern island due to nuclear testing.

On September 4, we were arrested by a Border Guard vessel and brought back to their anchored mother ship before being let go six anxious hours later.

The next day, September 5, we went up the Murmansk Fjord and our Northeast Passage was completed.

We were welcomed by Nicolai Babich of the Murmansk Shipping Company, who had done so much for us. We asked why he sent the big ice-breaker to help us. 'Because last year you helped us, when you saved the Dutchman,' he said.

There, Slava, now 'friends forever', Rory and Colm left. We still had 1,900 miles to do to get home to Ireland.

Arriving in Norwegian waters, off Vardo, we radioed in. 'Welcome to Norway.' That was it. What a contrast to the Russians, no paperwork, no 'problema' here. Wonderful.

Over the next five weeks we worked our way down the coast of Norway, being joined in Tromsø by Brendan, Tom and Eoin, crossing the North Sea, going through the Caledonian Canal and arriving into Westport on October 12, our polar circumnavigation completed.

31

The Cottage by Mannin Bay, Connemara

Around 1911 all changed in Mannin. The government Land Commission bought out Brown, the landlord, and distributed the land to the tenants, 16 in number. One of these was Paraic 'Dan' Conneely. In 1927 he sold to Joe Gorham, a local man returned from America, who, as referred to earlier, built a fine cottage. The date of building is well remembered locally because during the course of construction its gable wall was blown down by the 'Great Gale'. That was on the night of October 28, 1927, when 45 fishermen were lost – the Cleggan Disaster.

The cottage later came into the ownership of an English lady, Mrs. Hueston, who put in a toilet and 'wired' it for bottled gas. In 1976 she remarked to my father, who was her tax advisor, that she no longer used it and must sell it. I bought it for £3,000, about my annual salary at the time.

It stands at the end of the road on an acre and a half of partly reed marsh, and looks across towards Slyne Head Lighthouse, flashing twice every 12 seconds at night. Swinging one's gaze around towards the northwest is Dooloughan and False Bay, good for surfing at half tide. In the far distance lie High Island and Inis Boffin. Out of sight to the north, two fields away, is Mannin Bay, with its rocky coves and sandy beaches.

The village of Ballyconneely is three miles away, the distance to the main road being two and a half miles, mostly single track and macadamed, but with grass centrally for the last half mile approaching the cottage.

The Cottage, Slyne Head is in the distance. The beach on Mannin Bay is a couple of fields to the right, out of picture.

And this is where I like to be. Happily, so too does Mary and our youngsters and friends, young and old.

Over the last 40 years, some extensions and improvements have made it more comfortable, particularly in winter, though still it retains its character, whitewalled outside and the open turf fire within.

The kids love the freedom, no traffic, barefoot across the fields to the beach, their own 'space' back in the house, *Seomra na Buachaili* and *Seomra na gCailíni*.

I love the run on the *machair* grass and along the beach, the Twelve Bens for the occasional high ground walk and cycling on the roads (except in too-busy summer traffic). When the *Saint Patrick* was around, I moored her in Roundstone, 10 miles away. Now, when not travelling, that's where I base *Ar Seachrán*.

Long may it last and too, hopefully, for our *Sliocht Shleachta* to follow.

32

South to Azores, 2007 and North to Lofoten, 2009

After the return from the Northeast Passage I must have been 'played out', not surprising I suppose.

On the work front, with Dun Laoghaire Council I was put to supervising a construction job on the busy Rock Road; with difficult traffic management and an even more difficult contractor. Fortunately, I had the good head office support of John McDaid and his director, Eamonn O Hehir. With me on the job were engineers Marcella Murphy and Fergal Connolly. Eamonn had been instrumental in the official Dun Laoghaire County Council welcome home given to our *Northabout* team.

All was well in Belgrave Road, Mary connecting with, and on Sunday dinners, feeding whichever of our youngsters were around – all now young adults making their own way – not to speak of minding myself and all the while being active as a volunteer in a caring organisation.

In the Spring of 2006 I suggested to my normal sailing pals a non-demanding sail around Ireland.

Communications from the boat, technically, were by now much more advanced than 20 or 30 years previously. I still was inclined to the 'when yer gone, yer gone' style, in contrast to the 'running commentary', but had learned that something in-between was far better. Whether on long trips or short, some sort of communication with home, say twice a week, seems to me about right.

'I've given up setting objectives,' I said to the lads. 'We'll sail whichever way the wind blows us.' They smiled as they do when I say, 'We'll only be out in good weather.'

This easy life must have been over-exhausting because the following year we were bound for the Azores Islands. These are nine in all, located about 1,000 miles off the coast of Portugal and 1,200 miles south of Ireland. This trip would be no big deal but demanding nonetheless in that it would be *Ar Seachrán's* first ocean passage, her previous history being largely racing or coastal.

With Sean and myself on the outward leg were Ruaidhri, two friends of his and Mike Alexander. I had first met Mike, an early-retiree Aer Lingus pilot, at a distance in Dublin's Grand Canal Basin during 2002 as I worked on *Saint Patrick* and he on his green steel boat. I hadn't realised that he was preparing this boat for a trip to the other side of the world. Even as we waved to him from our mooring, as he moved down the Liffey, I presumed that he was merely going out into Dublin Bay.

Mike Alexander – he had sailed his own boat around the world to Australia.

Five years later, having sailed across oceans to New Zealand and visited the most wonderful of places, he now had moved from Malahide to being a neighbour in Blackrock. In the Breffni pub, where a few of us would meet on Wednesdays, and still do, he proved good company and adroit at marking his position on whatever the topic might be. On one Wednesday, when he had first joined us, he had been impressed that we were discussing the Council of Trent, or maybe it was the Synod of Whitby!

The passage outward to Azores was uneventful and pleasant, mostly. Closing the islands, in fresh following weather (the log succinctly noted 'wild tonight') we did contrive to put a good tear in the mainsail, thus arriving in Praia da Vitória, Terceira under headsail only. Still, not a bad passage of seven days.

However, worryingly, a knocking of the rudder bearing had developed. Whatever it was, this would certainly need attention before going again to sea.

Being skipper on a boat at sea imposes a different mindset than being crew. As crew, you do your stint – and that's it. As skipper, you're all the time 'on duty', mentally aware. 'Who's on watch now?' 'Did I tell them …?' Even with the finest of crew, sometimes ahead of yourself in ways, the timing of some move is for you to call. You're never 'off'.

With the best of friendly help in Terceira, a sailmaker was organised and a mechanic for the rudder problem (top bearing worn, new one to be flown in from Lisbon). Thus relaxed, we dined well and stayed too long in the Bar Mexicano, our Portugese improving all the while!

Ken Price from Dalkey, an engineer, climber (former) and stoic, joined us. I had first met Ken with the Saturday Walkers. On a crowded weekend trip across the Irish Sea to Wales in 1987 in *Saint Patrick* I had assigned him a berth right up in the bow. He emerged the following early dawn, somewhat shattered. I had completely forgotten about him as we battered our way across, his location within the boat being at the worst end. 'I just tied myself down,' he uncomplainingly remarked. 'Sorry,' was all I could say. Ken, when not engineering or climbing, had taken to sailing in the racing Howth 17s, but latterly was cruising with us, good bachelor company.

For two weeks we enjoyed the islands and its people. We climbed the volcanic Mount Pico and were again ready for sea. Sean had left and for the trip homeward we were joined by my brother Fred and Sligo cattleman Brian Mullan.

For a couple of days after leaving the warm green islands of the Azores it was lovely. Then it changed, and how. The wind and seas rose – bigger and bigger, fortunately from astern. Uncomfortably, increasingly so, we

Ken Price – a noted climber in his younger days, latterly he had come to sailing.

were forced to hand steer and, with only a tiny amount of foresail set, were blown northwards. Seven and a half days on we arrived in Roundstone. Fred, who had been knocked out of his high-level bunk against a bulkhead with his face closely missing a coat hook, described the trip as 'memorable'. Brian, in Sligo, still dines on it.

I recovered in the cottage in nearby Mannin and in early September sailed, northaround, back to Dublin. That otherwise nice trip was blighted with the bad news, received by us off Donegal, that good friend Louis Purton, ailing with cancer for some time, had died. We hurried on back.

Two months later, while I was in China on a retirement holiday with Mary, we got a further shock, also not unexpected, but a bitter blow nonetheless. Cancer had finally got the better of Pat Redmond. Silently, I cried.

          ε   ε   ε

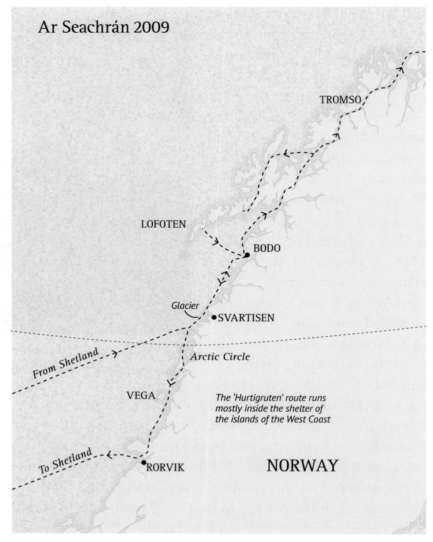

Ar Seachrán 2009

TROMSO

LOFOTEN

BODO

Glacier •SVARTISEN

From Shetland →

Arctic Circle

VEGA

The 'Hurtigruten' route runs mostly inside the shelter of the islands of the West Coast

To Shetland ←•RORVIK **NORWAY**

Norway/Lofoten

The prospect of a 2009 trip to Norway, floated in autumn 2008, attracted sufficient interest to outline a four-stage plan: Dublin to Shetland, two weeks; Shetland to Tromsø, two weeks; Lofoten two weeks; and from Bodø, southward to Roundstone, three to four weeks.

With Norwegian prices in mind, duty-free drink was taken aboard. The 'hard food', bought mostly in Aldi, was bagged and labelled, ring-fenced for each stage (to avoid untimely diminution of 'the nicies').

Mike, Ken and Liam Ó Muirlithe sailed, headsail only, in a brisk westerly wind from the Liffey to Clogher Head Pier in Louth. Next day they reached Glenarm in Antrim where Kevin and I joined.

Liam is an Irish language writer in prose and poetry, and as we went north brought to our group a nice Munster atmospheric. Each placename passed was discussed as to meaning, origin and antiquity. I once asked him whether modern poets ever 'tip the hat' to each other? 'Tip the hatchet, more likely,' he said.

Longtime friend and mainstay sailor, particularly in our earlier days, Kevin would now probably have preferred to be casting his rod in search of the ever elusive trout or salmon, but he enjoys the company on the boat and what we do.

We now had a policy of staying a minimum of two days in any place we stopped so as not to be rushing too much. We called to Craighouse in Jura and the island of Eigg. There the previous year, on a May trip, Liam had met the piper Donna and given her a generous tip to 'pipe us away'. She had earned it. We went aground, but bravely she had played on until half hour later we floated and left on the rising tide. Liam composed a 'Lament for the Grounded Boat'.

In Skye, beautiful but with high unemployment, I read an advert, looking for fish farm workers for Norway:

> Successful applicants must have stamina, be physically and medically fit, flexible in their approach, commercially aware and who understand the importance of meeting deadlines – the work involves long hours, in sometimes harsh conditions and only individuals capable of dealing with these levels of pressure should apply.

Would you dare put that in 'Crew Wanted'?

In Orkney, near Stromness, we visited the former home of John Rae. It was he, working for the Hudson Bay Company, who in the 1850s had discovered remnants of the lost Franklin Expedition. In Shetland we saw the remains of the wartime 'Shetland Bus', so called as the wintertime passage, braving gales and Luftwaffe, when Norwegian fishermen had run the gauntlet of the German occupiers of their country to bring supplies to resistance groups.

There we crew changed and aboard came Paul Cooper, Tom Leonard and Mark Lennon. Paul, from Howth, had sailed on *Shardana* with John Gore-Grimes, repeatedly. Enough said. For that you had to 'cut it' and how he did. For twenty years or so past he had been a regular, with Pat Colleran, on *Saint Patrick,* and laterally *Ar Seachrán*, during May Weeks. Paul could fix anything. And as John Gore-Grimes had written, 'When Paul fixes something, it stays fixed'. And he's a very good cook.

From Lerwick to the Svartisan glacier, well up the coast of Norway, we covered 550 miles in three days. We coasted up the inside Hurtigruten route, past the Arctic Circle and to Tromsø. It was for the mountains the next men were here to join ship: Harry Connolly, Paddy O'Brien, Peter Gargan, Rory Walsh and Frank Nugent.

Frank has been introduced earlier; Paddy and Peter have featured as well. Frank I had met in 1993, after he had come home from the successful Everest expedition. He, like myself latterly, had the

'Hurtigruten' is the name of Norway's coastal waterway inside (most of) the rocks and islands and also of the ferrys who work this waterway; a five day run from Bergen in the south to Kirkenes in the north.

benefit of a state job, Fás in his case, where he was a training manager. This allowed him the flexibility – in other words the time off – to pursue long distance climbing objectives. Also, like myself, he had the good fortune to have a generous and supportive wife, Carol. From 1994 onwards, Frank and I have sailed, hiked and climbed over short weeks in Scotland and longer, twice in Patagonia, Newfoundland and of course the big trips to Shackleton's Antarctic and the Northwest Passage. If something needs doing on the boat, he's first out of the bunk. And to boot he's hugely social. No

Peter Gargan – he did tremendous metal work for our boats

strangers in the room with Frank – first up to dance or sing a song – and considerate too. While slogging with difficulty up a soft crevassed, snowslope in Chile I asked him, 'When do we turn back?' He replied, 'When either of us wants to!'

And I got to know Peter and Paddy too around the early 1990s. From Rathfarnham, they were friends of the late Pat Redmond and, like Pat, bring energy into all they came into contact with. We've sailed and hill-walked round Ireland and Scotland, weekends and May Weeks, and more recently to East Greenland. They're cyclists too, recreational not racing, but damn competitive and fast as I find when trying to keep with them when walking the hills, as is Maurice O'Hara.

For two weeks we sailed and climbed on the Lofoten Islands. Reserved as were the local Norwegians, we still managed to knock a bit of *craic* out of them in the evenings, even with beer at 70 kroner, that's €8.00! To conclude that fortnight we visited the Polar Museum in Bodø. There, apart from the general polar exhibits that you'd expect, are some of Roald Amundsen's original documents, including the telegrams when he finished the Northwest Passage and after reaching the South Pole.

Sailing pleasantly southward over the next month we had old friends aboard, and were now joined by young men, brothers Ruairc and Darrach Ó Tuairisg, sons of Ruaidhri, who as boys had been to the Baltic with us in 1996.

'Ar Seachrán' in Lofoten

Frank Nugent and Harry Connolly climb in the magical islands of Lofoten in Norway

Frank and Harry did this article for **Mountain Log.**

33

A Spell in Ethiopia

'Rapid Response Team' said the Irish Government advertisement of July 2007 seeking applications. This sounded interesting; a specialised civilian team to respond to disasters, worldwide, at short notice. I would be retiring from Dun Laoghaire/Rathdown County Council in September and had no plans. A spell of this, now and again, might be just the job; something exciting with 'doing good' added on. Voluntary, no pay – fine, my pension would be coming in.

'Not a hope of getting selected' was the judgement at home. This was for ex-Army and Garda men, active doctors, nurses and electricians, not aged Council engineers. Nonetheless, the interview seemed to go well. My time in Malawi, adventure background, stable work history and domestic record – together, I suppose, with the spring in my step and enthusiasm – got me in. About fifteen of us did a one week course, lectures first then several days practical stuff in the Curragh Military Camp. And these Irish army guys were impressive. I suspected that some of them were Rangers, the elite. We learned about recommended behaviour if taken hostage, minefield escape and gunfire protection ('sandbags are way better than brick walls').

It was a year later, September 2008, when I got the call. It was for Ethiopia where the United Nations World Food Programme (WFP) was active and they needed a civil engineer to oversee construction of food warehousing for a three-month stint. This wasn't quite the dramatic stuff that I'd envisaged, but okay anyway. On the phone from Dublin I spoke to my Dutch UN boss-to-be in Addis Ababa. Would I need a tent? No. A sleeping bag? Definitely, and light because I'd be in the hot lowlands near Somalia. War-torn? Yes, but low intensity. Suddenly this was interesting. I didn't tell Mary of the location. She wasn't very keen anyway.

From the early morning Addis airport bus going into town I saw a group of runners, just loping along, at speed. We were in the 'land of runners' all right. The WFP office was less impressive, five-story, glass-fronted, with lots of idleness within it seemed to me. But I did notice that taking the stairs left me somewhat breathless. Why? I was reasonably fit. Because Addis Ababa is 2,300 metres above sea level, that's why.

I met my people, the local engineer who had prepared the drawings, a good guy but I wondered what I was doing here. I met my Dutch boss, one of the contractors and a few others. There would be induction that Friday afternoon. About a hundred people of all nationalities filled the room as our facilitator began. A late entry crept in the back door. 'Out,' shouted our man on the stage. 'Come back on Tuesday.' What a jerk, a power-hungry bureaucrat. I was seeing aspects of the aid industry in action.

The 10-man plane swung in over Gode, 300 nautical miles southeast of Addis – I tend to think in nautical miles; for kilometres, double that figure. Below through the sand and scrubby bushes ran a muddy river. Single story buildings spread for a mile or so around. A few unsmiling ground staff waved us through the tin shed of an airport. Dennis welcomed me, WFP second in command here, a Bosnian. He seemed glad to have some company I reckoned, as we drove the dusty road back into town. A guard opened the compound gate as we approached. Within was nice – palm trees, brick single story buildings, a central building and a mess hall. It looked good to me.

My billet was a simple clean room, one of a terrace of eight. It had a bed, table and a few hangers. I was surprised that there was no mosquito net over the bed – apparently not considered necessary.

Dennis was a full time WFP man, as were most of them, some Europeans and others from all over, Sudan, Burkino Faso, China.

'Not very competent' would be an under-description of Dennis's view of them.

My work, to call it that, took about an hour and a half a day, just walking around the site of the new food warehouse under construction, nodding here and there, a word to the foreman, making a few notes, calculations perhaps of materials required, emailing Addis and that would be it. And so I took to having a run outside the village each morning at dawn. That half hour was the best part of my day. Dennis was good company, though a little heavy on the evening beers at which I felt obliged to keep up – no hardship.

There was a serious food shortage in the 50 mile area around us, and God knows what further out. The WFP had plenty of food in Addis, but apparently couldn't decide by which of the two roads to send it to us. A month later, both roads were out of use for 'military reasons'. So instead of 20-ton loads coming in by road, 4-ton loads were being flown in at considerably greater cost.

I also worked on warehouse construction in a couple of other locations, flying to Jijiga City and Degeh Bur, but it was the same story as Gode but without the good company of Dennis. For some reason, I came to be regarded as a 'security expert'. It must have been to do with the 'troubles' in Northern Ireland. I was asked to do a protective blast-wall around the WFP glass-walled building in Addis, so I 'designed' a mixture of the RUC Newry Barracks wall, that I had seen driving by, and a two-story high reinforced concrete wall we had built on the Dundrum Bypass!

And then there was the Great Ethiopian Run. Conveniently for me, it coincided with a WFP meeting I had in Addis. Together with 32,000 others, I lined up at the front where I had inveigled my way – big mistake. The elite runners, as always at these events, were a couple of hundred metres ahead. A line of police, just in front of me, held the start line. A surge and away we went, swept along. Arms out I fell, and was being trampled on by those coming from behind; they couldn't help it. I managed to get back on my feet, scraped and bruised. To keep up I had to run like bejasus, flat out. No room to slip sideways out of the way to get my breath. About a kilometre later, knees and hands bleeding, I managed to get to the side of the road. Passing now were teams of chanting Ethiopians, Kenyans too I think, and the odd white guy. I limped on, up and down hills – Addis is a hilly place – and heard 'come on grandfather, you can do it' from runners passing. At about the 8 kilometer mark an African running beside me said, 'Brother, we can do it'. And we did. My breath back, together we ran, stride for stride, and eventually downhill into the finish for a time of 57 minutes. And a medal for being one of the first thousand in. Dennis and I drank some beer that night.

On the work front, my very short connection with the town of Warder was probably the most satisfactory feature. Warder lies close to the Somali border. WFP had been making the odd food delivery, but needed a secure compound. Would I be prepared go and sus one out? The four-man UN plane swept in. 'We have an hour and a half,' the pilot said. I was met by a Médicins Sans Frontiéres guy (MSF are everywhere, mostly where others dare not).

We drove past the radio station and the abandoned Chinese roadbuilding site into the crowded town, dense with camels, goats and people. He showed me the sheds where WFP had made their deliveries, surrounded by thatched wattle buildings. Fire hazards, ambush and hide hazards. No way. 'How about back out near the airport?' he said. Not good, the radio station and the airport are always first to go if there's trouble.

'Where are MSF?' I asked. We drove there, half mile outside the town, a clear view in all directions. 'What's that low walled area, overgrown, with some decrepit stone buildings?' Our time was nearly up. Hurriedly I stepped the wall around, took photos and some GPS readings. This place would do.

Back in Addis, I submitted my report and recommendation. At last I might have done something worthwhile.

I was home in Dublin for Christmas; in January I submitted my expenses. For my 'voluntary' effort I would, to my great surprise, be getting the same allowances that Irish Civil Servants get for their trips to Brussels, amounting in total to some €15,000. Welcome, of course, but ridiculous.

34

Newfoundland, 2010 and The White Sea, 2012 in Northabout

'Arrest me so,' said the bold Mick Brogan to the Canadian Im-migration honcho, armed and dressed in black, on the quay at Halifax, Nova Scotia. It was June 2010 and it was my fault for arriving without a passport. But what a big deal these guys made of it. 'Command and Control' wasn't in it, as a half dozen of them sur-rounded us, threatened confiscation of the boat and arrest of us all. Mick and Matt Molloy, arriving to greet us and full of post-closing time joy, seemed to threaten their iron grip on the situation.

We had sailed 1,600 miles from Horta in the Azores – Jarlath, three pals and myself. I bunked in my usual berth, now with a Dromoland Castle sticker on the cabin door. The fourteen day pas-sage was without incident. We met the fog on the Grand Banks, which confirmed that our journey was nearing its end. However, I had 'found' that my passport was missing, probably left in Horta where I had cleared Portuguese immigration. A message home had Mary performing heroics with the Irish Passport Office, including some forgery of my signature on the replacement application form. Frank joining ship in Halifax, brought it out arriving a day later than *Northabout*. Now all was well.

How people treat their own is an indicator of how civilised is a place. In this regard Halifax was tops. Cars stopped for pedes-trians; joggers and cyclists had right-of-way, or seemed to; people smiled at strangers. We were driven to Lunenburg, former base of

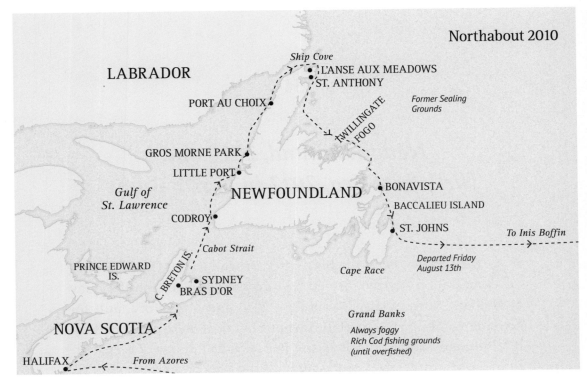

Newfoundland

the schooners who fished the Grand Banks. We visited the *Bluenose 2*, undergoing a $12 million rebuild. In his shed we met a dory-builder, lanky and slow-spoken, with all the time in the world to talk schooners, dorys and the fishing which was now gone, fished out. Evenings were pleasantly musical. We were in the land of 'Four Strong Winds' and folksinger Stan Rogers. The Scottish background, giving the area its name 'Nova Scotia', seemed little evident.

From Halifax we sailed north, able to see nothing in the fog, so thank God for radar, GPS and plotters. On the southern end of the island of Cape Breton we entered the canal leading to the 45-mile-long wonderlake of Bras d'Or. The coastal fog does not extend here inland, a different and pleasant world. Musically we were disappointed. Cape Breton, supposedly rich in Scottish tradition, was somewhat minimal in that regard, until we got to the former coalmining town of North Sydney. There Matt connected with a family group, the Barra MacNeils, and what a night. Days later, as we sailed the 100 miles across Cabot Strait towards Newfoundland, the music still rang in our ears. The 'Barra' part of their name was because their antecedents had come from the island of Barra in the Scottish Hebrides.

With Jarlath and myself now were Kevin Cronin, Wally McGuirk and Mike Alexander. Up the 300 mile west coast of Newfoundland, pronounced 'New*fund*land', we sailed. We were in every night, to anchor or at piers, meeting generous, talkative people. Sparse population makes for that. The cod fishing had been closed by the government, leaving thousands without a livelihood. Emigration was widespread, to the cities of Montreal and Toronto and to the shale oil mines of Saskatchewan. The logging and paper industries had also been greatly reduced.

Frank and myself, boots on, hiked up the mountain of Gros-Morne. Going north the trees grew sparser and the town names were French, legacy of days when the fate of colonies were often decided by battles and wars in distant Europe.

It was in Port au Choix that we experienced our first Shed Party. Strolling through the town, a couple of us got talking to some people clearing nets and ropes out of their shed. A smell of cooking wafted out. 'Yer off an Irish boat, ya must come.' About fifty of the Cornick family and neighbours gathered, eating, talking, drinking and singing. It was a summertime family reunion of those visiting from the mainland and those at home. And we were treated as family.

In the Strait of Belle Isle we saw some icebergs and the distant shore of Labrador.

L'Anse aux Meadows was different. It was here that Norsemen in their great longboats had landed long ago. The physical remnants are dated at about 1,000 AD. We anchored in the shallow water off-shore and dinghied ashore to the newly built mock Viking village. It was a little 'kitsch' but, nonetheless, with actors dressed the part, weaving, blacksmithing, baking and talking to us (we were lucky to be in before the tourist crowds), most informative.

St. Anthony, capital of the north, was rough. The writer Annie Proulx, who set *Shipping News* in this area, critically had it about right. We now were joined by Brendan Minish, communications wizard, and Castlebar men Rory Casey and his brother Gerry, big and energetic both. The fortnight south to St. John's would be about 250 miles, many more if we were to go into the many bays and outports of this broken coast.

With the Casey brothers aboard the tempo was lifted. In my journal of the trip I see that I aspired to an 'alcohol-free night', which was to be again and again denied, though never disappointingly! In summer these islands and outports are socially great.

In Twillingate we met George, fingerless from frostbite and with a leg injury too. He talked non-stop. He was one of the last who had gone to the ice in the spring, after seal pelts. It had been a brutal business, hard on the employed men, cold and underfed, who had to go to sea in the vessels of the merchants of St. John's. Put onto the ice, they bludgeoned the seals and skinned the pelts. Those pelts, when cured, would be shipped out to fashion houses for the vanity of well-off women. George said that at the finish of this trade they had stopped taking the 'white coats' – the very young pups – and were doing no harm at all. There were plenty of seals, no matter how many taken, however bad publicity had put an end to this and yet another source of livelihood for Newfoundlanders had been lost.

Fogo Island was very Irish. The Foley family collected us and brought us to their shed, where with instruments already unboxed it was straight into the singing, a mixture of Newfie and Irish. We extricated ourselves about 2.00 am.

Sailing southwards towards Greenspond we saw dozens of big humpback whales, jumping out of the water, their white fins showing brightly. The place names were descriptive: Seldom Come By, Burnt Island Tickle (tickle is 'newfie' for rocks) and the Dildo Run – I kid you not!

We went inside the island of Baccalieu, infamous for shipwrecks. There's a song:

We were bound home in October, from the shores of Labrador
Trying to head a strong nor'easter and snow too,
But the wind swept down upon us, making day as black
    as night
Just before we made the cliffs of Baccalieu.

And on it goes, men hauling frozen ropes, decks steeply tilting, mainboom bending, snow falling, cliffs ahead, until eventually their ship cleared that dreaded island.

We had none of that, but enjoyed a grand sail and later made it through the narrow gap into the fine harbour of St. John's. This was to be our last Newfoundland call. Unfortunately, we would not see the 'southern shore', very Irish they say; nor Brigus, home of the great Arctic sailor Bob Bartlett; nor Burgeo, home for years of the environmentalist and writer Farley Mowat. 'Always leave something for next time.'

We had seen enough of St. John's and were to leave for Ireland, Jarlath, Mike and myself on board. The forecast was good, but it was Friday, August 13! Now we're not superstitious, but…. So we waited until about seven in the evening, when, five hours ahead, it would already be next day in Ireland, and then left.

The passage home took two weeks and was pleasant and unremarkable, arriving in Inis Bofin to have grub and a pint in Murray's.

The White Sea, 2012

We had unfinished business in Russia.

In doing the Northeast Passage in *Northabout* we had intended routing through the White Sea and from there into the Baltic and home. However when approaching its entrance from its eastward side we reckoned that it would be shorter, and certainly faster, to take the seaward route via Murmansk and Norway, which we did.

So now, seven years later, 2012, we were going back, for 'one last big trip'. We left Westport on June 21, mid-summer's day, sailing for Skye, Cape Wrath and Orkney. From Shetland we crossed to Trondheim in Norway, that city and its people looking resplendent in the sun. Following the inside coastal route, in undemanding manner, we reached Honingsvaag near North Cape, a magnet for tourists. Here, well north of the Arctic Circle, the days were long, just dulling for a few hours at night. Joining Jarlath, myself, Matt Molloy and Pat Hartigan would be Mick Brogan and Gary Finnegan, camera equipped, coming in on the ferry from Tromsø.

Matt and I swam in the cold sea, briefly. Then for a few days the wind blew and the rain lashed. Matt played a few tunes, lovely sounds from forward in the boat.

On July 23 we left, initially with a good sailing wind and then, in a flat windless sea, going under engine. From Moscow we had the required permissions, but nonetheless were glad not to meet any Russian border patrol boats. We kept well out to sea to avoid their coastal guardships. Our designated port of entry was Archangel, so even had we wished to, we couldn't land on the barren Kola Peninsula.

For four days we travelled east and I considered various previous journeys here. I had read of *The Voyage of Othere*, a ninth century journey undertaken by a wealthy hunter (he owned 600 deer).Englishman Richard Chancellor, seeking the Northeast Passage, had left Gravesend on May 12, 1557, reaching Archangel on July 13. In 1701 a vessel of war left Gothenburg on June 6 and was attacking Archangel on July 6. Some fast passages those, done entirely under sail. In *The House by the Dvina*, Eugenie Fraser of a Scottish merchant family describes her life married to aRussian counterpart in Archangel. During World War II Allied convoys to Murmansk and Archangel carried war material to 'our brave allies the Russians'. We were far from being the first to go this way.

Going southwards into the White Sea we re-crossed the Arctic Circle, feeling strong tides in the narrows of The Gorlo (The Throat). Along the shore, trees came into view, then shipping and then the Archangelisk Number One Buoy. Going inward, dereliction appeared along the riverbank; collapsed jetties and abandoned warehousing. Only the big timber yards seemed active. On sandy edges youngsters swam and oldsters fished.

The White Sea

Entry formalities were surprisingly friendly and efficient. Then Colm Brogan, our Russian speaker, was at our berth to meet us. And an excellent berth it was, clean and central, in this rebuilt concrete city of 300,000 people, called after the Archangel St. Micheal. The sights, few in number, were some museums, fairly threadbare, some remaining seventeenth and eighteenth century merchants' timber houses and for me, the Biblio Café. The people were helpful, as is so often the case of those living in thin conditions.

On July 30 we left for Solovetsky Island, formerly a monastery, more recently a gulag prison 'so far away that the screamscould not be heard', as Solzhenitsyn described it. The town was a broken, impoverished place among the grass and flowers in the sunshine. But the gem, the reason we were here, was the monastery, truly wonderful. It is bounded by stone fortress walls, within which are several magnificent churches. In the former living quarters I sat alone, contemplatively, in a stone-walled timber-floored monk's cell. How lucky we in *Northabout* were.

A forecast gale, 20 metres per second, had us away for an overnight dash to Belamorsk on the mainland, the entrance to the Belomore Canal. As we arrived the weather blew up, but we were

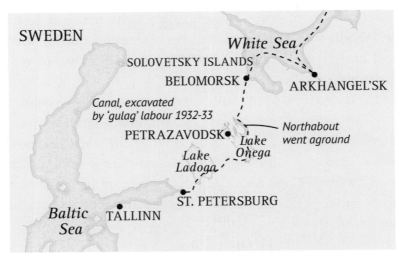

The White Sea Canal

sheltered within the huge concrete entry lock. Some phone calls were made by the lady lock-keeper and up we went in the lock and into a different world, a sylvan lakeland. The nearby town of 12,000 people consisted of ugly four-story blocks with some shops on each ground floor, some lumpy school buildings, and a library among timber houses and sheds of charm and dilapidation. What was lovely was the river, 50 metres wide, rushing over rocks between grassy edges – and on one bank, an attractive small wooden church.

We taxied out the dirt road to see the petroglyphs. In a forest clearing, etchings of hunters and animals, several thousand years old, were carved into the rock floor. The locals call them 'the devil's footprints'.

The 450-mile waterway linking Belomorsk on the White Sea with St. Petersburg on the Baltic is largely composed of lakes and rivers, with 100 miles of it, the northern end, being major canal works. These include 19 locks and five dams.

The Belomor Baltica Kanal (BBK) was built in 1932/33 on Stalin's instructions. It was to be done quickly and cheaply. In this first gulag-labour project men and women worked, half-starved, in atrocious conditions. Tens of thousands died of injuries, the cold, starvation and execution. The canal banks are their graveyard, unmarked. We later learned that those who lost, say, a left arm would be put to work with one who had lost a right arm and be treated as one labour-unit. Engineers had been arrested on the streets of Moscow and given a choice of BBK on pick and shovel or working as canal engineers.

But for us going into the BBK, first there was the Russian hassle factor – bureaucracy and money. Having dealt with that, we were on our way. For three days we travelled southward on the canal. The locks were superefficient, though a no-photos policy is strictly enforced by black-clad, Kalashnikov-carrying police. The Karelian landscape of woods and lakes was wonderful, but one just couldn't get away from its terrible history.

The canal enters Lake Onega at the town of Povonets, with its broken-down pier and the town not much better. By road we travelled 10 kilometres out to a forest graveyard called Sandemark. Here, near a railway line, there were many, many marked graves. We couldn't understand the distance from the canal – why take them so far, these Turkish, Germans, Ukranians, Jewish and Russians? We were later to find out.

Lake Onega has 20 miles of shallow going before becoming deeper. In the shallows we went aground – my fault. I was navigating and got it wrong. For 12 hours we were stuck on a stony bottom and worried. Passing vessels, in the channel a mile away, paidour distress no attention. We dinghied out to a couple of guys in a small angling boat. Colm explained our situation. Most helpfully, they got on their phone and within a few hours assistance arrived. A big rigid-inflatable boat (RIB) pulled us off, out to their parent vessel in the channel. Their diver checked our hull and propeller for damage – all this was going to be expensive we feared. They gave us paper clearance to proceed and a good navigation chart. 'Best Wishes', they said, and no charges. You never can tell!

Sixty miles later, in Petrazavodsk, the capital of Karelia Province, we struck gold in the person of historian/archaeologist Yuri Dmitri, who had unearthed the burials at Sandemark. Some 15 years earlier a Karelian hunter had discovered human bones in a badger sett. Yuri had been nearby on the Canal and was sent for. He excavated and found the first of 7,000 human remains, victims of Stalin's purge of 1937/38, unrelated to the canal. Russian authorities are good record keepers (don't we know their bureaucracy!) and Yuri had got access to the records in Moscow. They had been sent by train for execution: poets, writers, musicians and other 'threats to the state'.

In Petrazavodsk also we strolled the Embankment and admired the walk of so many women and, it seemed, the general sense of well-being.

At the southern end of Lake Onega we entered the Svir River, 200 miles long and surely one of the world's most scenic. It winds through deciduous forest, widening into lakes, with occasional timber villages on its banks. All this beauty was helped by a two-knot flow in our direction – it might not have felt so wonderful had we been going the other way. Helping greatly now was the company of Russian sailor Vladimir, to whom we had been introduced in Petrazavodsk and who had previously lived for three years in Bristol. The Svir River is busy, it being part of the Volga Waterway through western Russia. We got lots of toots and waves, yachts of any nationality being a rarity.

After Lake Ladoga we entered the Neva River; forty miles to go to St. Petersburg. As we drew closer, good looking industrial units and road traffic showed, as did some terrible looking kitzy houses, displaying the wealth, and bad taste, of the 'New Russians'. Alexander, our designated pilot, came aboard. Weren't we glad to have him as we made the night passage in convoy through the many opened bridges, meeting vessels anchored and travelling against us, the difference not always being apparent.

For three days we 'touristed', then cleared with the authorities and went out into the Baltic Sea, which I had last sailed in *Saint Patrick* in 1996. In the following fortnight we visited Tailinn (where Mike, Wally and Ken joined), Marihamn, Stockholm and, 50 miles south, Skanssundet. There I left ship and flew home via Ryanair.

Northabout continued with fresh men through the Gota Canal across to Denmark, the North Sea, through the Caledonian Canal and was back in Westport at the end of September.

35

Iomramh, 2011, Following the Celtic Monks to Iceland

The idea came from Dr. Breandán Ó Ciobhán, scholar from Ventry, County Kerry, to venture by boat to places where early Irish monks had left their mark, physical or literary, and to gain some appreciation of their spiritual values.

It was his neighbour, my old friend and shipmate, farmer/fisherman/writer Danny Sheehy from Ballyferriter who had put it to me, and away we went on a magic carpet of delight – planning, making contacts and getting our own crew together, or rather team, because we would be a mixture of archaeologists, poets, historians, musicians and sailors.

We'd start at Skellig on the feast of St. Brendan, May 16, and then go up the Irish west coast to the Inner Hebrides, Orkney, Shetland, Faroe and the south coast of Iceland. We'd return by St. Kilda and the Outer Hebrides and finish on McDara Island on his feastday, July 16.

But first we had a 'May Week' of sailing and hill-walking on the Iveragh and Dingle Peninsulas, climbing Mount Brandon and walking down *Cosán Na Naomh* (The Saints' Way).

The 'Imram' team gathered, or 'Iomramh' in modern Irish. This is the name given to the peregrinations of those who, following the Old Testament and then North African Christian practice, sought solace and hardship in the desert. The Irish, not having sandy wastes, took to the 'desert of the ocean'. Unlike those, we were not going to 'let God steer' and our comfort, frugal enough on the yacht *Ar Seachrán*, was in a different league.

We were to fail on our first three intended destinations. The weather was too rough to land on Skellig, and similarly for St. Feicin's High Island and then Inis Glóra off Mayo. On board with Breandán, Danny and myself were Donal De Barra (farmer, historian and a first cousin of mine), archeologist Finbarr Moore with others. At Burtonport, Donegal we had to shelter for eight days in desperate weather. Burtonport, once busy, now was in sad decline. There was little stirring other than the ferry over to the island of Arranmore. Rory Walsh continued to cook for us as he would at sea. Rory is a good swimmer but, by his own admission, is not at all a sailor. He compensates by being active in all other ways, whether walking the hills or cooking. He has a particular attraction for the Irish language, at which he can readily change dialect as we travel. No rural townland is strange to him, nor anyone in it. His memory of these is encyclopaedic. In particular he has bachelor hill farmers as friends, with whom he makes a connection every opportunity – a great travelling companion.

We left on May 27, our programme now in bits. Scottish antiquarian Dr. Ian Fisher had beenwaiting for us in Colonsay for the last week and, a patient man, was still there when we landed. He is the author of *Early Christian Archaeology in Argyl*. Colonsay, and its adjacent Oronsay, had for us the special interest that it may well be the famed Hinba,where, geographically uncertain, St. Colmcille (called by the Scottish, St. Columba) is recorded as meeting St. Brendan, so written byAdomnán, later Abbott of Iona.

Even though the weather now was fine, the sea was running too high to make a landing on Oileán Na Naomh, the Garvellochs. Nonetheless, Ian, unfazed and in delightful manner as we drifted by described the beehive cell, other constructions and his excavations there.

Iona was to have been our next stop, but the anchorage would have been too exposed. In any event we had been there many timesso we continued north to Kerrera, opposite Oban. There Ian

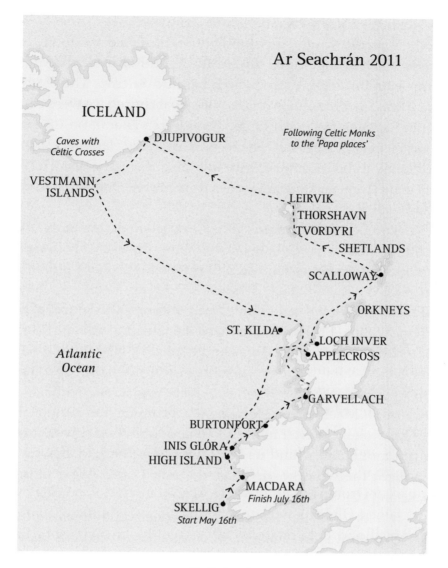

To Iceland

took us out behind the Richardson Monument to view Clyvernoch, a monastic settlement – the name deriving from the Gaelic 'Cladh A Bhearnóg', from 'Mearnóg', better known to us as 'Port Mearnóg', yes, 'Portmarnock', County Dublin.

Danny, in his ramblings, had met the Canon over at Oban Cathedral and told him of our 'pilgrimage'.

'Do ye pray together?' asked the Canon.

'No, but we drink together,' said Danny.

The forecast was for continuing poor, unsettled weather. Nonetheless, we had a glorious sail up the Sound of Mull and around to the island of Eigg, with its high basaltic outcrop, The Sgurr. In Eigg it was for Killdonnan's early medieval church we were bound. Within its walls Ian expounded. This church is built on the site of an earlier one, where St. Donnan was martyred. Ian made it seem as of today as he recounted, carefully distinguishing historical fact from conjecture, and ancient stones from newer, Donal in particular taking it all in.

Back on board, our minds abuzz, we sailed across to the mainland, the Cuillin a jagged skyline to the northwest. At Mallaig harbour and rail terminus, Ian and others took the train for Edinburgh. Ken Price joined.

From Mallaig we sailed pleasantly through the Sound of Sleat and under Skye Bridge. Nearby was the island of Pabay. This was the first of many Papays, Papas and Papils, all having their names given by the Norse Vikings when they came upon the *Papar* monks or signs of their presence. We had to skip Applecross, with its monastery of St. Mael Rubha, because of upcoming bad weather and were glad to take shelter in the good harbour of Loch Inver, mighty Suilven mountain behind us but invisible in the rain and clouds. That night the wind howled and the rain lashed. Next morning Breandán Ó Ciobhán said he was leaving.

A day later we left Loch Inver, in ideal conditions, with 180 miles to Scalloway in Shetland, now intending to skip Orkney because of lost time. However the weather turned bad again, as we passed Papa Westray in Orkney, but the 'roost', as they call the big tides, was with us. Waiting to come on board in Scalloway was our friend, Kerry musician Brendán Begley. John Smith, Shetland Heritage Officer, and Adalene Fullerton of Papil, West Burra also were expecting us.

Between them, they did us proud, John showing us Papil churchyard and the incised Celtic cross-slab, a copy, the original having been taken to the Scottish National Museum. That Saturday evening, in their restored croft-house, we had storytelling, singing and music, theirs and ours. We had hoped to land on the nearby islands of Papa Staur and Papa Skerry, but Faroe, 200 miles distant, was calling and the immediate weather window looked good.

We had an easy crossing to begin with but then it blew up as we reached Tvordyri, the main town on the southern island of Suderoy. ('Oy' meaning island, and 'Suder' presumably meaning south). Then the rain lashed and wind blew around us in this tree-less place – we could see why no trees would grow, much less survive.

Rory Walsh and Kevin Cronin coming ashore.

Dr. Steffen Stumman Hansen, Senior Danish Archeologist, now living in Faroe, arrived in off the Thorshavn ferry. Over the winter we had been in contact, discussing our Iomramh tour of Faroe and where we might go, never realising that he, Steffen, was going to guide us all around. In the various places, he set up transport and had local experts waiting for us. Hans and Fionnbjorn took us to their village of Hovi, showed us their museum, the Field of the Irish (monks) and fed us Faroese food.

From Thorshavn, the capital which you could walk end to end in 20 minutes, Steffen brought us out to Brandanvik, where there are remains of an old church and it is the bay where St. Brendan had landed. Brendán had to have a swim, to honour his namesake. The water was freezing – I know, because I went in too.

We now had been joined on board by Dr. Jonathan Wooding from the University of Wales. In Leirvik, site of both Norse and early Irish monkish presence, the discourse between Steffen and

On board with us along the south coast of Iceland was Lutheran minister Rev. Gunnthor. He also played harmonica.

Jonathan took wings. Some of us were distracted by the hospitality in neighbouring Eric's house. Later, when we filled the boat's fuel tank with many hundreds worth of diesel, Eric picked up the tab saying it would be charged to a Nigerian fish company that he did business with!

It got colder as we sailed and engined northwards to Iceland. We got into Djupivogur on June 14, and there were met by the Reverend Gunnthor Ingason, a Lutheran minister. We also met Frank Nugent who, with his son Ciaran, had been hiking. 'Too early in the season,' he said. 'Many of the mountain passes still were snow-blocked.'

Gunnthor, looking forward to sailing, couldn't do enough for us. At Thorberger Cultural Centre we stayed overnight for a conference on Pre-Viking Christian Settlement, Jonathan being the principal non-Icelandic speaker. Danny spoke of Christian and pre-Christian beliefs on the Dingle peninsula. Frank sang and Brendán played.

The 200 mile passage along Iceland's bleak and iron-bound south coast to the Vestmann Islands went without incident. Gladly, we had no need of the 'refuges for shipwrecked mariners' marked on our charts. In Heimay, population 4,500, the town on Vestmann, we were met by photographer/journalist Gisli Oscarson. Enthusiastically he showed us early Norse buildings, the Irish Well and a Celtic Cross carved into the rock behind the town.

The highlight for us was a visit to the Seljaland Caves over on the Iceland mainland. Within these caves are carved many crosses of a uniquely Celtic type. Recent excavation of the middens and analysis have established an occupation date of 795 AD, that is, 79 years earlier than the first Norse settlers are recorded in Iceland in 874 AD. In Iceland, these dates are quite 'political', as most of the Icelandic population has a preference for Viking ancestry. It was these Vikings, of course, who raided Ireland and took as slaves our fairest women, now 40 per cent of Icelandic DNA.

Gunnthor and Jonathon left for Reykjavik, and Brendán too. Liam Ó Muirlithe, Aosdána poet and sailor, arrived so we were five aboard for the journey southward. Our plan was to make for St. Kilda, 500 miles to the southeast, with its Cill Bréannain.

The first two days we made good and pleasant progress. Then, late on day 3, the wind changed to strong southeasterly. We lay hove-to for the night and decided that the open anchorage of St. Kilda would be untenable, even if we could get there. With two reefs in the mainsail we lay off for the Butt of Lewis. Our autopilot packed in so, hand-steering all the way, we had sore arms several days later when we got into Stornaway. What day was it? Sunday. Never the best in that dour town.

Pleasantly we coasted southward, sailing in sheltered water inside the Outer Hebrides, calling to Loch Maddy and next to Boisdale on South Uist. On Papey Island nearby, to which one can walk at low tide, we scrambled around the monastic ruins with diminishing enthusiasm. We'd had about enough of that. Some local people invited us to a 'house céilídh'. It was very nice, but not unlike a meeting of the parish council.

Normally, one would never pass Barra, but with a good forecast and the usual 'end-of-cruise-itis' we kept going onward for Tory, then Boffin, Clifden and Roundstone. On July 16, McDara's Day, a gale blew away any chance of the Annual Mass being held on the island. A few of us met in Carna anyway, and in Seamus Breathnach's house had a drink and a few tunes. So much to digest.

36

Camino, 2014 and East Greenland, 2015

In a currach, my friends Danny Sheehy, musician Brendán Begley, stonemason Brendan Páid and artist Liam Holden were going to row a Camino-by-Sea. From St. James Gate on the River Liffey to Santiago de Compostela they would go, down the Irish Sea, across to Wales, over the Bristol Channel to Cornwall and then to Brittany, row coastwise southwards down France and then westward across the north of Spain. They had done this sort of thing before, but never on such a scale. This would be a multi-year trip, taking five weeks each summer.

We in *Ar Seachrán* had occasionally kept them company, out to Skellig in Kerry and then in Iona in Scotland. Now we would do so again, Ken, Mike and myself to begin with.

A half dozen currachs went down the Liffey with them, including myself and Liam Ó Muirlithe in his. From Dun Laoghaire on it was southward with the tide, six or seven hours each day, making about 20 miles daily before they would pull in and pitch their tents. The crossing of the Irish Sea, from Carne, near Rosslare, was 43 miles plus several more on the Welsh side, caught by strong tides there. It took them 23 hours of hard pulling to get to Skomer Island, off the coast of Pembrokeshire, quite gruelling. There in *Ar Seachrán* rowers and ourselves slept well.

Around the corner near Tenby stands the magnificent Manorbier Castle. My cousin, and historian, Donal had written that this was the original Barry family premises from which, in 1169,

Strongbow, and the Barrys had invaded Ireland. He suggested that I should repossess it but unfortunately I could find no help!

Every day brought us to interesting places, some notorious: Lundy Island, Hartland Point, Tintagel and the Doom Bar outside Padstow. There was even a saying: 'From Hartland Point Point to Padstow Light, is a watery grave by day or night.' I took a seat in the currach for a long day of rowing. My hands and, worse, backside, weren't the better for it.

Liam, Kevin and Austin Duke joined us on *Ar Seachrán*. Austin has been aboard with us many times, since first he 'swung a business trip' to meet us in Boston in 1986. More than any of us he would need to get to a phone, as he would have 'things going on', business. Never was anyone less of a sailor, and of top of that, seasickness was never far away, but he must have enjoyed the company because he has kept coming back for more.

The crossing of the English Channel from Newlyn was to be 60 miles, about three or four days. The plan was that each evening the lads would come aboard *Ar Seachrán*, eat and then sleep, while we would keep station, more or less, and they would restart in the morning. This worked well for the first day and night. But then the weather blew up and with the currach in tow we motored across until, about 10 miles offshore, land was sighted. Out into the currach they climbed and rowed into L'Abervrach. All were hugely relieved to have that behind. With the tides, in the following days they rowed south, to finish in Duarnenez. Well satisfied, there the currach, or *naomhóig* as it is called in Kerry, was put into storage and we all sailed back to Dingle.

Over the winter, Danny and I agreed that from now on they would be going more or less headland to headland, and so would not need the cover of *Ar Seachrán*.

East Greenland, 2015

This we knew to be a cold and barren place, much different from the relatively green and populated coast of west Greenland, and far less visited.

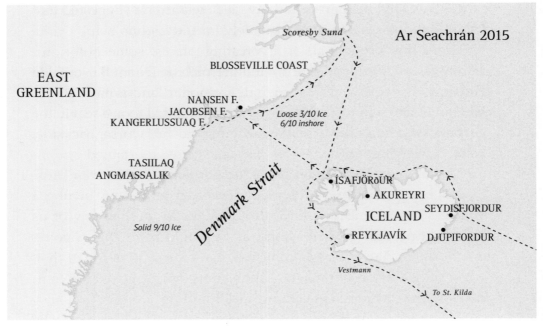

East Greenland

It was climber Gerry Galligan who proposed it to me. I circulated 'a modest proposal' to likely friends, got a good response, and it became a 'goer', an expedition with a small 'e', as Frank put it. *Ar Seachrán*, unlike *Northabout*, was not built for expeditions, much less for banging into ice, but with organisation and care it could work. We prepared, loaded and left.

The first leg of two weeks was to Stornaway in the northern Hebrides. This route was familiar ground and with familiar people, old friends. To spice things up, Ruaidhri had brought some turf sods from his bog in Indreabhán which were to be placed in locations where there had been an Irish monkish presence – a follow-on from our Iomramh journey of 2011.

In Craighouse, Jura, we looked the mile over at Eilean Bríde, but it was too rough to venture over with our sod in the dinghy. On Iona, on a fine mid-summer's night, we lit a small fire on the beach, placed a turf sod on it and passed around the Jameson bottle. Some visiting Australians, whom we invited to join us, thought they were in heaven!

Going northward the conversation flowed freely. Bonny Prince Charles was condemned by some –'he ran, while his people were being slaughtered' – Henry VIII was right when he closed the monasteries, and even Stalin got a good mention despite having killed 300 Ukranian poets for 'spreading dissension' – 'but he had a lovely singing voice'.

Pleasantly we sailed northward and into Stornaway for a full crew change. But first we were met and were entertained around the island of Lewis by Malcolm Maclean, joint author with Theo Dorgan of *An Leabhair Mór/The Great Book of Gaelic*.

Stornaway to Isafjordur, Iceland, July 1 to July 26

Our next crew were new to me, and for the most part to each other. This would be refreshing in its own way, but also interesting, not least in their view of my own style, whatever that might be.

I had met Rob Ó Foghlú, in his thirties, while I was making currach sails in west Kerry. Ciara Ó Flynn, his partner, also a muscician, had done a little sailing in her native Cork Harbour. Frank Spiers, retired graphic artist, sails a Folkboat in Dun Laoghaire. His friend Willie Finnie from Kildare was mainly a racing sailor.

On the isolated island of Rona we saw monastic remains. In Suduroy, first landing in Faroe, it was lashing rain. On the main island we hiked out to Brandanvik, St. Brendans Bay, and there planted a turf sod together with a medallion, one of several cast by Willie from mud near St. Brigid's Well near his home. We met Steffen Hansen, scholar, again.

A strong following wind gave us a fast, if uncomfortable, passage to Seydisfjordur on Iceland's east side. There we were joined by old friend Harry who has sailed and climbed with me over 20 years, me taking him and others to some out of the way places, he dragging me up mountains I had no right to be on.

Going anti-clockwise around the north Iceland coast it was foggy, but not particularly windy; it was a poor summer, as described by the people we met in the small fishing ports. In Akureyri, second city of Iceland, a big town really, Willie left and climber/sailor

Even with the stove lighting Paddy and Ronán were cold in the cabin, hats and gloves on (photo by Harry Connolly).

Paddy O'Brien joined. My hero Bill Tilman had written, 'Even in summer the Icelandic climate can be a little harsh', and yes, so it continued as we made our way to Isafjordur (pronounced *Ee*safjordur, as is *Ee*sland).

Isafjordur to East Greenland to Reykjavic, July 26 to August 15

The plan for these three weeks was to sail across Denmark Strait to the Kangerdlussuaq area, 150 miles north of the Arctic Circle, to spend a week or so there climbing coastal mountains, then go southwest for more of the same, visit Tasiilaaq/Angmagssalik and then sail back to Iceland. This is an exceptionally isolated and barren area, with the density of the coastal sea-ice being the major unknown. We equipped ourselves well, with backup for our 'mission critical' kit, two dinghies, two outboard engines, plenty of good ground tackle and two 100 metre spare lines. For shore-going/climbing, we had a full range of hardware, tents, ropes, stoves and such. In tanks and jerrycans we had 600 litres of diesel. Drinking water we could replenish from glacial streams or melted ice.

With our 'satphone' we could talk to 'baseman' Paul Cooper back home, who would advise on weather and sea-ice updates and be contactable in emergencies, if necessary.

With seven aboard we left, including Peter Gargan and a new man, Cork blacksmith and gunnery man Rónan Ó Caoimh. Our crossing of Denmark Strait proved uneventful, however our attempts at landing were not. Going in, mountains resplendent, sharp brown and rocky below, white ice and snow above, the fairly loose sea-ice initially proved no impediment. A polar bear rose from sunning himself, or herself, on a floe. But, going into our targeted Nansen Fjord, the ice thickened. Not to be easily thwarted, we weaved, banged and wound our way inwards. The propeller rang out a few times with ice impact – we had a spare, but…. Eventually, it became apparent that even if we could get to an anchorage, the density of the ice wouldn't allow launching of the inflatable dinghy, much less getting it ashore. We retreated out to sea.

For the next couple of days we tried to get into Mikis Fjord, but no go. Kangerdlussuaq Fjord was a no go as well. Then, weaving through the sea-ice, about a mile away, we saw a yacht mast. Quickly I grabbed a radio and called her. She answered in French, seemingly reluctantly. Harry, living in French-speaking Luxemburg, got on our radio. Ah, yes, now they were more talkative. They were the steel expedition yacht *L'Vlimouse* and a day earlier had been in Jacobsen Fjord, about 30 miles northward, almost ice-free. Wow, and thank you. 'A rub of the green,' Gerry called it.

We got in to Jacobsen Fjord, anchored near its head and there we had a wonderful week of scrambling and climbing – always leaving two to mind the boat as there were ice-floes, potentially dangerous, floating about. We sat by driftwood timber campfires on the sandy shore, placing turf sod and medallions on one – perhaps some monks had been swept this way?

The climbers did one mountain whose summit, almost certainly, had never before seen the boots of man.

Taasilaaq, we had heard, was ice-bound and inaccessible. Three weeks earlier an Icelander had his boat crushed nearby and his

We met a French expedition yacht, L'Vlimouse, *who told us where they had found an ice-free fjord (photo by Gerry Galligan).*

crew were fortunate to have been helicoptered to safety. So instead we went northwards for Scoresby Sund and there, even while shaking out our least dirty shoregoing clothes, frustratingly failed to get through the ice to the settlement.

We had a great downwind sail back to Iceland, which was just as well as our diesel stock was low and wouldn't have got us there. South through the Westfjords we went and into Reykjavic, well satisfied. The lads, outgoing and incoming, treated me to dinner.

Incoming to join Harry and myself were his friend and all-round sportsman Wilf Williams, Mick Delap, once BBC's African correspondent and Theo Dorgan, writer and sailor. We had a pleasant passage around to Heimay in the Vestmay Islands. There we waited, and waited, for there was a stationary low-pressure system giving us head-winds from the southeast. Eventually we went anyway, diesel tanks full but not looking forward to it. Nor did we enjoy our passage to Saint Kilda one bit, other than the relief of getting there. In the dark, one dim light showing from the shore, we dropped anchor in Village Bay and slept.

Our shore visit was interesting, but all too brief. I've always wanted to see the north side of Hirta, St. Kilda's main island, but that remains for another day? We had a spanking sail in the sun the 40 miles to the Sound of Harris, past familiar Hebridean islands, into Oban in the rain, and on to Jura. There, this time, we did 'land and plant' our sod and medallion on Eilean Bríde, carried our spinnaker down to the Irish Sea, and got into the Liffey on the last day of August.

St. Brigid's Cross. We carried medallions of baked mud, by Willie Finnie, from near her County Kildare home. The veneration of Brigid, saint or goddess, is widespread thoughout north west Europe.

37

Towards a Warmer Place – And Now?

Last year we had a May Week around Sheep's Head and Bantry Bay. There was less intensity than in previous years – I can't imagine why! – and on June 4, *Ar Seachrán* left Baltimore, bound across Biscay for the north of Spain, a warmer place than Ireland and certainly than Greenland, west or east.

Based in Gijon, Asturia, Frank, Paddy O'Brien and myself hiked the Cordillera Cantabrica and the Picos; the lads also doing some real climbing. With some new men we then coasted westward and into Galicia to meet up with the currach crew.

Yes, in this, their third year out, they were almost at journey's end, A Coruña. We could see their hands hardened and blistered, their faces scorched by salt, sun and sea. Their arses were sore (no, we didn't examine them!). From there to Santiago de Compostela, 60 kilometres inland, the currach, oars and sail went on the roof of a car owned by an Irishman living in Spain, their tents and bags inside. They, sensibly, took a lift in another car.

On Sunday, June 26, we helped carry the boat up the steps and into the Cathedral – well, not quite, the security guys wouldn't let handbags in, not to mind a boat. But the lads, in the full church, got pride of place on the high altar and deservedly so. We helped them celebrate, within, and later, without.

In the following three weeks we enjoyed sailing *Ar Seachrán* on the Rias of Galicia which are like the bays and inlets of West Cork and Kerry, but warm and sunny. In Xufre Boatyard, Ria de Arousa, the boat was lifted out for winter storage.

'I've had enough of this'

And Now?

I'm tiring of the work required keeping and maintaining such a big and complex boat as the Frers 45, *Ar Seachrán*. I'm going to sell her. I've bought a 27-foot open timber gleoiteóg called *Cailín Dubh*, a small Galway Hooker, and have her in Roundstone. This will do fine for me, and will see me out as far as boats are concerned.

And I know this boat. I had a loan of her for a year in 1987/88 when she was *Cú Uladh* and *Saint Patrick* was being rebuilt. She has for some years been in the ownership of my friend Paraic Ó Tuairisg of Aran, who in recent years has had her entirely rebuilt. His son Liam, who works abroad, will share her with me. I've had her re-rigged over the winter and have got a boom-tent made up for a sleeping shelter.

I can't wait.

The family are in good order: Cathal, a property lawyer, married to Julia, with lively baby girl Sierra to keep them busy; Caoimhe, an aid worker, married to Carl, with Fionán and Ferdia; Muireann, a yoga master, lecturing in Media in Limerick; and Bairbre, a Gaelscoil Teacher, living in Galway with Lorcan bringing up Cliodhna and Art. Mary puts up with me – feeding, minding and all. I'm a lucky man.

And to conclude, I've occasionally said this but now I mean it:

Everything I want in the way of pastime is to be found between the Mizen and Malin Head, 10 miles inland or out; the hills for walking, the roads for cycling and a pub to quench the thirst. Offshore, there is the sea for sailing, more hills for walking and you never know who'd be knocking about, maybe with some tunes!

That'll do.

P.S. The vessel *Ilen*, which we last sailed in 1998, is nearing the finish of a complete rebuild in Liam Hegarty's West Cork boatyard. Could there be the odd sail in her?

Index